# THE ROMAN
## SOLDIER

# ASPECTS OF GREEK AND ROMAN LIFE

*General Editor: Professor H. H. Scullard*

# THE ROMAN SOLDIER

G. R. Watson

**CORNELL UNIVERSITY PRESS**
ITHACA, NEW YORK

CORNELL UNIVERSITY PRESS
1969

Standard Book Number: 8014-0519-X

Library of Congress Catalog Card Number: 69-11153

PRINTED IN ENGLAND

# CONTENTS

# LIST OF ILLUSTRATIONS

# PREFACE

MANY BOOKS, though perhaps not so many in English as in German, have been written on the Roman army, and no doubt there will be many more. (Indeed, while this preface was actually being written, Graham Webster's *The Roman Imperial Army* was announced for publication at the end of the month.) So far as those which have appeared in the past have one common factor, they have for the most part been concerned with the Roman army as a collection of fighting units, and this, after all, was the army's primary function. It is this link which unites such studies as G. L. Cheesman's *The Auxilia of the Roman Imperial Army*, which is still a standard work, though published as long ago as 1914, and H. M. D. Parker's *The Roman Legions*, of which the original edition was in 1928, with a corrected reprint in 1958. With these works the following pages are not meant to be competitive. Rather they are an attempt to describe life in the Roman army from the point of view of the soldier, in which the main emphasis is laid on the ranks below the centurionate, the ranks in which the majority of the men would continue to serve for the whole of their careers. Thus the bulk of the work is concerned not with the organization of the army and the officer corps, but with such matters as the procedure of enlistment, basic training, field-service training, and conditions of service. No apology is made for treating the latter topic in perhaps disproportionate detail, since the prospects of promotion, the adequacy or inadequacy of pay, and the nature and frequency of rewards and punishments, were all subjects of profound concern to the individual soldier. The problems of religion and marriage, especially the latter, were also of importance to the soldier, and, particularly towards the end of his service, the question of his discharge and resettlement.

Ramsay MacMullen in his *Soldier and Civilian in the Later Roman Empire* (1963), also concerned himself with the soldier, but he concentrated upon the soldier's relationships with the civilian, or, in his own words, 'the army at peace, the spare-time doings of a group with a defined character, consisting of between a quarter and a half million men'. Since this particular aspect of the soldier's life has been so fully dealt with by MacMullen, much less is made of it in this work.

Some explanation is perhaps required of a practice adopted in these pages: translations from the ancient sources into English are provided in the text, while the Latin sources, but not the Greek, are given in the original language in the notes. The book is intended to appeal not only to the student, but also to the general reader 'with little Latin and less Greek'. Moreover, as far as the notes are concerned, students rarely appear to check references, and when the texts are occasionally hard to come by the temptation to take them on trust seems to be irresistible. In any case, the convenience of readers is surely helped by having the texts immediately accessible.

I must here acknowledge my very great debt to Professor Eric Birley, who first inspired me as a teacher more than thirty years ago, and under whose encouragement and guidance I first became interested in the problems of Roman military history. To Eric Birley and his colleagues at Durham, especially Dr John Mann and Dr Brian Dobson, who read the greater part of the typescript and gave me invaluable advice and criticism, I owe a great deal. I also owe my grateful thanks to Professor J. F. Gilliam, of the Institute for Advanced Study, Princeton, for his most generous advice and encouragement. To my colleagues Professor E. A. Thompson, Mr H. B. Mattingly and Mr W. R. Chalmers, I offer my heartfelt thanks for the help that they have given me, especially Mr Chalmers, who read the whole of the proofs. To Professor H. H. Scullard, the General Editor of this series, I should like to express my appreciation of the advice which he has so readily given me. I must, however, myself lay claim to all the errors and omissions which remain. Lastly, I should like to acknowledge my gratitude to Mr Stanley Baron, of Thames and Hudson, for the patience and forbearance which he has shown.

*The University*
*Nottingham,*                                        G. R. WATSON
*January, 1969*

# CHAPTER I

# INTRODUCTION

## SCOPE OF WORK

THE AIM AND PURPOSE of the present study is to reconstruct the life and training of the Roman soldier from enlistment to discharge, and to assess the impact of the serving soldier and veteran upon the society in which he found himself. Upon this general framework two limitations have been imposed: the one of time, the other of rank. Some limitation of time is inevitable if an acceptable degree of internal consistency and coherence is to be achieved, since, in spite of the conservatism of the Roman army and its high regard for tradition, the resemblance between the army which was defeated by Hannibal at Cannae and that which lost the battle of Adrianople nearly six centuries later is hardly more than superficial. As starting point the foundation of the Empire has been chosen, as terminal date the accession of Diocletian. Both dates are natural termini, the earlier because up to that time the Roman army had never been properly secured upon a permanent footing, however professional some of its members may be considered to have been,[1] the latter date because the reorganization of the army under Diocletian and Constantine reached such a point that a separate account would be required.

It is true that the establishment of the standing army was a gradual process which can hardly be assigned to a particular year. It would be fair to say, however, that the process was in all essentials complete by 13 BC, in which year Augustus laid down the period of ordinary legionary service at sixteen years, which was to be followed by a further four years as a veteran exempt from routine duties, living in special quarters under the command of an officer called the *curator veteranorum*.[2] The latter type of service was called *sub vexillo*, from the special standard or *vexillum* which distinguished the veterans' unit from the main legionary body. Doubtless very many soldiers had completed as many as, or even more than, sixteen plus four years of service during the previous two centuries, but their service had not been on so formal a basis. Equally, this choice of starting point is not invalidated by the fact that the conditions of service were changed as early as AD 6, when the years of service were increased to twenty plus five.[3] The important point is that in 13 BC service in the Roman army could at last be regarded as a career.

It is equally true that the accession of Diocletian did not cause a sudden transformation of the army into something very different from what it had been before. The army of the fourth century did not owe all its distinctive features to the genius of Diocletian, but, as modern scholars have shown, was merely the culmination of a long process of reorganization begun by the innovations of Septimius Severus, and continued by Gallienus and Aurelian in particular, and by the majority of third-century emperors to a lesser extent.[4] The Roman army, like the river of Heraclitus, was constantly changing, however slowly; with Diocletian the rate of change merely gathered momentum.

The second limitation is of rank. A study of the ranks of the Roman army may be tackled in one of two ways, from the top downwards, or from the bottom upwards. The great German scholar, Alfred von Domaszewski, used mainly the former method in his fundamental work, *Die Rangordnung des römischen Heeres*,[5] and most subsequent writers have followed much the same plan. Yet this method, though it is attractive and logical, has two obvious disadvantages, the one of arrangement, the other of perspective. The fault of arrangement is that by beginning at the top, and then proceeding downwards by a method of division, an overall plan tends to be presented which perhaps never existed in its entirety, and which in its details is generally late rather than early. Thus Domaszewski was induced by his method to present a plan, which, if it is to be ascribed to any period at all, must be assigned to the third century. Domaszewski himself, with his pronounced bias against the emperor Septimius Severus and with his belief in the *Barbarisierung* of the army in the third century, may have felt that the complex organization which he records existed before that date in full perfection, and then gradually decayed as illiteracy increased.[6] But this belief is now discredited: the Diocletianic reorganization is no sudden change, no Phoenix rising from the ashes, but merely the end-product of a prolonged series of minor alterations.

The fault of perspective is that this method is the reverse of experience, for whether every private soldier has a fieldmarshal's baton in his knapsack or not, at any rate he does not normally begin his service as a general and end as a private. Thus the gradual sense of the extension of the horizon of career is liable to be lost in a formalized tabulation of ranks.

### ROMAN MILITARY FORCES

At this stage it may be appropriate to set out in simplified form the Roman military system. Like Caesar's Gaul, the army of the early Empire was basically tripartite. The kernel was that portion which was stationed in or near Rome, and which consisted of the praetorian guard, and later the *equites singulares*, the urban cohorts, the *vigiles* or fire-brigade, and the fleets of Misenum and Ravenna. The latter unit alone was stationed at any great distance from the centre. All these forces were much more immediately under the emperor's control than any of the units stationed in the provinces.

The second segment of the army comprised the legions. Of these there were never at this period more than thirty, and more usually twenty-eight, each with an establishment of perhaps some 5,500 men.[7] This gave a total legionary strength of about 160,000, or approximately fifty per cent of the armed forces as a whole. Historically, the legionaries held pride of place in the armed forces: in practice, the praetorians held higher status and received higher pay. A certain resentment is noticeable as early as AD 14, when the mutinous Pannonian legionaries expressed their jealousy of the privileges of the Guard.[8] The legions were distributed mainly along or near the frontiers: Tacitus gives us the Order of

Battle for the year AD 23, a time when the number of legions had
fallen to as few as twenty-five:[9]

| Rhineland | 8 | Germ. Inf. I, V *Alaudae*, XX *Valeria*, XXI Germ. Sup. II *Augusta*, XIII *Gemina*, XIV *Gemina*, XVI |
|---|---|---|
| Spain | 3 | IV *Macedonica*, VI *Victrix*, X *Gemina* |
| Africa | 2 | III *Augusta*, IX *Hispana* |
| Egypt | 2 | III *Cyrenaica*, XXII *Deiotariana* |
| Syria | 4 | III *Gallica*, VI *Ferrata*, X *Fretensis*, XII *Fulminata* |
| Pannonia | 2 | VIII *Augusta*, XV *Apollinaris* |
| Moesia | 2 | IV *Scythica*, V *Macedonica* |
| Dalmatia | 2 | VII, XI. |

The major subsequent change was that necessitated by the
conquest of Britain, in which initially four legions served, though
the number was later reduced to three. Even this smaller number
meant that Britain had one of the largest military garrisons in the
Empire, a garrison quite out of proportion when we consider
the comparative populations of Britain, the Rhineland and the
Danubian provinces. An indication of the Order of Battle at the
end of the reign of Antonius Pius is given on two columns at
Rome, which clearly belong to the same monument; to these
there have been added at the end the legions created by M.
Aurelius and Septimius Severus.[10]

| Britain | 3 | II *Augusta*, VI *Victrix*, XX *Victrix* |
|---|---|---|
| Germ. Sup. | 2 | VIII *Augusta*, XXII *Primigenia* |
| Germ. Inf. | 2 | I *Minervia*, XXX *Ulpia* |
| Pann. Sup. | 3 | I *Adiutrix*, X *Gemina*, XIV *Gemina* |
| Pann. Inf. | 1 | II *Adiutrix* |
| Moes. Sup. | 2 | IV *Flavia*, VII *Claudia* |
| Moes. Inf. | 3 | I *Italica*, V *Macedonica*, XI *Claudia* |
| Dacia | 1 | XIII *Gemina* |
| Cappadocia | 2 | XII *Fulminata*, XV *Apollinaris* |
| Syria | 3 | III *Gallica*, IV *Scythica*, XVI *Flavia* |
| Judaea | 2 | VI *Ferrata*, X *Fretensis* |

| Arabia | 1 | III *Cyrenaica* |
|---|---|---|
| Egypt | 1 | II *Traiana* |
| Africa | 1 | III *Augusta* |
| Spain | 1 | VII *Gemina* |

*Later additions*

| Noricum | 1 | II *Italica* |
|---|---|---|
| Raetia | 1 | III *Italica* |
| Mesopotamia | 2 | I *Parthica*, III *Parthica* |
| Italy | 1 | II *Parthica* |

It will be noticed that over a hundred years later three legions, III *Augusta*, III *Gallica* and V *Macedonica*, are still stationed in the same provinces. Only III *Augusta*, however, had had an unbroken spell.[11]

The third large category of the armed forces was the *auxilia*, the auxiliary forces. These had their origin in the practice of the late Republic by which the traditional Roman deficiency in cavalry and light-armed troops was made good by the recruitment of specialist units raised outside Italy. The number of such regiments increased greatly during the Civil Wars and from this rather heterogeneous collection of units Octavian created an important section of his standing army. It would have defeated his purpose to have made them homogeneous, and so they remained units of varying type and function. Inevitably, however, the Roman desire for order and standardization tended to minimize their differences as time went by. The basic division was into *alae* and *cohortes*. The *alae*, or cavalry, were the élite troops, and enjoyed higher pay and status. They were organized for the most part in regiments 500 strong (*alae quingenariae*), but a limited number were of double size, 1,000 strong (*alae miliariae*). The cohorts were similarly divided into units 500 and 1,000 strong, with the smaller size again predominating. Some cohorts of both classes were part-mounted, or *equitatae*. The mounted men in these units were not so much cavalry as mounted infantry.[12] The total number of auxiliaries was probably only slightly lower, if at all, than that of legionaries.

The auxiliary soldiers were originally recruited from *peregrini*, and their veterans, at least from the time of Claudius, received the citizenship on discharge. From as early as the reign of Augustus, however, recruitment of citizens for the *auxilia* began to be practised, at first into special units such as the various *cohortes civium Romanorum*, and eventually quite generally.[13] The long-term effect was the gradual elimination of the most obvious distinction between the legions and the *auxilia*.

There will always be a place, however, in a military system for irregular units, and the Roman army was no exception. By the time of Trajan and Hadrian the regularization of the *auxilia* had proceeded so far that it was found necessary to recreate the very type of unit which the *auxilia* had formed in the beginning. Regiments were raised from less romanized provincials who brought to the army a measure of the élan which the standardization of the *auxilia*, however much it inspired *esprit de corps*, had almost eliminated. These new regiments were simply called *numeri* ('units'), and were allowed to fight in their own native styles, with their own native weapons, and using their own native tongues. Many of the *numeri* serving in Germany were from the newly conquered areas of Britain.[14]

*The praetorian guard*

The praetorians were established as a permanent corps by Augustus in 27 BC. During the middle and late Republic it had been customary for generals to have a bodyguard to which the name *cohors praetoria* was given. Apart from the name, however, there was little in common between these bodyguards and Augustus's new creation, which was nine cohorts strong. Three of these cohorts were billeted about the city, while the other six were stationed in nearby Italian towns. For some time they continued to be a real bodyguard, inasmuch as Augustus kept them under direct control, but in 2 BC the command was entrusted to two *praefecti praetorio*, who were regularly of equestrian rank. This command made the prefecture of the praetorians the pinnacle of the equestrian career, though the full potential of the post was not realized until Sejanus became, first, joint prefect with his father on the accession of Tiberius, and then sole prefect (AD 16 or 17). By AD 23 he had so far modified Augustus's conception of the praetorians as to concentrate the entire praetorian force in one large barracks near the *porta Viminalis*. This action made the commanders of the praetorians the effective masters of the city.

In spite of the history of the praetorians under Tiberius, when Sejanus came near to exercising the imperial power, Gaius further increased the praetorian forces by raising the number of cohorts from nine to twelve. The size of these cohorts has been disputed, but Durry is perhaps right in believing that until AD 69, when they were transformed by Vitellius, the cohorts were each 500 strong.[15] In the fighting of AD 69 the praetorians had supported Otho, and Vitellius naturally had doubts about their loyalty. He therefore took the rather drastic step of dismissing the existing guard and replacing it with a fresh guard of sixteen cohorts each 1,000 strong, which he formed from soldiers from his trusted Rhineland legions. This increased the establishment of the force from 6,000 to 16,000, and meant that Vitellius had the equivalent of about three legions immediately to hand. Even this proved inadequate, however, and his successor Vespasian reduced the guard to its Augustan establishment of nine cohorts, at the same time restoring their previous strength. Later, Domitian added a tenth cohort, and after his reign there was no significant change in establishment until the final disbandment of the praetorian guard by Constantine in AD 312.

As befits a metropolitan force the praetorians were regularly recruited from Italy and the more romanized provinces. Except of course under Vitellius, this policy was continued until the accession of Septimius Severus, who scrapped the existing guard, which had offered its support for sale at the famous auction of the Empire, and in its place substituted a new guard recruited from the Illyrian legions which formed his chief support.

The cohorts were divided into centuries in much the same way as legionary cohorts, but there was not the same complicated hierarchy of centurions as there was in the legions. Instead, all centurions of the guard were of roughly equal rank, differing only in seniority, apart from the two most important, who were

entitled *trecenarius* and *princeps castrorum*.[16] Service in the Guard
was of great advantage to the ambitious soldier, quite apart from
the pay and donatives which were much higher than in the
legions.[17] Some of the more successful praetorians, in fact, had
impressive military careers. Enlisting in the praetorians as young
men, they served their sixteen years, and then as *evocati Augusti*
they were promoted to legionary centurionates, and often
beyond.[18]

Even more successful, naturally enough, were those who
reached the centurionate in the Guard itself.[19] They might
become *primi ordines* or *primi pili* in the legions, and then proceed
to a succession of tribunates in Rome, first as tribunes of the
*vigiles*, then of the urban cohorts, and finally of the Guard itself.
They might then proceed to a second primipilate, satisfactory
completion of which would open the door to many higher
appointments in the procuratorial career.

### Equites singulares imperatoris

The need for cavalry as a supplement to the Guard was satisfied,
probably in Flavian times, by the creation of a corps of *equites
singulares*. They were recruited chiefly from Germans and Pan-
nonians, and served as a mounted bodyguard for the emperor.
They were commanded by two praetorian tribunes and were
stationed in their own barracks near the Lateran. Their establishment was at first 500 and later 1,000 men. As was proper for a
cavalry unit, their internal officers were decurions, the senior of
whom was called the *decurio princeps*.[20]

### The urban cohorts

The existence of the urban cohorts as a completely separate entity
from the Guard probably dates from the appointment of L. Piso
as the first permanent *praefectus urbi*.[21] The three urban cohorts,
like the nine praetorian cohorts of Augustus, were at first billeted
partly in Rome, partly in neighbouring towns. When the praetorians were moved into one large barracks under Tiberius—the
*castra praetoria*—the urban cohorts moved with them. They
remained, however, under the command of the *praefectus urbi*.[22]

Like the cohorts of the Guard, the urban cohorts were commanded by tribunes.

*The vigiles*

The *vigiles* occupied a peculiar position in the structure of the Roman army. Originally they were founded by Augustus to serve as a city fire-brigade, and were largely recruited from freedmen. Their creation formed part of the reforms of AD 6 and undoubtedly served to fill a long-felt need. They were organized from the first on a para-military basis and had military ranks and drill, but that they were regarded as *milites* at that time in any real sense of the word seems unlikely. Tacitus, for instance, omits them entirely from his review of the armed forces of the Empire for the year AD 23.[23] Their position would appear to have been not unlike that of many modern police forces and fire-brigades. They were divided into seven cohorts of 1,000 men each, and the cohorts themselves were each subdivided into seven centuries. The suggestion, however, that this was done deliberately to emphasize the non-military character of the corps overlooks the fact that there were fourteen regions of Rome at the time; the seven cohorts were each responsible for two regions of the city, and the number of centuries not unnaturally reflected the number of cohorts.[24] The first stage in the upward climb of the *vigiles* towards social respectability is marked by the passing of the *Lex Visellia* in AD 24, by which members of the corps acquired the citizenship after six years' service.[25] Later, the qualifying period was reduced to three years.[26] By the time of Ulpian in the early third century the *vigiles* had become soldiers in the fullest sense of the term.[27] It was probably the increase in the number of citizens serving in the *vigiles* brought about by the long-term effect of the *Lex Visellia* which raised the social status of the corps and encouraged freeborn citizens to enlist in it; certainly by the middle of the second century AD the freeborn members were in a considerable majority.[28] The *vigiles* were rarely called upon to function as a military force, but in this capacity they proved their value in the events which led to the downfall of Sejanus in AD 31.[29] The corps was commanded by a high-ranking equestrian officer, the *praefectus vigilum*, who ranked below the *praefectus praetorio*, the *praefectus Aegypti* and the *praefectus annonae*. From Trajan's time he was assisted by a sub-prefect. Each cohort was commanded by a tribune, who might expect his next promotion to be to a tribunate in an urban cohort.

## The fleets

The Roman navy was first placed on a permanent footing immediately after Actium in 31 BC.[30] The original base was at Forum Iulii in Gallia Narbonensis and this base remained in use even after the transfer of Gallia Narbonensis to senatorial control in 22 BC. Gradually, however, other bases at Ravenna and Misenum took the place of Forum Iulii, which after the completion of the pacification of Gaul and the Alpine areas was rather remote from the centre of affairs. Forum Iulii still existed as a base as late as AD 69, but after that date it lost all importance.[31]

Misenum and Ravenna had a much longer history as naval bases. Both became such early in the reign of Augustus, and remained in use as long as the Roman Imperial Navy existed. The establishment of neither the *classis Misenensis* nor the *classis Ravennas* is known with any certainty, though some indication is given by the fact that each fleet was able to provide enough men for a legion during the Year of the Four Emperors, the Misene fleet providing I *Adiutrix* for Nero, and the Ravennate fleet II *Adiutrix* for Vespasian. Starr estimates that the Ravennate fleet was considerably over 5,000 men strong, and the Misene fleet double that size.[32]

Each fleet was commanded by a prefect of equestrian rank, except that during the reigns of Claudius and Nero the commander's title became *procurator Augusti et praefectus classis*, and during this period at least three of the prefects were freedmen.[33] Vespasian reverted to the former designation, and from that time onwards the *praefectus classis praetoriae Misenensis* was one of the highest equestrian officials in the Empire, ranking immediately below the *praefectus vigilum*. The *praefectus classis Ravennatis* was of slightly lower rank. At least from the time of Nero a *praefectus* could be assisted by a *subpraefectus*, who was a minor equestrian official. Surprisingly, so far as is known, no *subpraefectus* ever reached the rank of *praefectus classis*.[34]

Besides the major fleets at Misenum and Ravenna there were minor naval forces stationed in various parts of the Empire. Of these the most important was the *classis Augusta Alexandrina*, to give the Egyptian fleet the title it held from the time of Vespasian onwards.[35] Because of its association with Egypt, and its not infrequent mention therefore in papyrological sources, rather more is known about this provincial fleet than any of the others. It would appear, however, to have been in any case perhaps the largest. A fleet is also attested for Syria, and these two eastern fleets maintained detachments at Caesarea Mauretania for police duties in the western Mediterranean.[36] Presumably, this function was considered to be unsuitable for the imperial fleets at Misenum and Ravenna. Other fleets served outside the Mediterranean, such as the *classis Pontica* which was created in AD 64 to patrol the Black Sea, the *classis Moesica* and the *classis Pannonica* which patrolled the Danube, and the *classis Germanica* which patrolled the Rhine. The *classis Britannica* guarded the Channel, and was based at Gesoriacum (Boulogne).

## The legions

The history of the legions in the early Republic is obscure. The first trustworthy account is that of Polybius, who described a legion divided into thirty maniples, ten to each of the three lines of *hastati*, *principes* and *triarii*.[37] There was still a property qualification, but it was by then reduced to 4,000 *asses*. This rather cumbersome organization was simplified by the Marian reforms near the end of the second century BC. In the first place, the property qualification was now done away with, and the entire citizen body was made eligible for service. The effect of this measure was that the legions became even more what they had already begun to be, that is, largely volunteer forces of semi-professional soldiers. There was as yet no permanent standing army, but there was rarely a shortage of opportunities for military service. The second of the Marian reforms was the presentation of an *aquila* to each legion. The eagle gave the legion a sense of corporate identity, and enabled it to build up *esprit de corps*. Thirdly, the legionary cavalry and the light-armed troops (*velites*) were discarded. This left the legion as a homogeneous body of heavy infantry. The duties which had been carried out by the legionary cavalry and the *velites* were handed over to auxiliary forces. The last, and perhaps most important measure, is that the cohort of six centuries permanently superseded the maniple of two centuries as the tactical unit.[38] This meant that the legion was now divided into ten cohorts each of six centuries. It is not clear what was the formal establishment, or even whether there was one. On the face of it, ten cohorts of six centuries ought to have meant a legionary strength of 6,000 men. In practice, the number of men in a legion during the period from Marius to Augustus when known appears to average around 4,000 men.[39] Either the centuries were nominal centuries, or they were generally under strength. The establishment of the century under the Empire was probably 80 men, except in the first cohort, which was of double strength. When to these there are added centurions and *principales* (non-commissioned officers), the legionary establishment during the Empire was probably in the order of 5,500.[40] Outside the first cohort the centurions were little different in status apart from seniority.[41] Their titles were *pilus prior*, *princeps prior*, *hastatus prior*, *pilus posterior*, *princeps posterior*, and *hastatus posterior*. Before each of these titles the number of the cohort was prefixed; thus the last centurion of the last (tenth) cohort was *decimus hastatus posterior*. The position of the first cohort was different. Though double the size of the others, it had only five centuries. Its centurions as a group were called the *primi ordines*, and in ascending order of rank were *hastatus posterior*, *princeps posterior*, *hastatus*, *princeps*, and finally *primus pilus*. Except in the case of the last-named, the number *primus* was not prefixed.

At the beginning of the Empire the legions were *legio* I (on one inscription called I *Germanica*), II *Augusta*, III *Augusta*, III *Cyrenaica*, III *Gallica*, IV *Macedonica*, IV *Scythica*, V *Alaudae*, V *Macedonica*, VI *Ferrata*, VI *Victrix*, *legio* VII, VIII *Augusta*, IX *Hispana*, X *Fretensis*, X *Gemina*, *legio* XI, XII *Fulminata*, XIII *Gemina*, XIV

*Gemina*, XV *Apollinaris*, *legio* XVI (sometimes called XVI *Gallica*), *legio* XVII, *legio* XVIII, *legio* XIX, XX *Valeria Victrix*, XXI *Rapax* and XXII *Deiotariana*.

It will be noticed that several numbers were duplicated. In AD 9, legions XVII, XVIII and XIX were annihilated in the Battle of the Teutoburger Wald and were never replaced or their numbers re-used. This loss reduced the number of legions to twenty-five. The former establishment was once again reached by the creation of XV *Primigenia* and XXII *Primigenia* in AD 39 and of I *Italica* by Nero in AD 67. The Year of the Four Emperors and the revolt of Civilis caused a certain amount of upset: the sequel was that various legions disappeared from the army list and others took their place. Legions I, IV *Macedonica*, XV *Primigenia* and XVI were disbanded: their place was taken by VII *Gemina*, IV *Flavia felix* and XVI *Flavia firma*, and by two legions created from marines, I *Adiutrix* and II *Adiutrix*.[42] This raised the number of legions to twenty-nine. Domitian increased the total to thirty in AD 83 by the creation of I *Minervia*, but the total fell again to twenty-eight by the end of his reign through the loss, first of V *Alaudae* in AD 86–7, and of XXI *Rapax* in AD 92.[43] Trajan therefore inherited the very number of legions with which Augustus had started. He successfully raised the number to thirty by the creation of II *Traiana* and XXX *Ulpia*, but the number was to fall once more through the loss of IX *Hispana* and XXII *Deiotariana*, both probably during the Jewish War of AD 132–5. Marcus Aurelius restored the number once more to thirty by the creation of two new legions, II *Italica* and III *Italica*, probably about AD 165. The number of thirty was finally passed by Septimius Severus, who created three new legions, I, II and III *Parthica* about AD 197.

In the beginning the legions stationed in the West were recruited mainly from Italy and Narbonensis, those in the East from the Eastern provinces. As romanization proceeded, the area of recruitment spread, until in the second century local recruitment became the rule. The legionary commander (*legatus legionis*) was regularly, except in Egypt, a senator of praetorian status. He was supported by a *tribunus laticlavius*, a senator of lower standing, and five *tribuni angusticlavii* of equestrian rank. The legions of Egypt were commanded by equestrian *praefecti legionis*, as were later the three Parthian legions raised by Severus.

## The auxilia

The *auxilia* served as a complement to the legionary forces. The legionary commander by virtue of his rank exercised a general supervision over the auxiliary units stationed in his area, none of which, of course, approached anything like the size and importance of a legion.[44] The majority of these units were in numerical strength about the size of a legionary cohort. When the legions in the early Empire were recruiting in the West mainly from Italy, Narbonensis and Baetica, the *auxilia* were recruited from Gallia Comata and Tarraconensis, which were not as yet so romanized. But just as in the case of the legions local recruiting came to predominate, and the *auxilia* gradually became less associated with the provinces from which they were originally recruited, and more and more assimilated to the legions.

## Alae

The title *ala* carries within itself the origin of the name: it originally denoted the troops posted on the wings. These were in Republican days *socii* (allies), and after the Social War invariably cavalry. Once Marius had abolished the citizen cavalry, allied replacements were essential. Caesar made extensive use of Gallic cavalry during his campaigns in Gaul. In the Augustan reorganization of the armed forces the cavalry units were called *alae*, and, like the auxiliary cohorts, were of two kinds, 500 strong (*quingenariae*) and 1,000 strong (*miliariae*). Each *ala* was commanded by a *praefectus equitum* (later *praefectus alae*), who was an equestrian officer at the peak of the *tres militiae*—the succession was *praefectus cohortis, tribunus militum, praefectus equitum*. Thus the command of an *ala*, which was normally the most important non-legionary appointment in any legionary area, was given to an experienced officer of higher standing than a legionary tribune.[45] The *ala* was subdivided, not into centuries, but into *turmae*, sixteen if the unit was 500 strong, twenty-four if it was 1,000 strong.[46] Each *turma* was commanded by a *decurio*, the senior of whom was the *decurio princeps*.[47]

## Cohorts

Auxiliary cohorts were mainly infantry regiments, but some were part-mounted and these were known as *cohortes equitatae*.[48] The infantry regiments were divided into centuries, of which there were six to a cohort 500 strong, ten to one 1,000 strong, while the mounted elements of a *cohors equitata* were divided into *turmae* commanded by decurions. The number of centuries and *turmae* in these cohorts is not clear. Hyginus states that in a *cohors equitata miliaria* there were ten centuries of *pedites* and a total of 240 *equites*.[49] If we assume 30 men to a *turma* this would allow for eight *turmae* in a cohort 1,000 strong and, again on Hyginus' reckoning, four *turmae* in a cohort 500 strong. Unfortunately, the cohort for which there is the most evidence, the *cohors* XX *Palmyrenorum*, which was stationed at Dura-Europos in the third century, does not fit this establishment.[50] This cohort, although 1,000 strong, had only six centuries and five *turmae*. It was not, however, a strictly typical unit, since it also contained *dromedarii* (camel-riders), and this fact may have caused complications. A *cohors quingenaria* was regularly commanded by a *praefectus*, who was an equestrian officer on the first step of the *tres militiae*. A *cohors miliaria* or a *cohors civium Romanorum*, however, was normally commanded by a *tribunus*, who counted for seniority as being on the second step of the promotion ladder.[51]

SOURCES

The sources on which this study is based fall naturally into three main groups. We have first the literary evidence, which itself may be sub-divided into three categories, works specifically written on military institutions, the legal Codes and the *Digest*, and general histories. Of the specific sources the most important is the treatise *De re militari* of Vegetius, which is the only ancient manual of Roman military institutions to have survived intact.

Since Vegetius's work is unique, it is all the more important that the date of its composition should be known. This, unfortunately, can be proved only within broad limits. A reference to the emperor Gratian in I, 20 as *divus* shows that the work was written after AD 383: a critical revision was produced at Constantinople by a certain Eutropius in AD 450. Nor is the fact that the work is addressed to a single emperor and not to a pair quite the help it might have been: Schenk believes the emperor to have been Theodosius I, whereas Seeck thought rather of Valentinian III. The former seems the more likely; if so, the work must be dated to the years 383–95, and perhaps even more closely, with Sirago, to Theodosius's stay in Italy from August 388 to June 391.[52]

Vegetius, however, was neither a historian nor a soldier: his work is a compilation carelessly constructed from material of all ages, a congeries of inconsistencies. To impress the reader with the weight of his learning he names some of his sources: Cato the Elder, Cornelius Celsus, Frontinus and Paternus, and the *constitutiones* of Augustus, Trajan and Hadrian.[53] This does not necessarily mean that these were the only sources which Vegetius used, or even that he used all these at first hand. The imperial *constitutiones*, for example, may well have been gathered from Paternus, who as a military jurist would have been bound to take them into consideration, and the citations from Cato may have been transmitted by way of Celsus, the encyclopaedist. Schenk, in his monograph on the sources of Vegetius, takes on trust Vegetius's account of his indebtedness, and is led thereby to the conclusion that since Paternus was the latest of the sources named by Vegetius, all additions later than the time of Paternus must come from Vegetius's own day and experience.[54] Such can hardly be the case, for it would mean that all the third-century material contained in the work had been introduced by Vegetius himself. That the *Epitoma* does contain third-century material is clear from the composition of the second book. H. M. D. Parker, for instance, has pointed out that the *antiqua legio* described by Vegetius belongs neither to the early Empire nor to the fourth century, and should be ascribed to the second half of the third century.[55] From this it follows that the epitomator must have had some source as late as the third century at least. Of the identity of such a source there is no clue, except possibly in a remark by the sixth-century writer Johannes Lydus in his work *On the Magistracies:* 'The authorities are Celsus, Paternus and Catiline—not the conspirator but another—and before them Cato the Elder and Frontinus, and after these also Renatus, all of them Romans.'[56]

It is not likely that Lydus had read all these authors himself, or even most of them, but he probably acquired the names of Cato and Frontinus from Vegetius (Renatus), and those of Celsus and Paternus either from Vegetius as well, or from the mysterious Catiline, whose date, if we are to judge from the order of the names in the sentence, which is otherwise chronological, must lie between that of Paternus, who was put to death in AD 183, and Vegetius.[57] It is, however, strange that both Vegetius and Lydus mention the military jurist, Tarruntenus Paternus, the praetorian prefect executed by Commodus, but not the military jurists of the two generations following, Arrius Menander and Aemilius Macer, both of whom, as well as Paternus, are cited in the *Digest.*

Apart from Vegetius the only extant specific treatise of importance is the incomplete work ascribed to Hyginus, the *de munitionibus castrorum*, a handbook of castrametation devised on a basis more theoretical than practical.[58] Its date is disputed and has been assigned to various periods, ranging from the age of Trajan to the beginning of the third century.

The juridical sources are more important. Though the *Digest* is a compilation of the time of Justinian, many of its citations are from the period of the Principate, and three of the jurists cited, Tarruntenus Paternus, Arrius Menander and Aemilius Macer, wrote specifically on military law. Paternus indeed wrote two books *de re militari* and was for Vegetius a main source.[59]

Moreover, not only do the legal Codes, and especially the *Codex Theodosianus*, contain many details that may safely be attributed to the early Empire, but their indirect evidence is often invaluable. For example, the establishment of a new standard for the height of recruits in *Cod. Theod.* VII 13, 3 confirms the statement of Vegetius (I 5) that the regulations were formerly more severe.[60]

Of the historians, Polybius, Josephus and Arrian have perhaps the most direct information for the student of military training. Polybius's account of the military system of the second century BC is invaluable as a guide to the extent of the system's subsequent development, while Josephus, who, like Polybius, looked upon Roman practice with the eye of an outsider, is our best authority for the order of march in the first century AD.[61] Arrian is of special value for cavalry training: the second part of the *Tactica* gives useful information, and the *Expeditio contra Alanos* is directly concerned with the order of march of the cavalry. The greater part of the *Tactica*, however, merely repeats the conventional treatment of the Macedonian phalanx, which had for so long been the stock-in-trade of the Greek military writers.

In the generality of Roman historians, however, the technical side of warfare is either ignored or, as Cheesman pointed out, left to the technical writers.[62] Such details were felt to be destructive of the elevation at which literary authors aimed; a famous example is the roundabout way in which Tacitus avoided calling a spade a spade.[63] From Herodian and Lucian we learn that a technical literature did exist: it is to be regretted that so little has survived. In spite of this deliberate avoidance of the straightforward it was inevitable, however, that a great number of details of military technique still remained in the accounts of even the conscious stylists such as Tacitus. The Roman historians are therefore often helpful despite their own artistic theories and personal inclinations.

The second main group of evidence is the epigraphical. The mass of epigraphic evidence is hardly capable of being summarized briefly, though there are two main types which are of especial interest, tombstones and the so-called *diplomata militaria*. To these we might add Trajan's Column and the Column of Marcus Aurelius which, though not strictly epigraphic, contain a large amount of material by way of illustration.[64] Tombstones often list the career of a person in whose honour the inscription has been made, and frequently give detailed information. Their chief disadvantage is that, if submitted to statistical treatment, they may give a distorted picture, either because they are essentially laudatory in their origin, or because the number of inscriptions recorded from any given area reflects also the influence of certain extraneous factors. These factors include the attitude of the inhabitants of the area to the erection of inscriptions, which itself, apart from sometimes being affected by a feeling of class-consciousness, is necessarily influenced by the availability of suitable stone in the neighbourhood and by the affluence of the region. Other important considerations are the subsequent history of the area and the re-use made of inscriptions in later buildings, quite apart from one other extremely variable factor, the comparative zeal of local archaeologists.

Not all inscriptions, however, are on stone. Bronze is best known from what are nowadays called *diplomata militaria*. (Their ancient title is not known.) These are small bronze tablets which record the privileges granted to a soldier on the completion of his service. They have been collected in *CIL* XVI and Supplement.[65] Building tiles and lead pipes yield their stamps, and sherds are a prolific source of receipts.[66] Waxed tablets were used mainly for wills, leases, sales, loans and birth certificates.

The third group of evidence is the papyrological. Under this general heading we should include parchment, though this material is rarely of importance in the military field, apart from a few examples from Dura-Europos.[67] The great majority of the papyri are in Greek, which, though widely used in the armies of the East, and often the mother-tongue of men in the Eastern legions, never displaced Latin as the official language of the army until after the fall of the Western Empire. The result of this bilingualism in the East is that such papyri as are in Latin are usually either literary, official or military, and even those which are civil appear to have been written in the Latin language merely in order to invest them with an air of authority. Cavenaile, in his recent and invaluable *Corpus Papyrorum Latinarum*,[68] lists a total of 345 Latin papyri (including ostraca, waxed tablets and parchments), of which about half have a military connection. Of these perhaps 68 are military documents, and therefore military by the strictest definition. Many others are of considerable indirect value, since they are concerned with soldiers in one way or another.

For Egypt itself the evidence has now been collected by Daris, who deserves the gratitude of all students of Roman military history for his *Documenti per la storia dell'esercito romano in Egitto*.[69] In this he prints a total of 108 documents (61 Greek, 41 Latin, 6 bilingual) which are all concerned with the Roman army in Egypt.

For the Empire as a whole it would hardly be feasible to put a definite number to the military documents so far discovered, since it is often a matter of personal opinion whether or not a particular piece of evidence is sufficiently military to justify inclusion. Nevertheless, a catalogue of 271 items (excluding military diplomas, for which the reader is referred to *CIL* XVI), will be found in an appendix (p. 232).

# CHAPTER II

# THE RECRUIT

## VOLUNTARY ENLISTMENT AND THE DILECTUS

Although recruitment to the Roman army was theoretically based upon conscription, there seems to have been little difficulty in normal times in maintaining the establishment by means of voluntary enlistment, especially in the western provinces.[70] The infrequency with which resort was made to the *dilectus* is remarkable. It may be argued that the establishment was deliberately fixed at too low a level, and that the number of legions and auxiliary regiments which had to be employed permanently in defence of the frontiers left little margin for emergencies, but the general effectiveness of Roman frontier policy during the first two centuries is evidence of the soundness of the system. The typical soldier was the volunteer. Further, although it was then and is now the essential duty and function of the serving soldier to engage the enemy in combat, during the Empire, as today, he was able to carry out this duty only under abnormal circumstances. The bulk of his military service was spent under conditions of peace. Any study of the life of the Roman soldier, therefore, should primarily be concerned with his experiences in time of peace.

We shall begin by considering a hypothetical volunteer, and tracing his career from the time that he first thinks of enlistment, through the various stages of his military career, to the day when if he survives he will receive his discharge.

1  Trajan's Column: battle scene of Roman soldiers fighting together with allied barbarians

2  Hunt's *pridianum*: the annual report of an auxiliary cohort (No. 157 in Appendix C)

3   Tile of *legio* XX, with boar emblem

4   Relief, standard with goat and Pegasus badge of *legio* II *Augusta*

5 Trajan's Column: firing of native dwellings

6 Trajan's Column: Roman auxiliary cavalry attacking mailed horsemen

## LETTERS OF RECOMMENDATION

If he is wise, he will first arm himself with a letter of introduction. This he will most easily obtain from his father or from one of his father's friends who has seen service in the type of unit which he desires to join. If no member of his family or circle has any close acquaintance with military connections, it will be much more difficult for him to obtain a letter of recommendation. This is one of the reasons why service in the Roman army tended to become more and more the privilege of a particular section of society. The letter of recommendation was not essential but it had considerable value, and this was true, as it is today, at all levels of society and in all walks of life. There are numerous examples in the letters of Cicero and Pliny: Pliny, in particular, was rarely reluctant to use his not inconsiderable influence in procuring appointments for his friends and acquaintances. One well-known instance is his securing a post as military tribune in Britain for the historian Suetonius. Suetonius decided that he did not want it, and actually requested that the appointment be transferred to a friend. Another example is his request to Falco for a similar post for a fellow-countryman of his from Cisalpine Gaul, a Cornelius Minicianus.[71] We may be sure that so eminently respectable a Roman gentleman as Pliny would not have made any such request had he thought it to be in any way improper or unconventional.

In the lower ranks of the army also, the use of testimonials and letters of introduction (*litterae commendaticiae*) was almost universal.[72] This we may gather from the general tone of a letter from a serving soldier to his father, a letter of the early second century in which the writer expresses in semi-literate Latin his dissatisfaction with service in the Alexandrian fleet, and a desire to transfer to an auxiliary cohort. 'I hope to live frugally, God willing, and be transferred to a cohort. But you can do nothing here without money, and it's no use having testimonials and references if you don't help yourself.'[73]

It is interesting to notice that this angry young man subsequently achieved a transfer, not to an auxiliary cohort, but to a legion, which represented a striking rise in status. His initial setback, which led to his having to join a unit towards which he felt no sense of *esprit de corps*, seems to have been due to an unsatisfactory report from one of his father's friends. How a satisfactory testimonial might read we may see from another second-century example.[74]

'To Julius Domitius, legionary tribune, from Aurelius Archelaus, his *beneficiarius*, greetings. I have even before recommended my friend Theon to you, and once again I beg you, Sir, to consider him in your eyes as myself. For he's just the sort of fellow you like. He's left his family, his property and his business and followed me, and in every way he's kept me free from worry. And so I beg you to let him see you, and he can tell you everything about our business. . . . Hold this letter before your eyes, Sir, and imagine that I'm talking with you. Goodbye.'

This letter was written in Latin, as such letters usually were, even when, as in this instance, the writer's command of the language was by no means perfect. Since Latin was the military language, the use of it was no doubt felt to give a letter an air of authority and officialdom. Another example of this type of letter is the following third-century one which aims at a rather higher standard of Latinity.[75]

'Priscus to Petronius, his father, greetings. I recommend to you a worthy man, Carus, *duplicarius*, son of Aper, *duplicarius*. If he needs your assistance in any way, I beg you to honour me by helping him in so far as you feel proper. I pray that you are in good health. Give greetings to all our friends. All our friends give greetings to you. Goodbye.'

### PROBATIO

Armed, therefore, with his letter of introduction, the would-be recruit had then to present himself for his interview. The technical term for this was *probatio*, and it was held in most provinces on the authority of the governor. In the special circumstances of Egypt, from which senatorial commands were excluded, the *probatio* was held by order of the Prefect. The *probatio* concerned itself in the first place with establishing the precise legal status of the applicant. This was essential because the legions, the *auxilia* and the fleets required different qualifications for entrance, and it was therefore necessary to discover for which branch of the services each applicant was fitted and qualified.[76] The legal requirement for admission to the legions was the possession of full Roman citizenship, though exceptions were commonly made for the sons of serving soldiers. These were technically illegitimate, at least until the reign of Septimius Severus, and many of them were given the domicile *castris* and enrolled in the tribe *Pollia*.[77] For the *auxilia* the possession of free non-citizen (i.e. peregrine) status was sufficient outside Egypt. In Egypt the auxiliary recruit had to prove his membership of the Graeco-Egyptian class of society: the native Egyptian could be accepted only by the Misene fleet.[78] The *probatio* also included a medical examination: the physical standards required for this are not known for the period in question, though a standard for height is mentioned by Vegetius, which in view of the conservatism of the Roman military code may perhaps be applicable to the early Empire. It is clear from the context that in Vegetius's own day this standard had long been unenforceable.[79]

'I am aware that it has always been the practice for a standard height for recruits to be laid down, with the consequence that only those of six feet in height, or, at the least, five feet ten inches, used to be accepted for service in the cavalry or in the leading cohorts of legions. But in those days the numbers were greater, and more entered the armed services. For the Civil Service was not yet enticing away the flower of our youth. Accordingly, if need presses, take not so much account of stature as of physical strength.'

Since the Roman foot was approximately one-third of an inch less than the modern measure, Vegetius's figures require conversion. The two heights given, the desirable and the shortest acceptable, are for us about 5 feet 10 inches and almost exactly 5 feet 8 inches respectively. The lower standard of the fourth century is clearly attested in the Theodosian Code:[80]

'The same Emperors [Valentinian and Valens] to Magnus, Vicar of the City of Rome. The levy shall be made of men five feet seven inches in height by common measure. 27th April, AD 367' (i.e. just above 5 feet 5 inches in our measure).

The manpower shortage which made this lowering of the height standard inevitable is reflected in another enactment of the same day. Military service was by then clearly unpopular.[81]

'The same Emperors to Magnus, Vicar of the City of Rome. By the decree of the Emperor Constantine of blessed memory, Your Sincerity is not to permit those who seek to avoid active service by amputation of the fingers to be protected by mutilation of the hand, in so far as perpetrators of self-inflicted wounds may still be of service in some public capacity.'

This order was repeated, with more and more drastic penalties prescribed for self-inflicted wounds, in paragraphs 5 and 10 of the same title. The latter order, of the year 381, allows the provincial administrators to furnish two mutilated recruits in place of an uninjured one:[82]

'Whosoever by shameful amputation of a finger shall seek to avoid the bearing of arms shall not escape the service which he shuns, but shall be branded with a mark, and that man shall be forced to perform military service as a labour who has declined it as an honour. Furthermore, the provincial administrators, who as a result of the impudent actions of these persons often suffer from a scarcity of the recruits they have to furnish, shall have the irremovable option of supplying to the directions of Your Eminence two mutilated recruits in place of an uninjured one at the time when the levy is being held, when recruits begin to be generally called in.'

During the early Empire, when military service was more attractive, the incidence of self-inflicted wounds can surely not have been so high. There is a striking instance, however, from the very beginning of the Principate. Suetonius tells us that Augustus sold a Roman knight and his property at public auction, because he had cut off the thumbs of his two young sons to prevent them from becoming liable for military service.[83] This case, however, would appear to be exceptional, and the indications are rather that a higher standard of physical fitness could be, and usually was, demanded. There is one document which has been taken to represent rejection on medical grounds, or perhaps discharge after provisional acceptance.[84]

'Copy of a certificate of discharge, signed and dated in the 12th year of Tiberius Claudius Caesar Augustus Germanicus Imperator, on the 29th day of the month Pharmouthi [24 April AD 52].

'This man was discharged by Cn. Vergilius Capito, Prefect of Upper and Lower Egypt:

'Tryphon, son of Dionysius, weaver, with weak sight owing to a cataract. On the list of those from the metropolis of Oxyrhynchus.

'Examined at Alexandria.

'Examined at Alexandria.

'The examination was carried out at Alexandria.'

The editors of the document are no longer of the opinion that it refers to rejection from the army, and they prefer to regard it as referring to a discharge from public service of some kind. A genuine army discharge after a medical examination on enlistment must in any case have given rise to a somewhat similar document. Probably, however, such a document would have been written in Latin. This particular document was written in Greek, and was presumably intended for production before the civil authorities in Egypt, where Greek was the official language at lower civil service levels. The complexity of the bureaucracy in Roman Egypt is shown by the triple check which is recorded on the document.

Tryphon was a weaver, and as such he would not have found approval as a recruit from Vegetius, who provides us with a list of desirable and undesirable occupations:[85]

'We must next inquire what are the trades from which we should select recruits, and from which we should absolutely reject them. Fishermen, fowlers, confectioners, weavers, and all those who appear to have been engaged in occupations appropriate to the women's quarters, should not, in my opinion, be allowed near the barracks. Smiths, blacksmiths, wagon-makers, butchers and huntsmen, whether of stag or boar, are fitted for association with the services.'

That Vegetius was not wholly fanciful in formulating these ideas is proved by a rather similar pronouncement in the Theodosian Code:[86]

'The Emperors Gratian, Valentinian and Theodosius: An Edict to the Provincial Administrators. We decree that to the regiments of our most excellent soldiers there shall be given for service no man of the station of slave, no man brought from an inn or from employment in a house of ill fame, or from the class of cooks or bakers, or from that category which is debarred from military service by the ugliness of its occupation, nor shall men be dragged from houses of correction.'

### POSTING

Once he had passed his *probatio* the recruit would receive an advance of pay and be posted to a unit. He would probably travel in a small party of recruits: such a party is described in a letter from the Prefect of Egypt, C. Minicius Italus, to the commanding officer of the Third Cohort of Ituraeans in the year AD 103 :[87]

'Copy of letter.

'C. Minicius Italus to his dear Celsianus, greetings. Order the six recruits passed by me to be entered on the rolls of the cohort which you command with effect from the 19th February. Their names and marks of identification I have appended to this letter. Farewell, dearest brother.

'C. Veturius Gemellus, aged 21 years, no mark of identification,
'C. Longinus Priscus, aged 22 years, scar on the left eyebrow,
'C. Julius Maximus, aged 25 years, no mark of identification,
'[?] Lucius Secundus, aged 20 years, no mark of identification,
'C. Julius Saturninus, aged 23 years, scar on the left hand,
'M. Antonius Valens, aged 22 years, scar on the right forehead.

'Received on the 24th day of February in the 6th year of Our Emperor Trajan, delivered by Priscus, *singularis*.

'I, Avidius Arrianus, *cornicularius* of the Third Cohort of Ituraeans, have certified that the original is in the record-office of the cohort.'

There are several points worthy of note in this document. In the first place, the day on which the posting order was received,

24 February, was probably also the day on which the recruits reported to the unit, as it is likely that the posting order accompanied the men. But that was not the day on which the recruits were to be placed on the nominal roll; instead, they were to be listed with effect from 19 February, which was presumably the day of the *probatio*. This makes the legal position of the men between these dates interesting, and the *Digest* contains a citation from Ulpian which covers this very point.[88]

'A man may make a will by military law from the time that he has been entered on the rolls, but not before; in the same way, those who have not yet been entered on the rolls, even those who have been selected as recruits and are travelling at the public expense, are not yet soldiers; for they have to be entered on the rolls.'

When Pliny was in Bithynia he was involved in a case which concerned two men who had taken the military oath but had not yet been entered on the rolls, when they were discovered to be slaves and therefore ineligible for military service. Pliny deferred passing sentence till he had referred their case to the emperor. Trajan's reply was that whether they had been entered on the rolls or not was immaterial, for they ought to have given a true account of themselves on the day of their *probatio*. They were liable for trial on a capital charge. Trajan also made it clear that if the fault lay with the examining officer he was punishable.[89]

A further point of interest in the Prefect's letter lies in the details provided of the recruits. They are all described by their names, their ages in years only, and by their distinguishing marks, if any. The names consist of the *tria nomina* without filiation, tribe or origin, and it is probable that they are not citizens. This of course is what we should expect among auxiliary recruits at this date; by the middle of the second century the situation had changed and far more auxiliary recruits were already citizens. It is likely that at the time of the *probatio* some other document was drawn up which described the men in greater detail; the information contained in the letter need not be taken to be exhaustive, for it was intended only to enable the recipient to have a rapid check made of the recruits on their arrival.

Finally, the document as we have it is a copy, at the end of which the *cornicularius* certifies that the original is in the record-office of the cohort. For what purpose a certified copy was required is not clear.

## THE VIATICUM

Other documents mention the payment which recruits received upon joining. The payment was called the *viaticum*. The term originally meant 'travelling-money', but it very early came in practice to be the Roman equivalent of the 'Queen's shilling', though it was much more valuable. The amount is well-attested. Surprisingly, it is invariably the same figure, 75 *denarii* or three gold pieces (*aurei*). In the well-known letter which Apion, a recruit from Egypt to the fleet at Misenum, wrote to his father in Egypt, we have second-century evidence for the fleet: 'When I arrived at Misenum I received my *viaticum* from Caesar, three gold pieces.'[90] For the auxiliary cohorts we have the repeated mentions of the identical sum of 75 *denarii in viatico* in the long pay accounts of *P. Berlin* 6866, which refer to the late second century.[91] There is no definite evidence for the legions, but since it appears probable that the amount of each basic *stipendium* remained at 75 *denarii* at least until the time of Septimius Severus, it would be quite consistent with Roman traditionalism if the *viaticum* remained at the same amount of three gold pieces for all arms of the service.[92]

## THE MILITARY OATH

We have seen already that before soldiers were placed on the rolls they had taken the military oath. The oath, or *sacramentum*, had in Republican times been administered in two stages in order to save time: first came the *praeiuratio*, in which a selected man recited the complete oath, then the remainder in turn came forward and subscribed to the oath by repeating the words *idem in me* ('The same in my case').[93] It is probable that the same procedure continued to be followed under the Empire whenever circumstances warranted it.

7 Tombstone of a veteran of *legio* VI *Victrix*, with his wife, son and daughter

8 'The standard-bearer of York': L. Duccius Rufinus, *signifer* of *legio* IX *Hispana*

9 Dedication slab from Lanchester fort

IMP CAESAR · DIVI TRAIANI PARTHIC FI
NERVAE N EPOS TRAIANVS HADRIANVS
PONT · MAX · TRIB · POTEST · XVII · COS III
EQVITIB ET PEDITIB QVI MILITAVER IN
ET COH VI QVAE APPELLSILIAG R ET IN NO
FRONTONET IVLI BRITTONOO ET I BRITANN
ET I HISPAN ET I BATAVOROO ET I AELIA GAESAI
OO ET II B RITTON OO ET SVNT IN DACIA PO ROLIS
SVB FLAVIO ITALICO QVINE TVI CEN PLVRIBVS
VE STI PEND EMERITIS D IMISS HON MISSION
QVOR NOMINA SVB SCRIPTA SVNT IPSIS LIBER
POSTERISQ EORC IVITAT DEDIT ET CONVB INM

CVM VXORIBVS INN CHIVNT SSENT
CVM EST CIVIT IIS DATA AVTS IQVI CAELIB ES
SENT CVM IIS QVAS POST EAD VXISSENT DVM
TAXAT SINGVLIS INGVLAS AD VI NON IVL

Q FLAVIO TERTVLLO    Q IVNIO RVSTICO COS
COH I BRITANN ICATOO         CVI PRAE EST
TI CLAVDIVS              FORTIS CAPVA

            EXPEDITE

SEPT FNESTO  RVI F      CORNON

DESCRIPTVM ET RECOGNITVM EX TABVLA AE
NEA QVAE FIXA EST ROMAE IN MVRO POST
TEMPLVM · DIVI AVG · AD MINERVAM

10   Military diploma from Dacia showing British units

11 Roman helmet of silver, from Emesa, first century AD

12 Bronze helmet of standard first-century legionary pattern

13 Skillet or mess-tin from Broxtowe (Nottingham), stamped ALBANVS

At attestation the number of recruits may occasionally have been small enough to justify individual swearing-in, but the shortened version must have been used at the annual renewal of the oath. During the early first century, at least, this renewal took place on New Year's Day, though later the ceremony may have been transferred, either by Vespasian after his defeat of Vitellius, or by Domitian after the rebellion of Antonius Saturninus, to 3 January.[94]

The terms of the oath may be gathered from references in Dionysius of Halicarnassus, Servius, Vegetius, and Isidore of Seville.[95] In a passage from Dionysius which refers to the period of Cincinnatus the men swear 'to follow the consuls to whatever wars they may be called, and neither desert the colours nor do anything else contrary to the law.' This is elaborated in his next book: 'For the military oath, which the Romans keep beyond all others, orders those who are about to serve to follow their generals wherever they may lead them, and the law has given commanders the power to put to death without trial those who disobey or desert the colours.' Servius's versions, which are late, but seem to be based on an earlier source, are 'that they would not leave except by command of the consul after they had served their time' and that they severally swore that they would act on behalf of the Republic, and that they would not leave until after they had served their time. Isidore's account closely agrees with that of Servius, though this may mean no more than the use of a common source. Vegetius's version of the oath is that of his own day, and shows how the Christianized *sacramentum* incorporated elements of the earlier practice.

'They swear by God, by Christ, and by the Holy Spirit; and by the Majesty of the Emperor, which, next to God, should be loved and worshipped by the human race. . . . The soldiers swear to perform with enthusiasm whatever the Emperor commands, never to desert, and not to shrink from death on behalf of the Roman state.'

If due allowance is made for the differences of date, which extend from the early Republic to the late Empire, these versions still show a similarity which is not altogether unexpected in view of the marked conservatism of Roman religious ritual.

Some historians add details. Livy, writing about the period immediately before Cannae, explains that this was the time when what had been a voluntary agreement became a formal one demanded by the tribunes.

'After completion of the levy, the consuls waited for a few days until the men from the allies and the Latins should arrive. Then, a thing which had never been done before, the soldiers were sworn in by the tribunes. For up to that time there had been no oath other than that they would assemble at the summons of the consul and not depart without permission; and whenever they met to form decuries or centuries, the cavalry in their decuries and the infantry in their centuries used to swear of their own free will that they would not run away in flight or out of fear, and that they would not leave their ranks except to pick up their weapons or to look for them, and to attack an enemy or defend a citizen. This now was changed from being a voluntary agreement between themselves to a formal oath made before the tribunes.'[96]

Polybius and Cincius Alimentus mention a further oath concerned with the maintenance of camp discipline. Polybius describes this merely as an undertaking to steal nothing from the camp, but Cincius includes also the surrounding country up to ten miles distant, and adds by implication licence to loot articles of up to the value of a *denarius* each day.[97] The looting of certain other articles on a specified list appears also to be permitted.

### THE MILITARY MARK

These oaths may be taken as peculiar to the Republic. In the late Empire there were peculiarities of other kinds. In Vegetius's day the recruit, before his name was finally entered on the rolls, was impressed with the military mark.[98] This sign, whether produced by branding or by tattooing, was intended to make desertion more difficult, and is itself an indication of the changed social conditions of the fourth century. In earlier days branding would have been considered an affront to the dignity of the soldier. The practice, however, must have proved to be of some use in the fourth century, for in AD 398 branding was made necessary

for the *fabricenses*, the workers in the Imperial armament fac-
tories.[99]

'Brands, that is, the national mark, shall be imprinted upon the
arms of the armament-workers, in imitation of the branding of
recruits, so that in this way at least deserters may be recognized.'

### DEPOSITED MONIES

To return now to our recruit, who has sworn the military oath,
received his *viaticum*, and has departed for his unit in a party under
the charge of a draft-conducting officer. An interesting papyrus
of AD 117 shows what happened when such a party was escorted.
The recruits handed over money to the draft-conducting officer
for him to take charge of it. This document contains the receipts
issued by the standard-bearers (*signiferi*) of the six centuries of the
First Cohort of Lusitanians to the centurion Tituleius Longinus.
They are all receipts for the deposited monies of recruits newly
arrived from Asia. (It should be sufficient to give the text of the
first and last receipts only: the others are similar.)[100]

'Longinus Longus, *signifer* of the *cohors I Lusitanorum*, of the
century of Tituleius, to his centurion Tituleius Longinus, greetings. I have received from you 423 *denarii* and 20 obols as
the deposited monies of 20 recruits from Asia assigned to the
century. In the 21st year of Our Lord Trajan, the Noble Caesar,
Thoth 6. [3 September 117]. . . . Quintus Herennius, *signifer* of the
*cohors I Lusitanorum* of the century of Longinus, to the centurion
Tituleius Longinus of the same cohort, greetings. I have received
from you 192 *denarii* 23 obols as the deposited monies of 23
recruits from Asia assigned to the century. In the 21st year of
Our Lord the Emperor Caesar Nerva Traianus, the Noble
Caesar, Thoth 6.'

The editors of the documents believe the receipts to be listed
in order of seniority by centuries. This is clearly correct. It
follows that the centurion Tituleius Longinus, who also appears
as the centurion of the first cohort, should properly be entitled
*centurio princeps*, or chief centurion of the cohort. It would be to
him in this capacity that the men's deposited monies, perhaps the

unspent portion of their *viatica*, were handed over by the draft-conducting officer.[101] Alternatively, the *centurio princeps* may have served as draft-conducting officer himself. Someone at any rate must have been in charge of the men, for a party of 126 must have been under some sort of command on their journey from Asia to Egypt. The *centurio princeps* would then see to the distribution of the money between the various centuries, and exact receipts from the respective *signiferi*. The *signiferi* were in charge of the regimental savings-banks, and the *signifer* of each century was responsible for the company chest.

## LITERACY AND NUMERACY

The *signiferi*, therefore, had to have a reasonable proficiency in writing and arithmetic. In these receipts, which are in Greek, it is perhaps significant that the spelling of Q. Herennius, *signifer* of the least senior century, is markedly inferior to that of Longinus Longus, *signifer* of the leading century. The Roman insistence on correct records meant that the question of literacy and numeracy had an importance in the Roman army which it rarely held in the armies of medieval times. Vegetius, indeed, writing in an age of collapse when illiteracy had become much more common but was as yet by no means universal, urged the deliberate recruitment of skilled clerks.[102]

'A number of offices on the establishment of the legions require men of good education: examiners of recruits, therefore, should not confine themselves to testing height, physical capacity, and mental alertness, but should in certain cases take into account skill in writing and experience in arithmetic and bookkeeping. For the entire state of the legion, details of duties, parade states, and pay, is entered daily in the *acta*, with almost as much care as the records of the revenue or other civil authorities are entered in the ledgers.'

## NOMINAL ROLLS

Once the recruits had reported to their units and been posted to centuries, their names would then be entered on the nominal rolls of the unit. These rolls were in the fourth century called *matriculae*, though this term is not attested earlier, and it would appear from the letter of Minicius Italus and other sources that in the early Empire the technical term was *numeri*.[103] If so, it was not surprising that the increasing employment of this same word in other military connections should have made a more specific term desirable. The details recorded, though not necessarily in the same document, would include the date of enlistment, the name of the officer responsible for the *probatio*, the recruit's origin and his father's name, his age, his marks of identification, and, as we learn from a Dura papyrus of AD 239, his height.[104]

'The two recruits whose names . . . and heights I have ordered to be appended . . . approved . . . in the Twentieth Palmyrene Cohort, Gordian's Own.'

# CHAPTER III

# THE SOLDIER

## BASIC TRAINING

At this stage, as Ulpian tells us, our recruit becomes a soldier. Now he begins his course of basic training. For the details of training Vegetius is our best guide. His first book is largely concerned with training methods, and a good deal of this material appears to be derived from as far back as Cato the Elder, though Vegetius probably took most of it from Cornelius Celsus, the encyclopaedist.[105]

### Marching

First comes marching: 'At the beginning of their training the recruits must be taught the military pace. For there is no point which must be watched more carefully on the march or in the field than the preservation of their marching ranks by all the men. This can only be achieved if by continuous practice they learn to march quickly and in time. For an army that is split and dis-arranged by stragglers is always in most serious danger from the enemy. Therefore, in the summer months, a march of twenty Roman miles must be completed in five hours at the military pace. When the full pace, which is more rapid, is employed, a distance of twenty-four Roman miles must be completed in the same period. Any further acceleration involves running, distances for which cannot be laid down.'[106]

It will be noticed that no mention is made by Vegetius of halts on the march. It is hard to believe that a route march of five hours during initial training would be made without a halt of any sort, and we must assume that such halts were in fact made. It is probable that the five hours are exclusive of halts; at any rate the

marching speed, if due allowance is made for the greater length of
the Roman hour in summer and the shorter distance of the Roman
mile, is at the military pace very similar to that which is normally
adopted in the British army, where three miles are covered in the
hour, with one halt of ten minutes included.[107]

## Physical training
Physical training also had its place among the exercises of basic
training. Vegetius mentions running, jumping (both the long
jump and the high jump), swimming, and carrying heavy packs.
The last item at least could hardly be begun before a certain
proficiency had been attained in marching without arms and
equipment. It may safely be concluded that all the exercises in this
category were practised first without arms and equipment, and
then, as the recruit became more proficient and accustomed to
using and carrying his weapons, the exercises were made progressively more difficult, until any exercise could be carried out
satisfactorily in full marching order.[108]

## Swimming
Swimming was to be practised during the summer months only.
'Every recruit without exception should practise swimming
during the summer months.'[109] 'If their quarters are near the sea
or a river, they must all be made to swim during the summer.'[110]
It seems that proficiency in swimming was regarded as desirable
rather than essential; certainly such notable achievements in
water as are recorded seem to have been performed largely by
auxiliaries, especially Batavians.[111]

## Weapon training
Our recruit next proceeded to weapon training, initially without
the service weapons. The exercises described by Vegetius illustrate
the thoroughness with which weapon training was carried out.[112]
    'The ancients (as we find in their writings) trained their recruits
in this manner. They made round wickerwork shields, twice as
heavy as those of service weight, and gave their recruits wooden
staves instead of swords, and these again were of double weight.

With these they were made to practise at the stakes both morning and afternoon. The employment of stakes is of the greatest benefit both to soldiers and to gladiators. No man has ever distinguished himself as invincible in armed combat, either in the arena or in the Campus, who was not carefully trained and instructed at the stakes.'

The mention of gladiators is interesting in this connection. We know from Valerius Maximus that Rutilius in 105 BC introduced the methods of the gladiatorial schools into military training, and from the author of the fourth book of the *Stratege-mata* that Marius was so impressed by the troops trained by Rutilius that he preferred them to his own.[113]

Valerius Maximus II 3, 2: 'The drill for weapon training was introduced to the soldiers by the consul P. Rutilius, colleague of Cn. Mallius. For he did not follow the precedent of any commander before him, but instead he summoned the trainers of gladiators from the school of C. Aurelius Scaurus and created in the legions a more sophisticated system of avoiding and delivering blows. He united courage with craft and craft with courage: craft was made bolder by the vehemence of courage, courage more circumspect by the awareness of craft.'

Frontinus, *Strategemata* IV 2, 2: 'C. Marius had the opportunity of selecting his army out of two already in existence, the army which had served under Rutilius and the one which had been under Metellus and which had subsequently been commanded by Marius himself. He chose the army of Rutilius even though it was the smaller, because he thought it was the better trained.'

The innovation of introducing gladiatorial methods of training can hardly have pleased the diehards, and the conservative opposition to it seems still to have been in evidence as late as the time of the younger Pliny, for in the *Panegyric* he commends Trajan for taking an interest in weapon training himself, instead of leaving it to a professional instructor.[114] Similarly Fronto, who disliked Hadrian intensely, deliberately misrepresented his training policy and criticized the army in the East for playing games with toy weapons instead of with real swords and shields.[115]

Vegetius continues: 'A stake was planted in the ground by each recruit, in such a manner that it projected six feet in height and could not sway. Against this stake the recruit practised with his wickerwork shield and wooden stave, just as if he were fighting a real enemy. Sometimes he aimed as against the head or the face, sometimes he threatened from the flanks, sometimes he endeavoured to strike down the knees and the legs. He gave ground, he attacked, he assaulted, and he assailed the stake with all the skill and energy required in actual fighting, just as if it were a real enemy; and in this exercise care was taken to see that the recruit did not rush forward so rashly to inflict a wound as to lay himself open to a counterstroke from any quarter. Furthermore, they learned to strike, not with the edge, but with the point. For those who strike with the edge have not only been beaten by the Romans quite easily, but they have even been laughed at.'[116]

When the recruit had attained a proper proficiency with these make-believe weapons he would begin training with the normal arms. This formal training culminated in individual combat, each recruit being assigned another as adversary. This more advanced stage of training had a name, *armatura*, which itself was borrowed from the gladiatorial schools.

Vegetius writes: 'The recruit should be instructed in that system of arms drill which is called *armatura* and is carried on by drillmasters. It is still partly kept up. For it is clear that even today those trained in the *armatura* are superior to the rest in all encounters. From this it should be realized how much better a trained soldier is than an untrained one. Those who have any experience of the *armatura* at all outstrip the remainder of their comrades in the art of fighting. With our ancestors so strict was the attention paid to training, that weapon training instructors received double rations, and soldiers who had failed to reach an adequate standard in those exercises were compelled to receive their rations in barley instead of in wheat. The wheat ration was not restored to them until they had demonstrated by practical tests, in the presence of the *praefectus legionis*, the tribunes or the senior officers, that they were proficient in every branch of their military studies.'[117] For these more advanced contests it appears likely that a special type of practice weapon was employed: a wooden sword of service weight tipped with a leather button.[118] The object of the button, of course, was to prevent the infliction of too serious injuries while ensuring as life-like a contest as possible.

By this time the recruit has completed his initial training with the sword; he has now to master the arm of next importance, the *pilum*. The same method of instruction was employed as before; practice *pila* of greater weight than service *pila* were used, and the same six-foot stakes served as targets. The purpose of the extra weight was to strengthen the arm. Vegetius lays great stress on this: 'For by this exercise the arms are strengthened and skill and experience in hurling missiles is acquired.' The advice is repeated in his second book: 'Let them also practise hurling their missile weapons at the stakes from a distance, in order to improve their marksmanship and to strengthen their right arms.'[119]

The *pilum* underwent a great deal of modification in the course of time.[120] The earliest description of the forms of the *pilum* is that given by Polybius of the *pila* of his own day (VI 23, 8): 'As well as these arms they have two *pila*, a bronze helmet and greaves. Some of the *pila* are stout, the others are slender. Of the more solid *pila*, the cylindrical ones are a palm square in cross-section. The slender *pila* resemble hunting-spears of commensurate size, and these they carry together with the others mentioned. In all these *pila* the length of the wooden haft is about three cubits, and to each there is fitted a barbed iron head of the same length as the haft. They make certain of its firm attachment to the haft and of its usefulness by fastening it into the wooden haft up to the middle point and bolting it with a number of rivets. The result is that the iron breaks before the fastening is loosened in use, even though at the bottom where the iron joins the wooden haft it is a finger and a half in width. Such is the care with which they make the fastening.'

This description of the 'heavy' *pilum* would appear to be incomplete, for, as has been shown,[121] a *pilum* with a shaft three cubits long and four fingers wide, and fitted with an iron head of equal length and a finger and a half wide where it fits into the

shaft, would have a probable weight of almost nineteen pounds.
This would be far too heavy to throw any reasonable distance.
Presumably, what Polybius has failed to mention is that the *pilum*
was thinner except where the head was fitted into the shaft. In
any case it is the lighter *pilum* which developed into the weapon of
the Empire, and which is important historically.

The chief disadvantage of the Polybian *pilum* was that the very
firm attachment of the blade to the shaft meant that even when the
blade was broken it was still not separated from the shaft. It was
possible, therefore, for a *pilum* which had missed its mark or
lodged in a shield to be re-used against its possessor. Marius was
responsible for a modification which was intended to correct this
fault.[122] By his day the rivets which held the head to the shaft
had been reduced to two in number. One of these he left un-
touched, but for the other he substituted a wooden pin. His idea
was that on impact the wooden pin would break and the iron
rivet bend, a combination of circumstances which would make a
*pilum* extremely difficult to extract from a shield that it pierced.
Ingenious though this was, apparently the modification failed to
work, and it was left to Caesar to make the necessary correction.[123] Instead of having the whole of the blade tempered,
the tempering was confined to the point. This ensured that the
neck where the blade was fastened to the shaft remained quite soft
and liable to bend. Henceforward, not only did the *pilum* become
useless on impact, but, as Caesar says, it made the shield to which
it remained fixed so unmanageable that it was often necessary to
abandon it. This model of *pilum* remained substantially unchanged
until towards the close of the second century AD, a striking testimony to its efficiency.

After the satisfactory completion of the exercise with the
practice *pila*, the soldier—by this time he could hardly be called
the recruit—began the next stage of training with the actual
service weapons. The procedure adopted was similar to that with
the sword. First came individual practice at the stakes, and then
mock fights were arranged between soldiers matched in pairs.
Here again, at the more advanced stage life-like contests were
made possible by the employment of *pila* tipped with a leather

button. These special weapons were known as *pila praepilata*.[124]

The sword and the *pilum* were the main legionary weapons. In the case of the auxiliaries these weapons were generally replaced by the *spatha*, or long broadsword, and the *hasta*, or thrusting spear, respectively.[125] Certain formations, of course, had their own special arms; the *cohortes sagittariorum*, for instance, as their name implies, were armed principally with the bow.[126] Slingers, however, do not appear to have been brigaded together under the Empire, although under the Republic slingers from the Balearic Islands had regularly been employed in their own units.[127] On the contrary, it appears from Hadrian's *adlocutio*, or parade-ground address to the army in Africa, that slinging formed part of the general training of all the auxiliary forces.[128] The legionaries too had their training with the sling as well as with the bow, as Vegetius tells us:[129]

'About a third, or perhaps a quarter, of the young soldiers, that is, those who are found to be the more suitable, should always be trained at these very same stakes with wooden bows and practice arrows. Skilled instructors must be chosen for this task, and even more adroitness must be employed to ensure that they hold the bow in the correct manner, bend it firmly, keep the left hand steady, draw back the right hand carefully, and keep the eye and the attention both upon the mark, so that they are taught to shoot straight both on foot and from horseback. This skill needs to be learned carefully, and to be kept up by daily practice and exercise.'

In a passage in the second book, Vegetius goes into greater detail:[130] 'The archers and the slingers used to set out *scopae*,[131] that is, bundles of twigs or straw, as targets; the consequence was that they used to hit their targets more frequently with their arrows, or at least with the stones they fired from their slings, even though the targets were six hundred feet away. Furthermore, they were in the habit of carrying out on the field without panic what they had invariably done on the exercise ground in practice. They had also to become used to whirling the sling only once about the head in firing the stone. Every soldier, however, used to practise throwing stones of up to a pound in weight by hand alone as well; since throwing by hand does not call for a sling, it is considered a readier method. They were also required to fire their missile weapons or their loaded javelins[132] in continual and constant practice; so much so that in wintertime they built riding schools for the cavalry and drill halls for the infantry, roofed with tiles or shingles, or if these were not attainable, with reeds, rushes or thatch.[133] In these in bad weather, or when there was too much wind, the army had arms drill under cover. But even in winter, if the snow or the rain had stopped, they were compelled to drill on the barrack square, in case the relaxation of discipline might weaken both their morale and their physical constitution.'

It is noticeable that Vegetius speaks only of stones in connection with slings, whereas the employment of leaden *glandes* is well attested for the Republic.[134] The reason for the comparative disappearance of these during the Empire is perhaps to be found in the de-specialization of the slingers. When they had been specialists, brigaded together in their own units, they had taken greater pride in their craft and materials, but in later days the 'amateur' legionary slingers tended to look down upon the sling as a barbarian weapon.

### Combining the skills

So far the soldier has gone through these stages of basic training— marching without arms, physical training, arms drill and weapon training. The next stage is to combine the skills already acquired. This is brought out clearly in one special form of physical training, vaulting on horseback. According to Vegetius this was practised not only as an essential preliminary exercise for the cavalry, but also as part of the general physical training of the infantry.[135]

'Not the recruits alone, but the trained soldiers as well were made to have constant practice in vaulting on horseback. This is a custom which has come down even to our own time, though now we have grown careless about it. Wooden horses were erected, under cover in winter and on the barrack square in summer; over these the young soldiers were made to vault, without arms at first, until they became proficient through practice, and eventually in full armour. Such attention was paid to this exercise that they learned both to mount and to dismount not only from the right, but also from the left, even with their swords unsheathed or grasping their lances.'

In this single exercise we may recognize the broad principles of training; the teaching first of the basic skill, then the variations of it, and finally its application in combination with skills already learned. The next step was to repeat the process on actual live horses. This further development was of course necessary for all prospective recruits to the cavalry, but whether it was carried out in the case of infantry recruits as well, would appear to be doubtful.[136] There always had to be, of course, a fair proportion of legionary soldiers with the ability to ride, simply in order to maintain the establishment of the legionary cavalry,[137] and presumably those legionary recruits who showed any marked aptitude at the exercises with the wooden horses were given the additional cavalry training appropriate.

### FIELD-SERVICE TRAINING

The soldier, his basic training now completed, would be ready for field-service training, which began with a route march in full marching order. Not for nothing were the Roman soldiers nicknamed 'Marius's mules' (*muli Mariani*).[138] Perhaps not until the First World War had such a weight of arms, equipment and rations had to be carried by the man on the march. But we must beware of exaggerating the amount. If he really had to carry the enormous loads which some German scholars have attributed to him, the Roman soldier might well have become a proficient porter, but there is little else that he would have had the will or the energy to do. Franz Stolle reckoned the total weight of the man's burden in full service marching order at the curiously precise figure of 41.259 kg. (=93.245 lb), assuming the minimum weight likely for each single article of the load.[139] Since it is in the highest degree unlikely that every item would weigh the least possible, this total would have to be increased by anything from ten to twenty per cent, and we should then have the soldier marching around with well over a hundredweight on his back. The absurdity of this as a regular occurrence does not bear thinking about. Around 66 lb (= 30 kg.) is generally considered to be the upper limit in modern armies.[140]

When we examine the basis for Stolle's figures, we find that the arms and equipment are items which must stand, since they are all amply attested, but to these he has added the weight of rations for seventeen days, depending essentially on evidence from Cicero, the Augustan History, and Ammianus Marcellinus.[141] Not one of these authorities provides evidence which is conclusive for our period by itself, though admittedly they gain weight in combination. Cicero is imprecise, and speaks of 'rations for more than half a month'. In any case he is evidence only for the Republic. The writer of the life of Severus Alexander in the *Augustan History* merely states that during the emperor's campaigns the soldiers were provided with supplies at each resting-place, and did not have to carry rations for seventeen days 'as they usually have to do', except in hostile country. Even in those areas he lightened their loads by making use of mules and camels. It is clear that all this is better evidence for the practice of the writer's own day, whenever that may have been, than for what actually happened in the lifetime of Severus Alexander, whose own practice is admitted to be different, or in the third century in general.[142] Ammianus alone provides good evidence: he speaks of 'the rations for seventeen days which a soldier going on a campaign carried on his back.' This, of course, is reasonably conclusive for the fourth century, though the past tense may be of some significance. There are no real grounds for assuming that the same practice was normal in the early Empire. It is a striking fact that Josephus, our only surviving first-hand authority on this question, is in direct conflict with Ammianus. In his *Jewish War* Josephus writes of the Roman soldier on the march: 'The picked infantry who form the general's bodyguard carry a lance (*lancea*)[143] and a round shield (*clipeus*), as well as a saw and a basket, a bucket and an axe, together with a leather strap, a sickle and chain, and rations for three days, so that an infantryman is little different from a beast of burden.[144] It was obviously not the intention of

Josephus to make the burden that the soldier carried appear to be lighter than it actually was, and if the soldier had had to carry rations for seventeen days, Josephus would certainly have said so. The evidence of Josephus must surely prevail for his own day, and probably for the early Empire in general.

Georg Veith made a brave attempt to reconcile the contradictions among the ancient authorities; he tried to show that the seventeen days' ration was a seventeen days' ration of hard tack (*buccellatum*), which was normally only a supplement to the corn ration (*frumentum*); by using it as an iron ration, however, a man with no corn could live on it for three days.[145] *Frumentum*, unground corn, was the staple diet, and, according to Veith, was at all times carried in the baggage train. The weight of *buccellatum* for seventeen days Veith estimated at about 3 kg., which is more than 11 kg. less than Stolle's figure for rations, 14.369 kg. By this means he managed to reduce the total weight of the man's burden to about 30 kg., or about 66 lb.

Veith's explanation depends upon there being a clear distinction between *frumentum*, the corn ration, and *cibaria*, rations in general. This distinction he discovered in a passage in which Caesar rewarded a cohort by presenting the men with double pay, corn (*frumentum*), clothing, rations (*cibaria*), and military decorations.[146] *Cibaria*, however, though the term employed by Cicero and the writer of the life of Severus Alexander, was not the word used by Ammianus Marcellinus, whose expression was *annona*, the normal fourth-century word.

At this stage it is worthwhile considering another passage of Caesar, this time from the first book of the *Civil War*: 'Afranius's men were hard pressed for food and had difficulty in finding water. The legionaries did have a fair amount of *frumentum*, for they had been ordered to carry a twenty-two days' supply from Ilerda, but the light-armed troops and the auxiliaries had none, for they had little opportunity of acquiring *frumentum*, and physically they were unsuited to carrying heavy loads.'[147] The numeral XXII has been doubted and a wide variety of emendations proposed, principally upon the ground that the weight of a twenty-two days' ration of *frumentum* would be an impossibly heavy burden. It is clear from the context, however, that the load was realized to be heavy, that it was not replenished and was steadily diminishing, and that the legionaries, but not the other troops, were expected to be able to carry heavy loads. The numeral must surely have been included for the very reason that the load was felt to be abnormally large: for that reason XVII is a most unlikely emendation, since that is one of the numbers that might normally have been expected, and the other figures suggested are all far too small to suit the context. There seems, therefore, to be no adequate reason to doubt the authenticity of the received reading.

If we are willing to abandon the idea that one particular number, either three or seventeen, was as fixed and immutable as the laws of the Medes and Persians, we can agree with those who, like Rice Holmes, thought of the three days' ration as the usual one to carry and the seventeen days' ration as an emergency measure.[148] The circumstances under which this would have to be carried are clearly stated by Ammianus: troops setting out on a campaign into hostile territory would not be in the same secure position as those marching through a friendly province.

Veith, however, would appear to have been on the right lines in suggesting that the seventeen days' ration was divided into two parcels. If we take this to mean that three days of the ration was an iron ration and was always carried on the man, but not necessarily in hard tack, and that the rest was normally carried in the baggage train, we shall have stated a rule that would cover most contingencies, but not every emergency. The upshot of this is that the weight of a man's burden on the march could not be fixed by regulations for all occasions, but it could within limits be varied to suit particular circumstances.

This lack of precision finds its counterpart and justification in Vegetius;[149] 'The young soldiers must be given frequent practice in carrying loads of up to sixty pounds, and marching along at the military pace, for on strenuous campaigns they will be faced with the necessity of carrying their rations as well as their arms. Let this not be thought difficult, if practice is given; for there is nothing which constant practice does not make easy.'

From the context it is clear that the loads to be carried are in addition to normal arms and equipment, and from this it follows that sixty Roman pounds, or just over three stones avoirdupois, represented the upper limit of the weight of rations.[150] Not all training marches, we may be sure, would be carried out under so heavy a load, and possibly only an occasional one in the later stages of training. In service conditions this weight of rations must have been decidedly uncommon.

One further point may be made in this connection. If Vegetius's sixty pounds represented the weight of seventeen days' rations, we should have to conclude that Stolle seriously underestimated the weight of the daily ration. His figure for seventeen days was just over fourteen kilos, whereas sixty Roman pounds come to just under twenty kilos. If, however, Stolle was right in his estimate (and in this the figures given by Polybius provide him with powerful support), sixty Roman pounds would account for rations for about twenty-three days.[151] If we allow for the variations due to humidity and other circumstances, it seems likely, therefore, that the twenty-two days' ration recorded by Caesar was simply the maximum weight permitted by regulations, a maximum which normally was rarely reached.

With route marches we mark the beginning of field training. The first essential was to have practice in camp construction. Since it was the Roman custom to build a temporary camp at the end of each day on the march, it was necessary to have a regular drill for camp construction. Hyginus's handbook contains the ancient theory of castrametation, but it was, of course, intended for the specialist.[152] Of more immediate benefit for our purpose are the remarks of Vegetius upon this subject, in which he tries to convince his readers of the advantages of this long neglected exercise.[153]

'The recruit should also be instructed in the construction of the camp. For nothing else is found to be so useful, so necessary in time of war. If a camp is properly built, the men spend their days and nights safe and sound inside the rampart, even if the enemy is besieging them. It is as though they carried around with them a fortified city wherever they go. But this science has been completely lost, for it is a long time now since anyone has built a camp by digging ditches and fixing palisades. The result has been, as we know, that when they have been attacked by the barbarians' cavalry, whether by day or night, many of our armies have suffered heavy losses.'

It is remarkable how thoroughly Vegetius is here imbued with the Maginot-line mentality. His account of siege operations in his fourth book is equally vitiated by an obsession with defence. Whoever is going to besiege a city, it is not going to be the Romans.[154] In another passage Vegetius gives a fairly complete account of how to fortify a camp. Here he is presumably following his source reasonably closely, and the defensive element is at first less prominent. He so arranges the description, however, that in the end the greatest weight is thrown upon the defensive aspect.[155]

'There are three different ways of fortifying a camp. If too much danger is not pressing, turves are dug from the earth all round, and from them a kind of wall is built, three feet high above the ground, in such a way that there is the ditch in front from which the turves have been cut; and then an emergency ditch is dug, nine feet wide and seven feet deep. But if the enemy force is more threatening, then it is worthwhile to fortify the circuit of the camp with a full-scale ditch. This should be twelve feet wide and nine feet deep 'below the line'. This is the technical term. Above this, placing supports on both sides, with the spoil from the ditch they raise a mound four feet high. At this stage the defences are thirteen feet high and twelve feet wide. On top of this mound they fix the stakes of stout wood which the soldiers always carry with them. For this task of entrenchment it is desirable to have always at hand entrenching tools, shovels, wicker baskets and other kinds of equipment. It is easy to fortify a camp in the absence of the enemy. But if the enemy is pressing, then the whole of the cavalry and half of the infantry are drawn up in line to repel an attack, while behind them the remainder of the men fortify the camp by digging the ditches. A herald marks out the task of Number One century, of Number Two, of Number Three, etc. Afterwards the ditch is inspected by the centurions, and measured. Men whose work is found to have been too negligent are punished. The recruit, therefore, should be trained in this task, so that when the need arises he may be able to fortify the camp without panic, quickly and carefully.'

Such practice field-works formed part of the manœuvres of the army in Africa when the troops there were inspected by the emperor Hadrian.[156] The unit that performed before the emperor, however, preferred to demonstrate its skill by fortifying the camp with stone. Practice camps have been recognized in Britain at various sites, including Haltwhistle Common, Castle Collen, Cawthorn and Woden Law.[157] At Cawthorn the men under training, probably young legionaries from *legio IX Hispana* at York, practised not only entrenchment but also the construction of *ballista* platforms, and of low internal banks of turf, which were intended to shelter tents. Even more interestingly, they had practice in the construction of field ovens.

How severe field training could be we learn from Appian and Tacitus. Both describe the measures taken by an energetic commander and a keen disciplinarian to restore the morale of undisciplined troops. Appian is concerned with the action of Scipio Africanus the Younger against the Numantines in 134 BC.[158]

'On his arrival he drove out all the merchants, the camp-followers, the soothsayers and the fortune-tellers, for the soldiers had been demoralized by their lack of success and were continually resorting to these people. He ordered that in future nothing except what was essential should be brought in, not even a sacrificial animal for the purposes of divination. He also gave orders for the sale of all wagons, and all their unnecessary contents, and of all pack animals, apart from a few exceptions which he made himself. No one was to have any cooking equipment apart from a spit, a bronze cooking-pot, and a single drinking vessel. He had their food confined by regulation to plain boiled and roasted meats. He forbade them beds, and he himself set an example by sleeping on straw. He did not allow them to ride on mules when on the march. "For what can you expect in wartime", he said, "from men who cannot even walk?" He made them bathe and oil themselves by themselves, for, as he said in scorn, only mules, which had no hands, needed others to rub them down. In this way he quickly restored their morale, and made them respect and fear him, by being hard to approach and grudging with his favours, especially those favours which were against regulations. He often said that generals who were strict and conscientious about regulations were good for their own side, but generals who were easy-going and free with privileges were a great help to the other side. For these latter generals, he said, had followers who were contented but contemptuous, whereas the former had men who were sullen but obedient, and ready for any emergency.

'He did not, however, dare to open his campaign before he had made his men fit by hard training. He went over all the low-lying ground nearby, and every day he had one camp after another first fortified and then razed, deep trenches dug and then filled in, high walls built up and then pulled down, while he himself watched over the work from dawn till dusk. On route marches he always had his men march in block formations to prevent them from straggling as they had done before, and nobody was permitted to leave the position assigned to him. He used to go up and down the column of march, and often visit the rear. If any men were sick, he would have them mounted in place of the cavalrymen, if any loads were too heavy for the mules he had them shared out amongst the infantrymen. Whenever he pitched camp he made those who had formed the vanguard during the day take up position after the march around the circuit of the camp, and a different squadron ride round on patrol. The rest were assigned their duties; some dug the ditch, others built up the rampart, others pitched the tents. He had the time required for these tasks measured and determined.'

Tacitus tells how Corbulo overcame similar difficulties with Eastern troops in the winter of AD 57-8.[159] 'Corbulo's major task was to deal with the idleness of his own men; the treachery of the enemy was less of an obstacle. The legions transferred from Syria, demoralized by long years of peace, did not take kindly to the discipline of a Roman camp. It was common knowledge that there were old soldiers in his army who had never been on guard or on watch, who paid visits to the rampart and ditch to look upon remarkable novelties, who possessed neither helmets nor breastplates, but were smartly dressed businessmen who had done all their service in towns. So he discharged those who were too old or whose health was bad, and called for reinforcements. Recruiting took place throughout Galatia and Cappadocia, and a legion was sent from Germany with its complement of auxiliary cavalry and infantry.[160] The whole army was kept under canvas, though the winter was so hard that the ground was icebound and needed excavation before tents could be pitched. The cold was so severe that many suffered from frost-bite, and one or two men were frozen to death while on guard. A case was reported of a soldier who was carrying a bundle of logs; his hands were frozen so hard that they became fastened to his load and fell off from the stumps of his arms. Corbulo himself wore little and went about bareheaded. He was constantly with his men both on the march and at their duties, congratulating the hardworking and comforting the sick. He was an example to all. When the harshness of the climate and the service became too much for many and they deserted, he looked for the cure in severity. Indulgence was not shown to first offenders, or to second offenders either, as in other armies, but any man who deserted the colours paid for it at once with his life. Experience showed that this course of action was salutary, and better than sympathetic treatment, for there were fewer desertions than in those camps where mercy was shown.'

The recruits are now ready for training in battle formations, the single line, the double line, the square, the wedge and the circle. Vegetius devotes a chapter to describing the usefulness of these.[161]

'There is nothing which has proved to be of greater service in action than for the men to learn by constant practice to keep their allotted positions in the line, and nowhere to close or to open their ranks disadvantageously. Men packed closely together have no room for fighting and merely get in one another's way. Similarly, if they are too scattered and there is too much daylight between them they give the enemy an opportunity of breaking through. Inevitably, if the line is cut through and the enemy attacks the fighting troops from behind, there is immediate panic and universal disorder. So the recruits should always be taken out to the square and drawn up in line according to the order of the nominal roll in such a way that, in the beginning, they dress in a single straight line without any bends or curves, and with every man separated from his neighbour by an equal and correct distance. Next they must be commanded to form a double line in quick time, and in such a manner that they take their dressing from the file they cover. The third stage is to order them suddenly to form a square. After this the formation should be changed to a triangle. (This they call a "wedge".) The last arrangement has been found to be extremely useful in action. There is also an order to form circles: well-trained troops have steadied themselves in this formation after the line has been broken by the enemy's attack, and they have prevented a mass rout and a serious crisis. If the young soldiers perfect these movements by constant practice they will more easily keep their ranks in real fighting.'

It is now time for the recruit to join the trained soldiers. Vegetius closes his first book, apart from a final chapter on the necessity of discipline, with an account of the *ambulatura*, the formal peacetime exercise of the Roman army.[162] There is a striking similarity between the general tenor of this account of the *ambulatura* and part of Onasander's monograph on *The General*, which was written about the middle of the first century AD and dedicated, almost certainly, to the Quintus Veranius who died while governor of Britain in AD 59.[163] The similarities should not be pressed, however, for the general principles of training apply to almost every army, no matter how organized, and although Onasander makes a point of stressing that his work is addressed to Romans, in practice he usually has in mind the Macedonian phalanx, in the tradition of the Greek military writers.[164] There is no indication that Vegetius even knew of the work of Onasander, though he may indirectly have absorbed some of Onasander's ideas by way of Frontinus, who quite probably used this work.[165] Frontinus, however, does not appear to have been used by Vegetius except in his third and fourth books, and the present passage with its reference to the *constitutiones* of Augustus and Hadrian would seem to be based on Tarruntenus Paternus, with some contribution, either direct or indirect, from Cornelius Celsus, who in his turn had used Cato.[166]

'It is a long-standing custom, and one for which provision is made in the regulations of the emperors Augustus and Hadrian, that three times in a month both the cavalry and the infantry are marched out to the *ambulatura*. This is the technical term for this type of exercise. The infantry, carrying their weapons and in full service marching order, were commanded to march out ten miles and then march back to the camp, mainly at the military pace but for part of the way more rapidly. The cavalry too, divided into squadrons and equally fully armed, covered the same distance; but in line with their cavalry drill they were part of the time to practise the pursuit, at other times the withdrawal, and then to reform and return with vigour to the charge. It was not only on level ground, but in hilly and difficult country as well, that the two battle lines were made to charge up and down. This was to ensure. that no emergency or accident might come upon them in actual fighting, which they had not already experienced through their constant practice as well-trained soldiers.'[167]

### PEACE-TIME DUTIES

With the completion of this course of preliminary training, which was continually being revised in the *ambulatura*, the soldier would have more time to devote to normal peacetime duties. To a certain extent these would vary according to his station, but the greater bulk of them would be the same everywhere and at all times. How similar many of these duties were to those of soldiers of today we may see from such duty-rosters as have chanced to be preserved. The best known of these, a papyrus from Egypt in the form of a tabulated chart,[168] contains the names of thirty-six soldiers from the same century in one of the legions stationed in Egypt, either III *Cyrenaica* or XXII *Deiotariana*. The names are arranged one beneath the other in the left-hand column, with ten more columns across the page, each representing a different day. The papyrus is torn along the right, and probably extended originally over a longer period. The headings at the tops of the columns show that these refer to the first ten days of October—here named after the emperor Domitian[169]—in a year that is not named but which may be AD 87. The majority of the entries are abbreviated, but in most cases the meaning is clear. The duties include such details as *stationes*, or guards, at the main gate, at the headquarters building (*principia*), or on the rampart; acting as batman (*ornatus Heli, ad calceamenta*); fatigues, for example *ad stercus*, cleaning of the latrines, *ballio* or baths fatigue; and various other duties both inside the camp (e.g., *strigis* or lines patrol, *armamentario* or armoury duty), and outside, including the patrolling of the main road, the *Via Nicopolitana*. Some men left the camp for duties further afield, to the granaries at Neapolis, a suburb of Alexandria; others were temporarily posted to other centuries. A surprisingly small number apparently remained within the century, and were available for training and parades.

This interesting document appears to be itself an expansion of a further one on the same side of the papyrus, a summarized parade state which lists the number of men available for duty:[170]

'REMAINDER 40
   of these
   free from duty
keeper of weapons [1]
requisitions clerk (?) 1
wagon-repairer 1
tribune's orderly 1
housekeeper [1]
bookkeeper and clerk 2
   Curiatius
   Aurelius
supernumerary 1
   Domitius
on guard 1
   Domitius

. . . .
   T[otal 9]
Remainder 31'

The forty men remaining who are mentioned in the first line are apparently all the soldiers of the century who were available for duty after a previous list had deducted those who were absent and those who for other reasons were unavailable.[171] Forty men remaining may seem rather a low proportion out of an establishment of about eighty, but perhaps the century was well under strength.[172] Even out of these forty there are nine who already have assignments. The remaining thirty-one are therefore available for general duties. The duties actually allotted to them are presumably those of the first thirty-one names in the tabulated duty roster of the first ten days of October.[173] The remaining five names out of the thirty-six which this duty roster contained may be accounted for in this way. M. Julius Felix, the thirty-second on the list, did not become available for duty until 6 October, and was then made gate guard. He had previously been part of the escort of the centurion Serenus and therefore unavailable. The remaining four men, the thirty-third to the thirty-sixth, had no duties assigned them at all during the first ten days of October, and presumably did not become available until later.

# CHAPTER IV

# CONDITIONS OF SERVICE

### PROMOTION

The next step to which the trained soldier will direct his attention is promotion. Before, however, we consider what prospects were open to our hypothetical soldier, there is need of a word of warning. The Roman army did not, at the beginning of the Empire, have all the non-commissioned ranks which are listed by Domaszewski in the *Rangordnung*; these developed gradually in number and especially during the second and third centuries. Sander would go further and hold that throughout the first century all posts below the centurionate were in theory of equal rank, but that some appointments in practice were more honourable than others.[174] Such posts as *signifer*, he would maintain, carried with them not a military rank, but only a function, a *munus* of the *miles gregarius*, the common soldier. Thus when Caesar reports that he censured certain standard-bearers and removed them from their positions, the punishment is a loss of office, not a loss of rank.[175]

*Immunes*
This interpretation seems to involve a number of contradictions. According to it, even being what was later described as an *immunis* or soldier who enjoyed exemption from general duty (*vacatio munerum*), would from this point of view, be a duty (*munus*). Words thus become meaningless. It would be simpler to say that in the first century AD soldiers in the Roman Army fell broadly into two main categories, those who had their own special jobs and those who had not. This is not strictly speaking a division

75

between private soldiers and non-commissioned officers, at least if we are to take the pay-scales as a guide, for the majority appear to have been on the same basic scale, even some of those who could be classed as *immunes*.[176] The real distinction was between the men who were available for general duties and those who enjoyed exemption from general duties because they had a more specialized appointment, which may or may not have been considered to be a promotion. To the latter category belonged all the 'tradesman' classifications in addition to what we should consider the non-commissioned ranks. To be appointed *immunis*, exempt from general duty, was, however, held to be a privilege, and to have one's *vacatio munerum* removed, to lose one's exemption, was looked upon as a form of punishment.[177] Tarruntenus Paternus, the praetorian prefect under Commodus, and a well-known military jurist, whose writings have survived in part in the *Digest*, and who was one of Vegetius's sources, defines the *immunes*, and then illustrates his definition by listing a wide variety of such soldiers. His catalogue is clearly not intended to be exhaustive and shows few signs of definite arrangement, though it does have some internal cohesion. His list may be taken as typical of his own time, the later second century, and may not necessarily be true of an earlier period.[178]

*Digest* 50, 6, 7: 'Certain soldiers are granted by their conditions of service some exemption from the heavier fatigues. These are men such as surveyors, the medical sergeant, medical orderlies and dressers, ditchers, farriers, the architects, pilots, shipwrights, artillerymen, glassfitters, smiths, arrowsmiths, coppersmiths, helmet-makers, wagon-makers, roof-tile-makers, swordcutlers, water engineers, trumpet-makers, horn-makers, bow-makers, plumbers, blacksmiths, stonecutters, limeburners, woodcutters, and charcoal-burners. In the same category there are usually included butchers, huntsmen, keepers of sacrificial animals, the workshop sergeant, sick-bay attendants [?], clerks who can give instruction, granary clerks, clerks responsible for monies left on deposit, clerks responsible for monies left without heirs, orderly-room staffs, grooms, horse-trainers [?], armoury sergeants, the herald and the trumpeter. These are all then classed as *immunes*.'

After the middle of the second century, therefore, the *immunes* were a clear-cut category of men, who were distinguished from their fellow soldiers not by a difference of rank but simply by being unavailable for ordinary duties, since they had special tasks of their own. The situation earlier is confused, but it would be difficult to trace the *immunes* as a definite class back before the reign of Hadrian, and it seems probable that it was during his reign that the situation recorded by Paternus first became crystallized.[179] Yet although men do not appear to have called themselves *immunes* before that date, their individual appointments certainly existed earlier. Thus in a particular century in an Egyptian legion during the reign of Domitian, there were, as we have seen, a total of only forty men on the parade strength after those absent, sick or on leave, had been accounted for.[180] Of these forty no fewer than nine already had assignments which made them unavailable for ordinary duties. These nine would, in the period after Hadrian, have been described as *immunes*.

## Principales

A soldier who was literate and had some knowledge of arithmetic would probably stand a good chance of appointment as *librarius*, or clerk. Many of these were no doubt recruited as such, as was urged at a later date by Vegetius.[181] A pair of letters written in Egypt in February and March, AD 107, reveal how one particular soldier came to be a *librarius*. Julius Apollinaris writes in his native Greek to his father:[182] 'I'm getting on all right. Thanks to Sarapis I got here safely, and so far I haven't been caught by any fatigues like cutting building-stones. In fact, I went up to Claudius Severus, the governor, and asked him to make me a *librarius* on his own staff. He said, "There's no vacancy at present, but I'll make you a *librarius legionis* for the time being, with hopes of promotion." So I went straight from the general to the *cornicularius*.' The *cornicularius*, the senior non-commissioned officer in charge of clerical duties, was next in rank below the centurionate. Apollinaris in this way secured an appointment which at a later date in the second century would more correctly have been described as that of an *immunis*.

But whatever good qualities he had apart from frankness, modesty was clearly not one of them, and in a letter to his mother he calls himself a *principalis*:[183] 'I give thanks to Sarapis and good fortune that while the others are working hard all day cutting stones, I am now a *principalis* and stand around doing nothing.' The basic definition of *principalis* is to be found in Vegetius at the close of a chapter in which he lists a number of military posts, including some which are assigned by Paternus to the *immunes*:[184] 'These are the soldiers who are *principales*, those who are protected by their privileges.' This should mean either that the *immunes* formed part of the *principales* or that there was no clear distinction between the two terms. There are, however, grounds for believing that Vegetius's definition is a reflection of fourth-century conditions. He lists his *principales* in accordance with the practice of his own time, and although there are certain indications of an earlier source, the general sense of the chapter must refer to the period which followed the reforms of Diocletian and Constantine.[185] We need not be surprised if some posts which had previously been counted as appropriate to *principales* had by that date been reduced in value. Sander saw another reason for the discrepancy: he contrasted the exact, legal terminology of the lawyer, who recognized the clear distinction between the *principales* and the *immunes*, with the matter-of-fact outlook of the soldiers, who looked upon inclusion among the *immunes* as a promotion, and therefore on the right side of the dividing line between the privileged and the majority, whether it was legally a promotion or not.[186]

The grade of *principalis* must have existed, at least unofficially in the *sermo castrensis*, as early as AD 107, since Julius Apollinaris could hardly have laid claim to a non-existent rank. The earliest epigraphic evidence is found a mere half-dozen years later, in an inscription of AD 113.[187] Sander, however, would maintain that the grade was at this stage still unofficial, and that it did not become official until the time of Hadrian.[188] This, however, is to ignore the papyrological evidence completely, and to overstress the negative aspects of the epigraphic evidence. The latter is itself unbalanced, since the great majority of inscriptions which mention *principales* and *immunes*, where they can be precisely dated, belong to the late second or early third century, long after the ranks concerned are known to have come into existence.[189] It is by no means impossible that these grades had their origin in Flavian times, or even earlier: witness the *opera vacantes* of the Geneva papyrus of the reign of Domitian, which included both a *librarius* and a *cerarius*.[190] This degree of specialization is remarkable at so early a date, but, and perhaps significantly, the term *immunis* itself is not used.

In the fully developed hierarchy of the *Rangordnung*, which would appear to have reached its greatest elaboration in the post-Severan period,[191] the *principales* can be divided into two main groups, the one within the century, the other at headquarters. The internal group was tightly knit, and consisted of the *signifer*, the *optio* and the *tesserarius*.[192] It was not uncommon to hold these posts in succession, and in any case it was normal to have held at least one of them before appointment to posts in the headquarters group or promotion to the centurionate. The *signifer* was the standard-bearer, and among his other duties, as noted above, he was responsible for the safekeeping of the men's savings.[193] The *optio* had more specifically 'military' functions, and he was commonly deputed to take command of the century during the absence of the centurion. It is usual to distinguish from the normal *optio* others who expressly state their qualification for the centurionate by such descriptions as *optio ad spem ordinis*, *optio spei*, *optio ad ordinem*, *optio retentus ad spem*, *optio retentus spe*.[194] Passerini, however, doubts that there existed a special category of *optiones*, and points out that the regulations of the *schola* of *optiones* at Lambaesis make no allowance for any such distinction.[195] All *optiones*, he believes, were hopeful of being made centurions. Those specially described are simply those whose names have been placed upon the promotions list. On the other hand, the order of posts in certain inscriptions suggests that there were at least some *optiones* who were senior to others.[196] The *tesserarius*, the third of these ranks, has duties which correspond roughly with those of an orderly sergeant today. His title is derived from the *tessera*, or 'watchword'.[197]

14  Dacian and Roman soldier: detail of a Trajanic frieze

15 Column of M. Aurelius: capture of a native settlement

16 Relief from temple of *Fortuna Primigenia*, Praeneste, showing a bireme with legionaries

17 Tropaeum
Traiani, Adamklissi:
*tribuni militum* in
undress uniform

18 Tropaeum
Traiani, Adamklissi:
a group of three
*cornicines*

19   Intaglio showing an eagle

The newly promoted *principalis* was, according to Vegetius, normally assigned to the lowest ranking cohort, and worked his way upwards from cohort to cohort until his next promotion, when once again he took his place at the bottom of the list. This is too formalistic a procedure ever to have been practical. So far as we can tell, if there was an established practice it was that men tended to be transferred from cohort to cohort *en bloc*.[198] Even so, there were many exceptions.

The headquarters group of *principales* was by no means so homogeneous. It can in fact be divided into two classes, one of the orderly-room staffs, who were in the main *beneficiarii* and who took their precedence from the rank of the officer on whose staff they happened to be serving,[199] the other of such soldiers as the *aquilifer*, who was responsible for the eagle, and the *imaginiferi*. If the *optio ad spem ordinis* was in fact of higher rank than the regular *optiones* he would be of equal rank with the most prominent in this class as the second-in-command to the centurion.

The *beneficiarii* as a class were later called *officiales*, because the *beneficiarii* and others on the staff of a particular officer together formed his *officium*. Within the legion there were several *officia*, ranging from the modest *officia* of the equestrian tribunes to the progressively more elaborate ones of the *praefectus castrorum*, the *tribunus laticlavius* and the *legatus legionis*. The largest and most complicated *officium* was naturally that of the provincial governor. This was normally headed by a centurion as *princeps praetorii*, supported by two or three *cornicularii*—the legionary legate had only one—besides *commentarienses*, *speculatores* and a large number of plain *beneficiarii*, probably as many as sixty. The higher officials sometimes had *adiutores*, or assistants. To provide the necessary support for so elaborate a structure, this *officium* also contained various minor grades, such as *stratores* (equerries), *quaestionarii*, *frumentarii*, not to speak of a great number of *immunes*, most of whom were *librarii*, *exacti* and *exceptores*, or clerks of different types.[200]

The *cornicularii* of the provincial governors were very important officials, and they could normally count on promotion to the centurionate. They appear to have had the privilege of being mounted.[201] *Commentarienses* are found only on the staffs of those officers who had judicial functions. Their duties were largely non-military (one is actually described as *commentariensis ab actis civilibus*)[202] and they were concerned mainly with the preparation of cases for jurisdiction. *Speculatores* had originally been scouts, but by the third century they had been transformed into executioners. The senior of them had the title of *optio speculatorum*.[203] Closely connected with the *speculatores*, but ranking below them, were the *frumentarii*, who had police duties. The *numerus frumentariorum* had its headquarters at Rome, and its members were seconded for duty with the staffs of provincial governors.[204] Of more or less equal rank with the *frumentarii* were the *quaestionarii*. These probably had the gruesome task of extracting evidence by torture. The *beneficiarii*, who formed the greater part of the *officium*, were less specialized in function, and they presumably had to be prepared to take upon themselves a great variety of tasks.[205]

The staffs of the legionary legates were much less elaborate. They lacked *commentarienses*, *speculatores*, *questionarii* and *frumentarii*, ranks found only where an officer had capital jurisdiction.

The highest ranking of the *principales* outside the *officia* was the *aquilifer*, whose sacred office gave him precedence next to the centurion. The post tended to be a position of honour for a man nearing the end of his service, as may be gathered from the number of veterans whose last appointment was in this grade. Sometimes, however, an *aquilifer* did achieve promotion to the centurionate.[206] After the *aquilifer* Vegetius mentions the *imaginiferi*, who carried the *imagines*, or standards containing medallions with the portraits of the reigning and deified emperors.[207]

## Centurions

No doubt the ambition of every man who enlisted in the Roman army was eventually to achieve promotion to the centurionate. By the time that he had reached the rank of *cornicularius*, *aquilifer*, or *optio ad spem*, the attainment of this ambition would be eagerly awaited. The man's change in status, if he succeeded, was quite considerable. As a *principalis* he was of non-commissioned rank, whereas legionary centurions were of officer rank: their records were maintained in Rome by the *ab epistulis* and his staff, and their appointment, promotion and transfer were all in the last resort subject to the Emperor's approval.[208] Moreover, there were two other channels which gave access to the centurionate: direct commissioning from civil life and elevation from the praetorian guard (either from the rank of *cornicularius* or after *evocatio*), so that the chances of the promotion of legionary non-commissioned officers were proportionately reduced. Nevertheless, at all periods the majority of legionary centurions were in fact men promoted from the ranks of the legions.[209]

Recommendations for promotion to the centurionate were no doubt made in the first instance by the legionary legates to the provincial governor, who might, if he approved the recommendation, either appoint the man directly to fill a vacancy which had arisen, or else pass the recommendation on to Rome. In either case, the man's name and service records would have to be sent there. Just as we saw in the case of the recruit the advantage which letters of recommendation brought with them, so now, at the threshold of the centurionate, the candidate for promotion would need all the support he could get. In most cases of serving soldiers, of course, the provincial governor's word would be sufficient, and if this were not forthcoming, the candidate could always look forward to a change of governor in the not too distant future. Where patronage can be seen to operate most clearly is in cases of direct commissioning. Juvenal implies that a commission had to be applied for—*aut vitem posce libello*;[210] and Pliny describes how he procured a centurionate for his townsman, Metilius Crispus, who set out with 40,000 sesterces to buy his kit and was never heard of again.[211]

Exceptionally, centurions were chosen by popular election: Tacitus records how Antonius Primus, after the Flavian success at Cremona, gave his legions the right of appointing new centurions to replace those who had been killed. The not surprising result was that the most undisciplined candidates were elected.[212] Their subsequent careers can hardly have been successful. This event occurred in a civil war, when normal procedures might well be upset. But an inscription does attest how

towards the end of the reign of Antoninus Pius—a comparatively
peaceful period—a man was elected centurion by the vote of his
legion and spent the next 46 years in that rank, completing a total
of 50 years of service.[213] This was a certain Petronius Fortunatus,
who may have come originally from Africa. At least it was to
that province that he retired, for the inscription was found there
at Cillium. His four years in the ranks were spent successively as
*librarius, tesserarius, optio* and *signifer*, and then, when he might
have been expected to be promoted a rather young senior
*principalis*, he found himself elected centurion by popular vote.
As a centurion he saw service in thirteen legions and in almost all
parts of the Empire. It is noteworthy that his son was commis-
sioned as centurion at the age of 29. After serving in two legions,
however, he died six years later.

Within the centurionate itself there was the possibility of
promotion, not however in quite so schematic and formalistic
a way as Domaszewski imagined.[214] He believed in a dual system
of *Staffelavancement* and *Stufenavancement*: the former was step
by step within each cohort in succession, the latter by jumps from
cohort to cohort. The first path was for the sluggard, the second
for the man marked out for advancement. A more general belief
now, though the evidence is not clear, is that the centurions of
cohorts II to X were equal in rank, if not in seniority, and were to
be distinguished from those in the first cohort, who were the
*primi ordines*, and constituted a superior grade of centurion.[215]
Within the *primi ordines* promotion was from *hastatus posterior* to
*princeps posterior*, and then to the top three grades of *hastatus*,
*princeps*, and finally *primus pilus*. Dobson believes that *primipilares*,
that is, men who had been *primipili*, received equestrian rank.[216]

The rank of *primus pilus*, however, was beyond the reach of the
great majority of legionary entrants, however ambitious their
dreams may have been. A good education and considerable skill
in administration were at this level even more desirable than
physical strength or skill at arms, and many of those who possessed
these qualities would have been more likely to enter the army
higher up the scale, either by way of the praetorian guard or by a
direct commission.[217]

## PAY AND ALLOWANCES

*The legions*

In the earliest times, when military service was often the annual duty of the able-bodied citizen, and the campaigning season began in the spring and ended before the harvest, the Roman army was strictly an amateur body. It was at the siege of Veii, when the campaign was protracted into the winter (396 BC), that we first hear of payment.[218] It is not until the time of Polybius, however, that any definite evidence on pay-scales becomes available. Polybius, writing of his own day (mid-second century BC), states that the legionary soldier received two obols a day.[219] He adds that the centurion was paid four obols and the cavalryman one drachma a day. What these amounts represented in Roman money is not made clear. The majority of scholars have assumed that an equation common later must have held good earlier and have made the Polybian drachma the equivalent of the *denarius*, which would give the legionary an annual rate of 120 *denarii* on the normal assumption of a 360-day year.[220] This would be all very well if it were an annual rate that was in question, but what Polybius is describing is a daily rate. The only daily rate that can emerge from this equation is the unlikely one of $3\frac{1}{3}$ *asses*. The daily rate must surely have been expressed in a payable form, one which did not involve fractions of the *as*.[221] Of possible equivalents of the drachma, the only one which produces a payable daily rate is the *quadrigatus* of 15 *asses*; if this equation is the right one we have the following equivalents: Polybius's two obols represent 5 *asses*, his four obols a *denarius*, and the cavalryman's pay a *quadrigatus*. So long as ten *asses* were reckoned to the *denarius* this meant an annual rate of 180 *denarii*, which on the retariffing of the *as* at sixteen to the *denarius* became an annual rate of $112\frac{1}{2}$ *denarii*. When Caesar doubled the pay the annual rate became 225 *denarii*,[222] and it remained at this level until the time of Domitian.

This theory has the advantage of accounting for the few pieces of clear evidence which we possess:

(i) that the rate in the time of Polybius was two obols a day;

(ii) that the *as* was retariffed at sixteen to the *denarius*, probably in the age of the Gracchi;[223]

(iii) that Caesar doubled the pay;

(iv) that in the time of Augustus the annual rate was 225 *denarii*.[224]

This would at first sight imply a severe reduction in the standard of living of the soldier during the period from the Gracchi to Caesar. Whether this actually took place or not depends not so much upon the gross amount of the pay, as on the net total remaining after all deductions had been made. Polybius tells us that stoppages were made for food, clothing and replacement of arms, and that these stoppages were made at source according to a fixed schedule.[225] The amount of these deductions is not stated, and it is not necessary to suppose that the total was the same in the case of every man. Nevertheless they may well have been substantial. H. M. D. Parker goes so far as to declare that it is possible that the soldier actually received considerably less than half his gross pay.[226] Still, we may assume that the amount remaining, whatever it was, normally sufficed to meet the soldier's needs. Had it been otherwise, we should certainly have heard of repeated mutinies and insubordination over this issue. Yet though mutinies are by no means uncommon at any period during the Republic, their causes when stated are usually quite different.[227]

Obviously, if no adjustment of the amounts deducted from total pay had been made on the occasion of the retariffing of the *as*, the men would have been placed in a position of hardship and, possibly, even one of debt to the treasury. There was, however, a *lex militaris* of C. Gracchus which allowed for a free issue of clothing.[228] This might go a long way, though probably not the whole way, towards compensating for the cut in pay caused by retariffing. Again when Caesar doubled the pay, he probably took some of the gilt off the gingerbread by cancelling the concession of free clothing. Certainly at the time of the Pannonian Revolt deductions for clothing were one of the complaints of the mutineers.[229]

It would appear, therefore, that there were three distinct periods in the late Republic so far as pay was concerned:

(i) from *c.* 170 BC to *c.* 122 BC the basic rate was 180 old-style *denarii* a year, with deductions for food, clothing and arms;

(ii) from *c.* 122 BC to the time of Caesar the annual rate was 112½ new-style *denarii* with deductions for food and arms, but not for clothing;

(iii) from the time of Caesar onwards the rate was 225 *denarii* a year, with deductions once more for clothing, as well as for food and arms.

Caesar's rates remained in force during the early Empire, and attempts by the mutineers of AD 14 to have them altered had no effect. The first improvement in the basic rate was made by Domitian, who increased the pay by one-third by the simple expedient of adding a fourth *stipendium*.[230] Previously payment had been made in three instalments, or *stipendia*, of 75 *denarii* each at the beginning of January, May and September: Domitian made the intervals three-monthly and thus increased the annual amount to 300 *denarii*. Some scholars have argued for an increase under Commodus, but for this there is no real evidence, and it would appear that the next increase was under Septimius Severus.[231] He raised the annual pay to an amount which is not precisely known, but which may have been 450 *denarii*, and at the same time he restored the former system of three four-monthly payments.[232] So far increases had been separated by intervals of more than a century, Caesar to Domitian, Domitian to Severus. Inflation now meant that the next increase had to come more quickly; Caracalla gave an all-round increase of 50 per cent, which brought the legionary total, probably, to 675 *denarii*.[233] After his time the effects of continued inflation led to a virtual abandonment of any attempt to make the actual pay more than nominal, and in its place there developed an increased dependence upon payment in kind, the *annona*.[234]

A considerable number of men, however, at all times received more than the basic scale. As in modern armies, the non-commissioned officers were rewarded for their increased responsibilities with higher pay as well as with disciplinary powers. This can most clearly be seen in auxiliary units, in which it was customary to designate ranks by terms which directly reflected pay, such as, for instance, *duplicarius alae* and *sesquiplicarius alae*, which came to mean simply that the men in question received double and one

and a half times, respectively, the basic rate of men in an *ala*.[235]
These terms were generally avoided in the legions, where the
ranks were more elaborately organized and the pay-structure
slightly more complicated.[236] Broadly speaking, legionaries who
were graded between the simple *miles* and the centurionate were
divided into *principales* and *immunes*, at least from the early
second century AD.[237] The *immunes*, who correspond roughly with
the 'tradesmen' of the British army, remained on the basic
legionary scale, and were rewarded for their special contributions
only by their *immunitas*, or exemption from the more menial
fatigues. The *principales*, however, did receive additional pay,
and the payment was fixed in relation to their position within the
hierarchy. The results may be summarized as follows:

(i) The *miles* and the *immunis* both received the basic rate.

(ii) Most *principales* received pay-and-a-half. This group probably included both those employed within the century, that is
to say, *signifer*, *optio* and *tesserarius*, and the majority of those
employed at headquarters.

(iii) Some senior *principales* received double pay.

(iv) Domaszewski believed that a small number of the most
senior *principales*, consisting of men already qualified for promotion to the centurionate, received treble pay. This remains
conjectural.[238]

20   Tropaeum Traiani,
Adamklissi: Roman legionary
surrounded by barbarians

21   Tropaeum Traiani,
Adamklissi: Trajan watches
the fighting, attended by two
guards

22 Tropaeum Traiani, Adamklissi: a group of standard-bearers
(two *vexilliferi* and an *aquilifer*)

23 Tropaeum Traiani,
Adamklissi: a mailed
cavalryman of Trajan's
army carrying a pike
(*contus*)

24 Housesteads Roman fort: latrine in S.E. corner

25 Bewcastle Roman fort: the underground strongroom

26  Corbridge Roman station: pottery mould showing the Celtic god Taranis

*The praetorian guard and the urban cohorts*

The evidence for praetorian pay in the reign of Augustus is not clear. Cassius Dio, referring to 27 BC, tells us that Augustus gave the praetorians double the pay which the legionaries received.[239] The latter were at the time earning 225 *denarii* a year. Dio's statement would imply praetorian pay of 450 *denarii*. Yet in another context Dio tells us that in AD 6 the scale of gratuities which Augustus proposed for time-expired soldiers contained a different ratio: it awarded 5000 *denarii* each to the praetorians and 3000 to the legionaries.[240] It was customary for gratuities and donatives to preserve where possible the same differentials as did the pay-scales;[241] it would therefore be natural to suppose that in AD 6 praetorian pay and legionary pay were in the ratio of five to three. Since the legionary pay was still 225 *denarii*, the praetorian pay on this reckoning would have been 375 *denarii*. It is most unlikely that praetorian pay was reduced at a time when other pay was steady, and it would seem more probable that the proper figure had been 375 *denarii* all along. In that case Dio's double pay for the praetorians was merely a very rough approximation for what on strict arithmetic should have been one and two-thirds.

Another line of reasoning would appear to support this conclusion. Festus tells us that the *cohors praetoria* of Republican days received *sesquiplex stipendium*, or pay and a half.[242] Though the praetorian guard of Augustus was essentially a new creation, and by no means a mere continuation of the earlier *cohors praetoria*, Augustus was certainly not indifferent to the claims of tradition, and usually preserved established customs as far as he could. *Sesquiplex stipendium* for the praetorians, however, would have meant the awkward sum of 337½ *denarii*. Since it was usual at the time for the payment to be made in three equal instalments, this would have involved payments of 112½ *denarii* three times a year. So far as we know, instalments of basic pay were generally, before deductions, expressed in round figures, and were theoretically capable of being paid in *aurei*, or units of 25 *denarii*.[243] We should suspect, therefore, that the actual instalments were either 100 or 125 *denarii*. The former figure would give us 300, the latter 375 *denarii* as the annual pay. Since 300 *denarii* would have been rather too close to the legionaries' 225, Augustus may well have settled on 375. This was probably the origin of the 5 : 3 ratio.

This ratio was, however, very quickly upset. It is generally agreed that in AD 14 the praetorians received 750 *denarii* a year, the men of the urban cohorts 375, and the legionaries 225.[244] How then did this change come about? The most likely occasion for this happening between AD 6 and 14 is surely the appointment of L. Piso as the first permanent *praefectus urbi*, probably in AD 13.[245] Up to this date the urban cohorts, numbered X, XI and XII, would appear to have been on a parity in pay and status with the praetorian cohorts, numbered I to IX; presumably the change in the command structure of the urban cohorts was the occasion for making a distinction in pay between the two bodies. Though the ostensible promoter of this move was Augustus, it is reasonable to discern in the doubling of praetorian pay the hand of Tiberius, who as the designated future ruler of Rome would find it desirable to secure the loyalty of what to an emperor was the most important section of the army.[246] The new differentials are apparent in the legacies of Augustus in AD 14, which gave the praetorians 250 *denarii* each, the men of the urban cohorts 125, and the legionaries 75.[247] It is noteworthy that each of these amounts is the equivalent of a single instalment, or *stipendium*. It is also in line with the gradual development in complexity of the Roman military system that whereas up to AD 6 there had been one scale for city troops and another for legionaries, by AD 14 there were separate scales for praetorians, for the urban cohorts, and for the legions.

During the Empire the praetorians and the urban cohorts presumably shared in the pay increases under Domitian, Severus and Caracalla.[248] The first of these would increase praetorian pay to 1,000 *denarii*, the second, if our reconstruction of the legionary increase is correct, to 1,500 *denarii*, and the third, probably, to 2,250 *denarii*. The actual pay, however of these highly privileged forces tended to be overshadowed by donatives, which for the praetorians, as the soldiers whose loyalty was indispensable to the emperor's immediate security, became more frequent and disproportionately greater. As early as the accession of Claudius the donative presented to each praetorian to secure the attachment of the Guard to the service of the new emperor, had reached the level of 3,750 *denarii* a man, or the equivalent of five years' pay.[249]

## The vigiles

There is no evidence about the level of pay in the *vigiles*, nor is it easy to make any estimate by assuming a precise relationship with the pay-scales of the other services. Baillie Reynolds believed that the pay of the *vigiles* was lower than that of the legions.[250] This most certainly must have been true in the first instance, when the corps was recruited from freedmen, and it may possibly have remained true later, even though the freeborn element had come to be in a clear majority. Yet by the time this stage had been reached it is hard to see how recruitment could have been maintained at a satisfactory level had its members been ill-paid, and in fact the legacies of Tiberius appear to place the *vigiles* already on an equal footing with the legions.[251] The round of the city tribunates, which became an accepted part of their career for ambitious *primipilares*, consisted of successive appointments as *tribunus cohortis vigilum, tribunus cohortis urbanae*, and *tribunus cohortis praetoriae*.[252] The round of the tribunates is often preceded at an earlier stage in the careers by successive centurionates in the *vigiles*, the urban cohorts and the Guard.[253] The *vigiles*, therefore, were firmly linked with the urban cohorts and the Guard in the public image. It is hard to believe that their pay still remained below that of the legions.

## The auxiliary forces

Legionary pay is simple, auxiliary pay more complicated. The legions were remarkably uniform in pay, status, organization and conditions of service: the auxiliary units show pronounced differences. There are *alae*, or cavalry regiments, and these may be either 500 strong (*quingenariae*), or, less commonly, 1,000 strong (*miliariae*): there are infantry cohorts, again either 500 or 1,000 strong, and some of these are part mounted, or *cohortes equitatae*. Finally, certain of the *cohortes civium Romanorum* appear to have been specially favoured.[254] With such wide differences it is not surprising that there were wide differences of pay. One of these differences is highlighted in the *allocutio* of Hadrian to the troops at Lambaesis: the *equites* of the *alae* are better mounted and better paid than the *equites* of the *cohortes equitatae*.[255] It is mainly from scraps of information such as this that the pay-scales of the auxiliary forces can be reconstructed. Only one document, a Berlin papyrus of about AD 192, gives a specific figure for auxiliary pay, and that the unlikely one of 84 *denarii* 15¾ obols.[256] This, of course, is a net figure, not a gross one, and the initial amount was probably 100 *denarii* exactly. It is noteworthy that this is precisely one-third of the basic legionary rate in force at the time.

Now we may reconstruct the scale. It was not unusual for a legionary to be appointed a senior *principalis* in an *ala*; from the fact that it was felt to be a promotion for a legionary to be appointed *duplicarius alae* we may safely conclude that the *duplicarius alae* received more pay than the legionary, i.e. more than 300 *denarii* a year in the period from Domitian to Severus, but considerably less than twice that amount, since otherwise the member of an *ala* would have had equal pay with the legionary. Moreover, there were at this date four *stipendia* a year, each of which normally consisted of a round number of *denarii*, a number preferably divisible by 25, so that the payment could theoretically be made in *aurei*. On these principles the easiest solution would be for the *duplicarius alae* to have received 400 *denarii* a year, which would give the *sesquiplicarius* 300 and the simple *eques* 200, assuming, as seems natural, that the terms mean exactly what they say.[257]

The members of cohorts received less than the members of *alae* of the same rank; moreover, the demand of the Batavians during the revolt of Civilis for the doubling of their pay and an increase in the proportion of mounted men implies that the auxiliary infantry received less than half the pay of the legionaries, and also that the *equites* in the auxiliary cohorts were somewhat better paid than the *pedites*.[258] These conditions are met by assuming that the *duplicarius eques* received the same pay as the *sesquiplicarius alae*, or the legionary on the basic rate, 300 *denarii* a year. The rest then falls into place: the *sesquiplicarius eques* received 225 *denarii*, the *eques* of a cohort two-thirds of this, or 150 *denarii*.

The *equites* of a cohort received more than the *pedites*, and therefore probably the same as the *sesquiplicarii pedites*. Hence the latter received 150 *denarii*, the *duplicarii pedites* 200, and the simple *pedites* 100. We may note that we have now reached by first principles the conclusion suggested by the Berlin papyrus, that the basic rate of the infantryman in an auxiliary cohort was exactly one-third that of the legionary.

*Conjectural Table of Auxiliary Pay in Denarii for the period from Domitian to Severus*

|  | ALAE | COHORTES | |
|  |  | Equites | Pedites |
|---|---|---|---|
| Duplicarii | 400 | 300 | 200 |
| Sesquiplicarii | 300 | 225 | 150 |
| Basic | 200 | 150 | 100 |

*The fleets*
There is no good evidence for pay in the fleets. It is clear that the internal pay-structure was, as might reasonably have been expected, similar to that in the other services, for there are references to *sesquiplicarii* and *duplicarii*, but the basic rate itself is not attested.[259] Arguments must therefore depend largely on comparisons of status. Status is most clearly indicated by the nature of recruitment and the statutory length of service. Starr has shown that Mommsen's supposition that the Augustan navy was manned by slaves and freedmen of the imperial *familia* was based on a misconception.[260] Though there were some freedmen in the navy, the majority of the sailors were in fact *peregrini* as early as the reign of Augustus, and the personnel of the fleets remained generally peregrine until the grant of citizenship by Caracalla to the greater part of the Roman world. The recruitment of the navy, therefore, was very much in line with that of the auxiliary forces, with the striking

exception that the native Egyptians, who were ineligible for the auxiliary forces, were accepted as recruits for the Italian fleets.[261] The Alexandrian fleet, on the other hand, still apparently remained closed to them.[262] The length of service in the fleets was first established at twenty-six years at a time when auxiliary service was for twenty-five years and legionary service for twenty years.[263] The diplomas show that at some time between AD 152 and 217 the period of service was lengthened to twenty-eight years.[264] The implication of all this should be that naval service was felt to be inferior to auxiliary service, but not appreciably so. We should expect, therefore, naval pay to be either on a par with auxiliary pay or slightly below it. Auxiliary pay itself was 100 *denarii* a year for the period from Domitian to Severus: Starr suggests that 'the sailors may have gotten the same pay as the auxiliaries', or, alternatively, that the *viaticum* which recruits to the navy received, three *aurei* or seventy-five *denarii*, represented an initial gift of one year's pay.[265] To the latter suggestion two objections may be raised. In the first place, the amount of the *viaticum* was apparently invariable irrespective of the particular service, and therefore can hardly be used as an index of the amount of the pay for any one service.[266] Secondly, the 100 *denarii* which the auxiliaries received represented the pay as increased by Domitian by the addition of a *quartum stipendium*: previously the amount had been seventy-five *denarii*.[267] It seems likely that Domitian increased the pay of all servicemen *pari passu*: if then the pay of the sailors was seventy-five *denarii* a year after the increase it should have been 56½ *denarii* a year before it. Such a fraction is absurd. We are thus driven to the conclusion that Starr's other suggestion, that the basic naval pay and the basic auxiliary pay were identical, is probably correct. The naval pay-structure was therefore probably identical with that of infantry cohorts of the auxiliary forces.[268]

## Stoppages

We cannot evaluate the standard of living of the men in the ranks by reference to income alone: it is necessary to examine expenditure as well. For this there are two pieces of evidence of the first importance. One of these is the celebrated passage at the beginning of the *Annals* in which Percennius summarizes the grievances of the men in the legions:[269] 'Body and soul are valued at ten *asses* a day; out of this we have to pay for our clothing, our weapons and our tents, out of this we have to find sweeteners for brutal centurions or else find ourselves on the roster for extra fatigues.' The expenses of which he complains fall into two distinct classes, the official stoppages for weapons, clothing and tents, and the unofficial back-handers made to grasping and venal centurions. With the latter of course we are not directly concerned. No doubt in any army this type of irregularity will at times exist under cover; it was probably the peculiarly Roman combination of an almost entirely amateur officer corps with a highly professional centurionate which gave such scope for it. The men's resentment eventually came to a head under Otho, who, being naturally reluctant to alienate his centurions, made arrangements for the *vacationes munerum*, as the customary privileges were called, to be paid for out of his own private purse. This became standard practice, Tacitus tells us, under all good emperors subsequently.[270]

Our second piece of evidence is less highly coloured. This, *P. Gen. Lat.* 1 (see Appendix A), is a document of AD 81—the third year of the emperor Titus—which contains the pay accounts of two Roman soldiers.[271] In these accounts deductions are made for a variety of items—*faenaria* (bedding?),[272] *in victum* (food), *caligas fascias* (boots and straps), *Saturnalicium k(astrense)* (regimental dinner?),[273] *in vestitorium, in vestimentis, in vestimentum* (all presumably meaning 'clothing'), and *ad signa*, which has been variously interpreted as a contribution to a burial club or the subscription to an annual ceremony associated with the standards.[274]

What is of prime interest in the present connection is that of the stoppages mentioned in Tacitus, for clothing, weapons, and tents, only one item, the deduction for clothing, is clearly indicated in these lists. Even this item is not constant in different pay periods, or even uniform for each man, but varies, and is successively 60, 0 and 146 drachmas for Julius Proculus, but 100, 0 and 146 drachmas for Valerius Germanus.

In the Polybian period stoppages had been made, as we have
seen, for food, clothing, and replacement of arms;[275] later in the
period from the Gracchi to Caesar the reduction in pay caused by
the retariffing of the *as* had to some extent been compensated for
by the issue of free clothing.[276] Rations and arms, unlike clothing,
appear never to have been made the subject of a free issue, except
in rare instances as a special concession. For example, after the
detection of the conspiracy of Piso in AD 65, Nero's reward to the
praetorian guard for their loyalty was 'sine pretio frumentum'.[277]
For this reason it would be wrong to assume from the absence of
food from the items listed in the complaints of Percennius that
it was a free issue at the time. It is far more likely that the men
were incensed not so much by deductions for food, which had
always had to be paid for, as by deductions for clothing, which
had for a long time—long enough to create a tradition—been a
free issue. What is more surprising at first sight is the absence of
any mention of stoppages for arms in the Geneva pay accounts,
especially in view of the complaints of Percennius and the fact
that arms had been a charge upon the soldiers throughout the
Republican period. There is no need, however, to consider any
*argumentum ex silentio*, for a document of about AD 175, which is
probably concerned with the *ala veterana Gallica*, has the sum of
103 *denarii* for arms against the name of one man in a long list of
names.[278] The conclusion to be drawn from taking both documents together is that payments for arms were only occasional
since a good set of weapons would with care last a man a lifetime
unless he had the misfortune to lose them. Since the two men
concerned in the Geneva pay accounts were not recruits, for they
already had balances to their credit, and probably had had not
many years of service, for their balances were by no means large,
it is likely that the weapons which they had had to buy at the
beginning of their service were still serviceable.

## The regimental savings-bank

The fact that the Geneva accounts show a running balance
confirms that a savings-bank system existed. This was already
known from Vegetius:[279] 'It was a provident institution of the

ancients, that of each donative that the men received one half should be kept with the colours and saved there for the men themselves to prevent it from being wasted by them through extravagance or the purchase of useless articles.' Moreover, Domitian prohibited the depositing of more than a thousand sesterces by any one soldier, because Saturninus in the revolt of AD 89 had found the combined savings of two legions in the double camp at Mainz were substantial enough to finance a revolution.[280] There is no confirmation in the Geneva papyrus of the practice mentioned by Vegetius of enforcing a compulsory saving of one-half of each donative. This may be simply because the men had not been in the army long enough to have received a donative, in which case they must have enlisted after the accession of Titus, or else for some reason not have been paid one.[281] Alternatively, the rule had not yet come into force.[282] There is, however, confirmation of the rule towards the end of the following century in another document concerned with auxiliary pay, P. Berlin 6866.[283] This document shows the balances of a number of auxiliary infantrymen, the majority of whom possess exactly 100 *denarii in deposito* and 75 *denarii in viatico*. Three men have more on deposit: a certain Pantarchus has the sum of 195 *denarii* 8½ obols, a soldier from Antaeopolis 206 *denarii*, and another from Oxyrhynchus 187½ *denarii*. The oddness of these amounts highlights the very preciseness of the 100 *denarii* which each of the others possesses: it would seem probable that they had received a donative on the accession of Septimius Severus, or possibly Pescennius Niger, and that the 100 *denarii* had been retained in the unit as a compulsory saving.[284]

To return to the Geneva pay accounts. It has sometimes been remarked that neither soldier draws any money at all to spend outside the camp.[285] This must surely be significant for the correct interpretation of the accounts. Granted that most necessities were probably provided for within the unit, it is unbelievable that the men did not wish to find entertainment outside, and that they never required money for this purpose. What then did they do for spending money? Perhaps they had large amounts left over from the previous year, which they kept hidden away in their barracks or secreted upon their persons? An unlikely tale. Or did they, as has been suggested, get along by demanding bribes, or exacting forced presents from the civilian population?[286] No doubt something of that sort went on, but it is hard to believe that the men could rely upon it as a regular way of life. They must surely have had some money of their own to spend. What is the explanation? The first point to observe is that the amount of each *stipendium*, or instalment of pay, was 248 drachmas. Now in Egypt the common coin of account was the tetradrachm, or four drachma piece, which normally passed as the equivalent of the *denarius*. On this equation, therefore, 248 drachmas would correspond to 62 *denarii*. The amount of each instalment, however, ought to have been 75 *denarii*. What has happened to the remaining 13 *denarii* in each instalment?

It is usually assumed that the 13 *denarii* must have disappeared in some manipulation of the exchange-rate by the authorities.[287] But another Geneva papyrus, which can be no more than a few years later in date, shows a figure of 297 drachmas for each instalment.[288] On the regular exchange-rate this would be equivalent to 74¼ *denarii*, which is near enough to the expected 75 *denarii*. In fact, the difference of three-quarters of a *denarius* is exactly the sort of amount one would be prepared and expect to lose on the exchange. Various attempts have been made to explain the discrepancy between the 248 drachmas of AD 81 and the 297 drachmas of three or four years later. It is known that in the meantime Domitian had increased the pay by adding a fourth instalment.[289] Some scholars, therefore, have suggested that it was not a fourth instalment which was added, but that instead each instalment was increased by one-third.[290] But the addition of one-third to 248 drachmas would give 330⅔ drachmas as the answer, and this is a good deal more than 297 drachmas. On this explanation, if the men had been swindled before, they were being swindled even more now. In any case, the papyrus gives clear indications, in spite of its mutilated form, that the sum of 297 drachmas was paid four times in the year, not three.[291]

How then are we to explain these differences? Once we admit that the soldier must have received at least a small part of his pay in cash to spend upon his purely personal pleasures, there is no longer any reason to suppose that he was in any way the victim of a semi-legal fraud. The procedure must surely have been somewhat as follows. Of the 75 *denarii* that were due each pay period, 62 were retained in the unit to cover the man's debts for whatever was supplied from official sources, and the balance, if any, was applied to his credit. Though in a few instances this method might lead to the soldier's being temporarily in debt to his unit, such a situation would be short-lived, and the long-term effect would be to build up a considerable nest egg which would be useful for his retirement.[292] The remainder of the pay-instalment, i.e. 13 *denarii* less probably a small amount lost on the exchange, was handed over to the soldier as pocket-money.[293] The soldier therefore received almost 52 drachmas as spending money three times a year at this period. In view of the Roman fondness for round numbers we may well suspect the actual amount received was 50 drachmas. We may even on the evidence of a letter from St Ignatius to Polycarp, which, though written in Greek, makes play with Latin military metaphors, go further and believe that the technical term for the amount actually received in cash in this way was *acceptum*.[294]

*Special allowances*

Tacitus mentions an allowance called *clavarium*, or 'nail-money', which was claimed by the Flavian forces marching on Rome.[295] We are not told that the claim was actually met, or for how much it was: the idea behind the claim was that the long march had caused unreasonable wear in the men's boots, which, as we have seen, could only be replaced against stoppages of pay. The fact that the allowance had a name seems sufficient evidence that it existed.

A similar allowance, possibly the same, is mentioned by Suetonius.[296] When the *classiarii*, who had regularly to march from Ostia or Puteoli to Rome, claimed *calciarium*, or 'boot-money', Vespasian with his customary dry humour is said to have required them to make the journey barefoot. According to Suetonius they still did so in his own day.

After the detection of the conspiracy of Piso in AD 65 Nero presented each member of the praetorian guard with 2,000 sesterces and free corn (*sine pretio frumentum*) as a reward for loyalty. Such is the story in Tacitus.[297] Suetonius simply tells us that he gave the praetorian cohorts a monthly allowance of grain free of cost (*frumentum menstruum gratuitum*).[298] Tacitus says that previously they had had to pay the market price (*ex modo annonae*). Whether this privilege continued after Nero's death is not clear. While it lasted it corresponded to a considerable concealed increase in praetorian pay.

Another form of indirect subsidy was initiated by Otho. The *vacationes munerum* of which the men had complained during the Pannonian revolt had by now become so expensive as to be the equivalent of an annual tribute paid to the centurions. According to Tacitus, as much as one-quarter of the regular strength of a unit might at any one time be on leave outside the camp, or even simply off duty inside the camp.[299] To secure the cash required for obtaining these privileges the men would resort to highway robbery, theft, or even part-time jobs of the most menial kind. The result was the gradual demoralization of men who had no money, and the equally steady impoverishment of those who had money, a continuous process which might have led to the complete collapse of morale. Otho decided to remedy the situation by paying the centurions for the men's annual leave directly from his own private purse. Tacitus had no doubt that this was a beneficial reform: it was continued by Vitellius and eventually became standard practice.[300]

## Donatives[301]

In the Republic it had been customary for a general to distribute part of the spoils among his troops at the conclusion of a successful campaign; by the first century BC the prospect of booty had become a major incentive to enlistment. Under the principate it was more convenient for the emperor to dissociate the payment of special bounties from the actual consequences of a campaign, and to make these additional payments in times of peace. Otherwise, he would very likely have been under constant pressure from the army to pursue an aggressive foreign policy. So in 8 BC Augustus paid a donative to mark the entry of his grandson Gaius Caesar into public life.[302] In his will, with a view to ensuring an easy succession, Augustus left the praetorians 250 *denarii* each, the members of the urban cohorts 125, the legionaries and those auxiliaries who belonged to the *cohortes civium Romanorum* 75 *denarii*.[303] The bulk of the auxiliaries and all the members of the fleets had no share in these legacies, which were thus confined to those elements of the armed services which possessed the citizenship and were the most fully romanized. This discrimination could have been justified on the ground that these donatives were the military counterpart of the *congiarium* which Augustus was at the same time leaving to the Roman people.

The succeeding emperors took pains to follow the precedent of Augustus, Tiberius so precisely as to leave to the army and to the people the very same sums as Augustus.[304] Gaius, however, in implementing Tiberius's will, doubled the amount due to the praetorians. This merely continued a policy of favouring the praetorians above the rest of the army which had been present from the beginning and which had been intensified on the fall of Sejanus. To recapture for himself the loyalty of the Guard, which had been Sejanus's chief support, Tiberius had granted 1,000 *denarii* a man to the praetorians.[305] Apart from this, there was one other significant change from the precedent laid down by Augustus: the members of the *cohortes civium Romanorum* were no longer included in the donatives—by now these units were being recruited from *peregrini*—and their place was taken by the *vigiles*, who since the *Lex Visellia* of AD 24 had acquired the right to the citizenship after six years' service, and whose social standing had correspondingly improved. With Tiberius, of course, it was also a case of recompense for services rendered: the *vigiles* had been of considerable assistance to him in his action against Sejanus.[306]

Claudius did not forget that he owed his accession to the Guard, and he rewarded them for their services with the immense sum of 3,750 *denarii* each.[307] Apart from his accession donative, Claudius again followed the example of Augustus and gave a *congiarium* to the people and a donative to the army to mark the entry of

Nero into public life;[308] to the praetorians alone he presented an annual bounty of 25 *denarii* each on the anniversary of his accession.[309]

Nero, on coming to power, repeated the size of donative which Claudius had given, and in general continued the policy of favouring the praetorians which had by now become established.[310] He gave them donatives after the murder of his mother, Agrippina, and again on the detection of the conspiracy of Piso he granted them as much as 500 *denarii* a head, in addition to a monthly allowance of grain free of cost.[311]

The dangers inherent in this policy were soon made manifest. Nymphidius Sabinus tried to buy the allegiance of the armed forces for Galba by promising the praetorians no less than 7,500 *denarii* a man, and the legionaries 1,250 *denarii*.[312] This was double what the praetorians would have been entitled to had the amounts of the gratuities been in proportion to the pay-scales in force at the time: the praetorians were being offered the equivalent of ten years' full pay and the legionaries a mere five years' full pay. The doubling of the amount due to the praetorians had a precedent in the action of Gaius on his accession. In the event, the promises of Nymphidius remained unfulfilled, for Galba was neither willing nor able to pay the huge sums involved, and the way was made clear for civil war.[313] The expenses of a lavish donative were too much even for Otho—though he was eventually forced to promise the praetorians 1,250 *denarii* a head[314]—but he had instead the ingenious idea of winning popularity with the army at a much lower immediate cost by paying for the men's *vacationes munerum*.[315] Vitellius was moved to do the same.[316] Vespasian returned to the practice of paying a donative, though in his case it was apparently a modest one. Tacitus says that he offered no more under conditions of civil war than others had done in time of peace.[317]

What Titus gave is not known, but whatever it was it was exactly matched by Domitian on his own accession.[318] In fact, according to Suetonius, Domitian had hesitated for some time on the death of Vespasian whether to offer a double donative in order to win the succession for himself.[319] There was a further donative on the occasion of the peace with Decebalus, though this may have been confined to the troops who took part in the war.[320]

Donatives were given on their accessions by Nerva and Trajan, and at twice the normal rate for the time by Hadrian.[321] Hadrian gave an additional donative on his adoption of L. Ceionius Commodus as L. Aelius Caesar. Antoninus Pius gave the usual *congiarium* to the people and donative to the army on his accession, and a second donative to celebrate the marriage of his daughter, Faustina.[322]

On the death of Antoninus Pius, Marcus Aurelius made L. Verus his colleague in the Empire, and in honour of their joint rule he promised a donative of 5,000 *denarii* to the praetorians.[323] This was probably equivalent to a bounty of five years' full pay in accordance with the scales in force at the time, and was therefore not altogether outside the bounds of precedent.[324] The immense cost would appear to have so depleted the treasury that to pay for the Marcomannic wars Marcus had to resort to a public auction of the palace valuables and his wife's clothes.[325] Certainly, the imperial finances were never particularly strong during his reign, and he refused to grant the further donative which was expected by the army after his victories in the wars.[326]

Commodus gave a *congiarium* to the people, and presumably the customary donative to the army, on his accession.[327] Apparently he had promised a second donative towards the end of his reign, for Pertinax found himself called upon to pay it.[328] Pertinax himself was hard pressed for money, and perhaps, following the example of Marcus Aurelius, held an auction of Commodus's effects and slaves.[329] With this help he was able to begin the payment of his own promised donative, 3,000 *denarii*, which he pretended to be the same as that paid by Marcus Aurelius and Verus.[330] The writer of his life in the *Historia Augusta*, however, reports that he had paid by the time of his death only half the amount due to the praetorians, and that the sums due to the rest of the army were never paid at all.[331]

We now come to the famous auction of the Empire by the Guard, with one of the rival bidders, Sulpicianus, inside the camp, and the other, Didius Julianus, shouting from outside.

Comical as the scene must have been, the participants would appear to have had both feet on the ground as far as money was concerned. The standard rate had long been set by Marcus Aurelius and Verus, who had offered the Guard 5,000 *denarii*: Pertinax had been unable to match this, but he too recognized the force of their precedent, and in fact pretended that his own donative was worth as much. We might have expected, therefore, the bidding to have started at 5,000 *denarii*, but it must have begun far below this level, for it was only after several rounds that Sulpicianus was the first to offer 5,000; at this stage Didius Julianus abandoned caution, raised him by 1,250, and won the day.³³² The sums involved hardly merit the censure of historians: Sulpicianus had merely offered the standard rate, and Julianus's offer of an additional 1,250 *denarii* was not unjustifiable in view of the inflationary effect of the wars and the plague since the accession of Marcus Aurelius and Verus. In real terms Sulpicianus's offer was on almost exactly the same level as that made by Claudius a century and a half before—five years' full pay. When it is also remembered that the regular pay had not been increased since the reign of Domitian, and that the wars and the plagues of the late second century had increased the cost of living, Didius Julianus's additional offer seems relatively modest.³³³

What Julianus actually paid is uncertain: the writer of the life in the *Historia Augusta*, who tends to be more lenient towards him than is Dio, reports that although he had offered only 6,250 *denarii* he actually paid 7,500.³³⁴ No reason is given for this change of mind, and whether we prefer to believe that it was due to Julianus's unbridled generosity or simply to a fondness for round numbers, Julianus would appear to be not so much a rogue as a fool. Herodian, who is perhaps even more hostile to Julianus than is Dio himself, so far from allowing the praetorians an additional, uncalled-for bonus of 1,250 *denarii*, says that Julianus did not even pay them the amount that he had bid.³³⁵ He describes Julianus as an out-and-out scoundrel, who did not possess and had never possessed the money that he had promised. The treasury was empty, thanks to Commodus, and so the poor praetorians would have got nothing had not Julianus, when

Severus was marching on Rome, made a last-minute effort to win the support of the soldiers by scraping together what money he could, and offering it to them. This move failed to have the desired effect, for the men looked upon the money, not as an unsolicited gift, but as no more than an overdue payment towards a debt.[336]

Severus owed his accession not to the Guard, which he promptly remodelled, but to the legionaries from the Danubian provinces. It was not unreasonable, therefore, that these troops should expect a donative on the scale that would normally apply to praetorians. Their demand of 2,500 *denarii* was in the circumstances modest.[337] They supported it by a historical analogy which some historians have found incredible: a reference to the 2,500 *denarii* which Octavian gave to his troops in 43 BC. That the rough provincial soldiery should concern themselves with antiquarian scholarship and should base their case on the events of some 230 years earlier was at first sight so surprising that Dio, an eye-witness, declares that many in the Senate had no idea what the men were asking for.[338] In fact, the men had no need to have very long memories, for Octavian's march on Rome and the payment of the 2,500 *denarii* occupied a great part of the third book of Appian's *Civil Wars*, which had been published only about a generation previously, and which surely must have been well-known to at least some members of the Danubian army.[339]

Severus was fortunate and managed to escape with the payment of as little as 250 *denarii*: presumably the leading spirits among the men were more than satisfied with their transfer to the remodelled praetorian guard.[340] It was to the new guard that he made his donative in celebration of his *decennalia*: this appropriately consisted of an *aureus* for each year of his reign and therefore amounted to another 250 *denarii*.[341] Neither of these donatives can have cost the treasury very much, still less his celebration of the conferment of the title of Caesar upon his sons Caracalla and Geta, when he simply gave his troops permission to sack the Parthian capital, Ctesiphon.[342]

His only other recorded donatives are of unnamed amounts before and after the campaign against Albinus.[343] It was left to

Caracalla, after the murder of Geta, to pay to the praetorians a donative of as much as 2,500 *denarii*.[344]

It is noticeable that in every donative known the number of *denarii* is a multiple of 25. In other words, every known donative could have been paid entirely in *aurei*. The probability is that donatives, since the sums involved were large, were normally paid in *aurei*. Now during the later part of the period under consideration the *denarius* was consistently depreciating in value: it has been estimated that the real value of the *denarius* sank during the third century to about 0.5 per cent of what it had been before the inflation.[345] The nominal relationship, however, between the undebased gold and the much debased silver remained unchanged, and there were still, officially, only 25 *denarii* to the *aureus*.[346] This must have led to the virtual disappearance of the *aureus* from normal commercial transactions, and it must have commanded a considerable black market premium. The gold issued by way of donatives, therefore, must have increased considerably the value of such donatives as expressed in *denarii*. In the same way, if an Englishman today had his salary paid in gold sovereigns at the rate of one sovereign for every twenty shillings, he would be receiving a great deal more in practice than the nominal value of his salary. The other side of the picture is that the importance of the soldier's regular pay, which continued to be paid in the debased silver, must have become negligible. Fortunately for the soldier the compulsory stoppages for rations, clothing and arms were probably not increased to keep pace with the rise in prices, and so eventually became of little importance. By the time of Diocletian they had been abolished altogether.[347]

### REWARDS AND PUNISHMENTS

*Decorations*

As early as the Republic there was a marked tendency to award decorations on a fixed scale and to confine certain of them to particular ranks, in much the same way as in the British Army the D.S.O. is granted to officers of field rank, the M.C. to captains and subalterns, and the M.M. to other ranks. By the time of

Claudius, Roman practice had crystallized and there was very little change until the age of Severus, when the conservatism of the Roman army was temporarily overthrown. The decorations available to ranks below the centurionate were *torques* (necklaces), *armillae* (armbands), and *phalerae* (embossed discs worn on the corselet). These lesser decorations disappeared in the time of Severus, but the *torques* were to reappear in the late Empire. Rather oddly, this reappearance of the traditional *torques* has sometimes been regarded as one of the signs of the 'barbarization' of the army of the late Empire.[348]

*Evocati*, who occupied a position midway in status between *principales* and centurions, were eligible for these minor decorations, if they did not already possess them, and also for the grant of the *corona aurea*, a plain gold crown.[349] Centurions could be granted, besides the *corona aurea*, or more often instead of it, the *corona vallaris* or the *corona muralis*, crowns given to the first man over the enemy's rampart, or over the wall of a besieged town, respectively. Just as the *evocatus* might be considered for the *corona aurea*, so the *primipilus* could be awarded the *hasta pura*, a silver spearshaft, which was the characteristic decoration of officers of the equestrian order. Beyond the rank of *primipilus* the scale becomes more precise: officers who did not pass the rank of *tribunus militum angusticlavius* usually had to be content with a *corona* and a *hasta pura*, whereas those equestrians who advanced a little further might expect a *vexillum* as well. This was a small standard mounted on silver, and is the characteristic decoration of the higher officers. Officers of senatorial rank were awarded sets of decorations according to their grade: those below praetorian rank, *tribuni militum laticlavii*, had regularly two *coronae*, two *hastae purae*, and two *vexilla*. Officers of praetorian rank, legionary legates, usually received three of each, while the quota for officers of the highest grade, those of consular rank, was four *coronae*, four *hastae purae*, and four *vexilla*.

Decorations, of course, remained a privilege of honour, and not a right, and it sometimes happened that an award was made which might appear ungenerous. Vettius Valens, for instance, who as a *principalis* of the Guard in Britain under Claudius was awarded *torques, armillae* and *phalerae*, and subsequently as an *evocatus* received the *corona aurea*, rose in rank steadily as far as *primipilus*, yet his only decoration later was a repetition of the award of *torques, armillae* and *phalerae*.[350] Repetition of an award, however, was a mark of honour; just as in the British army an M.C. and bar ranks higher than the primary award, and an M.C. with two bars even higher, so in the Roman army the iteration of a decoration implied a higher grade in the same order. This principle is well-attested in the earliest Republican times: the semi-legendary L. Siccius Dentatus, traditionally *tribunus plebei* in 454 BC, could hardly have worn his complete collection of decorations at one and the same time, if in fact they ever were awarded. A veteran of 120 battles, eight times champion in single combat, with forty-five scars on the front of his body and none on his back, he is reported to have been awarded no less than eighteen *hastae purae*, twenty-five *phalerae*, 83 *torques*, more than 160 *armillae*, and twenty-six *coronae*, of which fourteen were *coronae civicae* (crowns of oak leaves granted for saving the life of a fellow-citizen), eight *coronae aureae*, three *coronae murales*, and one the coveted *corona obsidionalis*, or *corona graminea*, the highest decoration for valour, a wreath of grass awarded to the deliverer of a besieged army.[351] Of this last honour, Pliny the Elder lists a total of only eight recipients, ending with Augustus. The *corona civica* remained in the Empire theoretically open to all ranks, though there is no known instance of its conferment after the reign of Claudius. Later, Septimius Severus created a *corona civica aurea*, or civic crown of gold, which was open to centurions.[352] The heroes of the Empire seem never to have had the opportunity for outstanding exploits on the scale of those attributed to Dentatus, and though there was still a fair amount of iteration the numbers involved are much smaller.[353] All these decorations were worn by soldiers on dress parades and festivals, and were normally awarded at the close of a campaign either by the emperor or on his authority.[354]

Not only individual soldiers, but sometimes entire units could be decorated. Again there was some discrimination in the choice of award for the particular unit. The praetorian cohorts might be awarded *coronae aureae*, which they could display upon their standards. The legions might similarly display *coronae*, but cohorts only *phalerae*.[355] Auxiliary units might even include their decorations in their formal titles, which occasionally became rather long-winded on account of these honorific additions, as in *Ala I Flavia Augusta Britannica miliaria civium Romanorum bis torquata ob virtutem*, or *Cohors I Breucorum civium Romanorum Valeria victrix bis torquata ob virtutem appellata equitata*.[356] The former of these units has been honoured in three different ways: in the first place, the name *Flavia Augusta* honours the *ala* in much the same way as the prefix 'Royal' does to a regiment of the British Army; secondly, the additional title *civium Romanorum* (usually abbreviated *C.R.*) shows that on some occasion on account of distinguished service the entire *ala* (or rather those members of it who were still without the citizenship) had been granted the citizenship as a mark of honour; thirdly, the phrase *bis torquata ob virtutem* records the decorating of the standards of the *ala* on two occasions after some meritorious action. Legions were honoured in the first two of these ways; legions II, III and VIII, for instance, are known as *Augusta*, while VII and XI were both named *Claudia* for their loyalty in AD 42. More commonly we find an additional title such as *pia fidelis*. Thus *legio I Minervia* was raised by Domitian in AD 83 as *legio I Flavia Minervia pia fidelis Domitiana*.[357] After Domitian's death the names *Flavia* and *Domitiana* were dropped, and its title remained as *legio I Minervia pia fidelis*.

## Punishments

The severity of discipline in the army of the Republic was almost legendary. It was, of course, always liable to be exaggerated by writers of the early Empire who tended to project the unrealized desires of the present into the past, and to colour their accounts, as Livy did, with Augustan idealism. This attitude was so ingrained that authors such as Valerius Maximus and the composer of the fourth book of the *Strategemata*, who may not have been Frontinus,[358] recount with evident approval tales of stern generals of the Republic whose only military virtue seems to have been their severity. Yet this gloomy picture was not completely false:

Polybius, who was able to take a comparatively detached view of Roman life, ascribed the Roman success in the military field to the strict system of rewards and punishments which was then applied.[359] We must not, however, stress the inevitability of Roman discipline. Messer pointed out that modern German scholars, no doubt influenced by the German military tradition, have tended to accept automatically the eulogistic generalizations pronounced by their predecessors as well as by the ancients.[360] He came to the opposite view, that mutiny and insubordination were surprisingly prevalent in the Roman army. He showed that at all periods in the Republic the Roman legionary arrogated to himself an independence of thought and action which was far beyond that with which the Roman soldier is generally credited. It was this individual initiative, he maintained, which made the Roman soldier so successful, and not any blind and unquestioning obedience. The truth, no doubt, lies somewhere between the two extremes.

It could be argued that an unyielding system of blind obedience might work in an age of universal conscription, and especially in times of national crisis such as the Hannibalic invasion of the Second Punic War, but that in the conditions of the Empire, with a professional army manned by volunteers, any attempt to continue the system would have had so disastrous an effect upon recruitment as to make the very maintenance of the army impossible. Yet the austerity of the Foreign Legion in modern times seems to have acted as no deterrent to the flow of recruits. Josephus, who is perhaps the only major historian of the Empire who may fairly be compared with Polybius in this connection, comes to much the same conclusion as Polybius did: Roman training methods, he says, are partly based upon fear.[361] The Romans have laws which punish with death not merely desertion from the ranks, but even a slight neglect of duty; their generals are even more fearsome than their laws. Discipline in the army of the Empire, therefore, was never generally relaxed.

Yet the overall impression remains that the discipline of the army of the Empire was, like that of the Republican army described by Messer, not quite so severe as some Roman writers were proud to believe. This seems to have been especially true of the Eastern legions, and at all periods, except when they were unlucky enough to have a Corbulo in command.[362] Significant for the West is the description by Tacitus of Aufidienus Rufus, the hated *praefectus castrorum* at the time of the Pannonian revolt: 'a long-service ranker, who was ultimately promoted centurion and was soon afterwards appointed prefect of the camp; he was for restoring the old-fashioned hard discipline.'[363] The implication is that such an attitude was out-of-date. Similarly, Corbulo in Lower Germany in AD 47 found his men showed keenness for little except looting.[364] His restoration of the 'traditional' discipline gave him the reputation of being a martinet, and led to a number of stories about him. Tacitus maintains that although these stories were no doubt exaggerated, and perhaps even invented, they must have had some basis in fact, and must have been inspired by Corbulo's strictness. We may fairly conclude that a Corbulo would not have been so remarkable had there been many others like him, and that the great majority of Roman generals must have been comparatively mild. The discipline of an army is bound to be affected by the thinking of the age, and during the first two centuries of the Empire the traditional Roman virtues were gradually being modified by a new wave of humanitarianism.

It is on account of this discrepancy between fact and fiction, between the punishments which an unreasonable officer could legitimately inflict and the more or less standard practice of the remainder, that it is important to note not only the legal penalties for the common offences but also the action usually taken.

(a) *Decimation* Of all the punishments that could be inflicted under the Roman system perhaps the most famous is decimation. This punishment was usually applied to a particular cohort, in which every tenth man was selected by lot to be clubbed or stoned to death by his comrades in the remaining cohorts.[365] A minor penalty, such as being fed upon barley instead of on wheat, was often given to the nine-tenths who survived.[366] Though this barbarous practice had been employed by Octavian as late as the Dalmatian War in 34 BC, examples of it during the Empire are

decidedly uncommon.[367] The earliest is a single instance under
Tiberius, when L. Apronius, who had succeeded Camillus in the
command against Tacfarinas, decimated a cohort. Tacitus himself
describes the penalty as rare and old-fashioned.[368] Caligula is
reported by Suetonius to have attempted to make use of decimation on the legions which had shared in the rebellion of AD 14,
at a time when he had them concentrated for his projected German
campaign.[369] This intended reprisal a whole generation later for
an incident of his childhood was easily thwarted by the unwillingness of the army to carry out the contemplated massacre. The
next successful decimation was accomplished by that inveterate
disciplinarian, Galba, who decimated some ex-marines whom
Nero had formed into a legion.[370] When Galba ordered them to
return to the fleet the men had refused and had instead sought
official recognition of their new status by demanding an eagle
and standards. Galba had them dispersed by a cavalry charge and
decimated. This action was carried out by him on his first arrival
in the city, and had the not unnatural result of making his troops
disaffected.[371] Yet by 22 December of the same year he had so
far been forced to change his mind as to make the force of ex-
marines into a *iusta legio* with the title *I Adiutrix*, as is shown on
three diplomas of this date.[372] Since this was the very result which
the marines had been demanding, and this demand the immediate
cause of their decimation, the unfortunate soldiers may not have
died in vain. These few instances of decimation show that its
appeal was to those who were obsessed with *nimio amore antiqui
moris*, like Cassius Longinus who in a senate debate in AD 61
supported the policy of executing all the slaves of a murdered
city prefect by the parallel of decimation in the army.[373] In this
case the appeal to antiquity won the day, and the sentence was
carried out in spite of a massive popular demonstration. Decimation itself, however, was ultimately doomed, for though the
army might be prepared to assist in the execution of innocent
slaves, professional soldiers could hardly be expected to cooperate
in the indiscriminate execution of their own comrades.

(b) *Individual execution* Desertion, mutiny and insubordination made the individual soldier liable to the death penalty.[374] In

practice, however, this sentence was commonly avoided: even in the case of desertion account was taken of such considerations as length of service, rank or appointment, place where stationed, the duties shirked, previous conduct, whether the desertion was independent, with a single companion, or in a party, whether any additional crime had been committed during the period of desertion, the duration of absence, the nature of the man's subsequent conduct, and whether the return to duty had been made voluntarily or under compulsion.[375] Special consideration was also given to young soldiers on the occasion of their first offence, though this did not mean, as it has sometimes been taken to mean, that a first offence went unpunished.[376] More often, therefore, than not, the actual penalty inflicted proved to be less severe than the maximum: the range extended from corporal punishment (*castigatio*), through a monetary fine (*pecuniaria multa*) or extra duty (*munerum indictio*), to relegation to an inferior service (*militiae mutatio*), or reduction in rank (*gradus deiectio*), or discharge with ignominy (*missio ignominiosa*).[377] It was left to a Corbulo to insist always on the death penalty.[378]

(c) *Discharge or disbandment* The ultimate punishment which could be inflicted on a unit was its disbandment. This could be effected in various ways:

(i) The three legions XVII, XVIII and XIX, which were annihilated in the battle of the Teutoburgian Forest in AD 9, were never reformed, and their numbers were simply not used again.

(ii) Sometimes legions just disappeared from the army list, as did XV *Primigenia* after the revolt of Civilis, V *Alaudae* after the defeat of Cornelius Fuscus in Dacia in AD 86, XXI *Rapax*, probably lost on the Danubian front in AD 92, and XXII *Deiotariana*, which may have been destroyed in the Jewish revolt of AD 132–5. The end of IX *Hispana* is obscure; it was thought for long to have met a mysterious end in Britain, either about AD 119 or as late as 130, but it now appears to have moved to Nijmegen c. 121, and later, perhaps, to the East. If so, it may have shared the fate of XXII *Deiotariana* in the Jewish War of 132–5, or even have survived to be lost in Armenia c. 161.[379]

(iii) Other legions were disbanded and reconstituted under a new form: after the revolt of Civilis *legio* I was probably incorporated with VII *Galbiana* to form VII *Gemina*: IV *Macedonica* was at the same time reorganized as IV *Flavia felix*; XVI (*Gallica*) was similarly reconstituted as XVI *Flavia firma*.

(iv) During the third century two legions suffered *damnatio memoriae*; III *Gallica* in AD 219 for opposing Elagabalus, to be restored after his fall, and III *Augusta* in 238, to be restored fifteen years later by Valerian.

Disbandment of units was not an innovation of the Empire. In 75 BC, for instance, C. Curio abolished the name of one of the five legions under his command in the Dardanian war, and distributed its members to fill out the other four, and during the Civil Wars Octavian disbanded a *legio* X with ignominy.[380] Similarly, Caesar all but disbanded his Ninth Legion before Placentia. He discharged them all in disgrace, and reinstated them only after earnest entreaties and the punishment of the ringleaders.[381]

A like threat was made by him to his Tenth Legion at Rome, when they were demanding immediate discharge and the payment of their gratuities, even though the war was still raging in Africa. In this case by addressing them as 'citizens' instead of 'soldiers' he brought them back to their senses. The disbandment did not then take place, but the most insubordinate were punished by the loss of a third part of the land and booty reserved for them.[382]

For the individual soldier discharge with ignominy became a more serious punishment as the army became professionalized. The loss of the *praemia militiae* which necessarily accompanied a *missio ignominiosa* was a heavy blow to men who had served for many years in the legions. So we find Caesar employing this measure against negligent soldiers, and dismissing two *tribuni militum* and three centurions before an assembly of his entire force.[383] Once Augustus had completed the process of professionalization by the establishment of the *aerarium militare* and the institution of the *praemia militiae* on a proper footing in AD 6, the threat of a *missio ignominiosa* acted as a very powerful deterrent to negligence and insubordination.[384]

The importance of the type of discharge had its effect upon the law, and eventually three categories were clearly distinguished, to which some added a fourth.[385] These were *honesta missio*, honourable discharge, which took place after due completion of service, or even before in certain cases; *missio causaria*, which corresponded more or less with our 'invaliding out'; *missio ignominiosa*, discharge with ignominy or cashiering. The fourth kind of *missio* was when a man who had not been qualified to serve in the first instance, but had enlisted to avoid some other liability to service, was removed from the army. The lawyers held that the type of discharge should always be stated, but that a discharge could be with ignominy even when this was not specifically expressed.[386] Hence soldiers took pains to make it clear, in inscriptions of all kinds, that their own discharge was honourable. The natural anxiety to demonstrate this seems to be the reason for the rather unusual wording of a diploma granted to an ex-marine, who was discharged from *II Adiutrix* on 7 March AD 70.[387] In this, though the recipient is described as a *causarius*, he is given an *honesta missio*. With this diploma we may compare an inscription of the early third century from Rome in which an ex-member of II *Parthica*, who had served for nineteen years, is described as *ex causa missus honesta missione*.[388]

It would seem on the evidence of these two documents that a man invalided out could still receive an honourable discharge if that were felt appropriate. Any rule to the contrary would have been obviously unfair. To that extent, therefore, the categories of discharge were not mutually exclusive. There is in fact some measure of disagreement between different definitions of *missio causaria* in the *Digest*:[389] Macer's is unfavourable to the character and reputation of the soldier, for it describes him as a man who has been made less suitable for service *vitio animi vel corporis*, 'through a weakness of mind or body', whereas Ulpian's is quite neutral and unbiased in tone, and simply ascribes his discharge to ill-health. This ambivalence would seem to correspond with the recorded cases: men discharged *ex causa* could, with a good record, receive a full *honesta missio* even before the end of their term of service, and Ulpian in the *Digest* describes the *honesta missio* as granted *emeritis stipendiis vel ante*, 'after completion of service or before'.[390] On the other hand, this indulgence would not be expected by men discharged for mental or physical weakness (*vitio animi vel corporis*). It is to men in the latter category that Nesselhauf would limit *missio causaria*.[391] This would save the tripartite division by leaving three fairly clear-cut categories of discharge: those who had completed their service together with the honourably incapacitated would receive the *honesta missio*; those who became mentally ill or physically unfit would become *causarii* and be discharged without privileges; those discharged by way of punishment would receive the *missio ignominiosa* with its attendant disadvantages. Yet this explanation, appealing as it is, fails to clarify why the men who received the *honesta missio* should have been described as *causarii*. Their discharge must surely have been *causaria* in the first instance, and subsequently upgraded after consideration to *honesta missio*. If so, discharges not so upgraded could, by implication at least, become *ignominiosae*. This is in harmony with the rule that a discharge could be with ignominy even in the absence of any express statement to that effect. The *missio causaria* would on this system be merely a temporary classification. Whichever of these two theories is correct, if either is, is not likely to be easily proved: there will never surely be a glut of dedications which lay claim to any discharge which is not strictly honourable.

(d) *Reduction in rank*   Before the army became professional there was no regular system of advancement: conversely, there could hardly be a regular system of punishment by demotion. Under Caesar, however, we hear of *signiferi* being stripped of their rank, and this punishment became more usual when the army became permanent.[392] Reduction in rank (*gradus deiectio*) was one possibility, another was transfer to a lower-ranking arm of service (*militiae mutatio*). A possible example of the latter punishment is contained in the *pridianum*, or annual strength return, of the *cohors I Augusta Lusitanorum equitata* for the year ending 31 August AD 156.[393] A decurion is recorded as returned (*reiectus*) from the *ala I Thracum*: since an *ala* is a superior arm of service to a *cohors equitata* this transfer is most reasonably considered as a case of *militiae mutatio*.[394] In the same document two soldiers are recorded as received (*accepti*) from *legio II Traiana fortis.*[395] This would appear to be another instance of the same practice. The best-known case, however, is that of P. Valerius Comazon. He began his remarkable career as an actor in pantomime but soon found his way into the army. It was while he was serving in Thrace, probably during the early years of Commodus, that he incurred the displeasure of the governor, Claudius Attalus, for some misdemeanour. It is not clear in what capacity his service in Thrace was, whether it was as an auxiliary, or as a legionary perhaps serving on the governor's staff, but the punishment is known: he was transferred to the fleet.[396] This disgrace did not succeed in ruining Comazon's career, for he subsequently rose to the command of the praetorians, to the consulate (in AD 220), and to the city prefecture, which he held three times.

(e) *Fines and deductions from pay* Fines as a punishment are attested by Polybius and were still employed in the time of the *Digest*.[397] One instance as early as 176 BC is of an entire legion which had its pay docked for a year, after the consul Q. Petilius had been killed in battle by the Ligurians.[398] Livy records a less severe example: a legion was put on half-pay for a year.[399] A different form of fine was imposed by Caesar, when he punished the insubordinate soldiers of the Tenth by depriving them of the third part of the booty and the land intended for them.[400]

(f) *Corporal punishment* Flogging was the punishment which made the name of the centurion feared. A disciplinarian such as Lucilius, the hated centurion of the Pannonian revolt, would use his *vitis*, or vine-staff, the symbol of his office, to such good purpose as to acquire the nickname '*Cedo alteram*' ('Gimme another') from his habit of breaking the *vitis* upon the backs of the men under his command.[401]

(g) *Other forms of punishment* Where corporal punishment was inappropriate, even more humiliating substitutes could be found. So, for instance, Octavian punished centurions guilty of minor offences by ordering them to stand all day long outside the *praetorium*, sometimes dressed in tunics and without belts, sometimes holding measuring poles or even a piece of turf.[402] Corbulo treated a *praefectus equitum* in much the same way.[403]

The same principle could be applied to entire units. To encamp outside the defences (*extra vallum tendere*) was a punishment which had been inflicted as far back as 302 BC, and again during the war with Pyrrhus, and which was used on more than one occasion during the Punic Wars.[404] Corbulo, who never showed reluctance to revive old-fashioned disciplinary measures, employed the same device against certain auxiliary units in Armenia.[405]

Finally, either as an additional punishment or as an independent one, men could be fed upon barley instead of on wheat. This punishment was laid upon certain legions for as long as seven years in the period after Cannae:[406] it is mentioned by Polybius in combination with encamping outside the fortifications as a penalty inflicted on the survivors after decimation:[407] it was used, however, without this added refinement by Antony in 36 BC and again by Octavian two years later:[408] presumably, by that date, encamping outside the defences was a punishment which had fallen into desuetude, at least until it came to be revived by Corbulo. A different reason for feeding men on barley is given by Vegetius. In his description of the training of recruits he declares that it was a practice of the ancients that men who had failed to reach an adequate standard in the *armatura* should be reduced to being fed on rations of barley instead of wheat, and that the wheat ration was not restored to them until they had demonstrated their competence in the necessary tasks to the satisfaction of the officers concerned.[409] If this was so, what had once been a punishment associated with collective disgrace had by now become a mark of personal shame for failing to pass a proficiency test.

Imprisonment was not in itself a form of punishment in the Roman army, but was no more than a convenient means of detaining men awaiting trial or execution.[410] This is reflected in the comparative unimportance of the camp prison, which, where attested, was generally under the charge of an *optio*,[411] with perhaps the occasional assistance of *clavicularii*, or turnkeys, though the inscriptions which record these are few in number.[412] The military prison is usually known as the *carcer*, and Domaszewski would ascribe only the *optio carceris* to the camp gaol, and would prefer to relate the *optio custodiarum* to the governor's prison.[413]

# CHAPTER V

# RELIGION AND MARRIAGE

## RELIGION

Practitioners of the art of war have not usually been noted for their religious beliefs. To this generalization there can, of course, be made numerous exceptions: many of those who took part in the Crusades may well have been motivated by a burning desire to win converts for Christianity; more of them, probably, merely wanted to win land for Christendom and, in particular, for themselves. Cromwell's army was, it is true, distinguished for its version of Puritanism, but this contained a strong political and social element. The armies of the Crusades and the Civil War were, however, peculiar in that they were raised for a special purpose, a purpose which was itself closely connected with religion. In a normal professional army there is not generally a unified religious outlook, but rather a diversity of religious beliefs. The Roman army of the early Empire was no exception to this principle. Freedom of worship was, within reason, permitted. Dedications survive to an enormous number of deities, ranging from those which were *di militares* in the narrowest sense to the most exotic, and from the traditional gods of the state religion to minor local gods and goddesses such as Cocidius and Coventina.[414]

### The cult of the standards

In such diversity a unifying element was essential. Tertullian found it in the cult of the standards:[415] 'The religious system of the Roman army is entirely devoted to the worship of the standards; oaths are sworn by the standards, and the standards are preferred to all deities.' We now know that Tertullian was guilty of exaggeration.[416] At Dura-Europos, a remote outpost on the Eastern frontier, amongst the records of the *cohors XX Palmyrenorum*, a festival list, the *Feriale Duranum*, was discovered during the excavation season of 1931–2.[417] The most striking feature of the list is that few entries are included primarily for their bearing on the army.[418] The great majority of the entries are such as would appear in any calendar of the official religion of the Roman state. What is most noteworthy is the exclusion of all foreign cults, which is all the more surprising since the garrison of Dura was composed largely of Orientals.[419] The clear intention of Roman army religion as shown in the *Feriale Duranum* was the promotion of romanization.[420] The army religion and the state religion were identical.

### The eagle

Nevertheless, Tertullian was not completely wrong. The cultivation of *esprit de corps* is a necessity for any military unit, and for this purpose the cult of the standards was ideal. In a sense, the standards formed the very identity of the unit to which they belonged. With the legions the eagle, *aquila*, was the object of special veneration. Tacitus describes how Germanicus, in the fighting against the Cherusci, took advantage of a fortunate coincidence:[421] 'He saw an excellent omen, eight eagles making for the woods and entering them. "Forward," he shouted, "follow the Roman birds, the legions' own spirits!" ' The other side of the picture was that the loss of the eagle was felt to be almost synonymous with the loss of the legion itself. Of all the disasters which could happen to a legion, this was by far the worst. The loss of the eagle was traditionally followed by the disbandment of the legion. This happened to the three legions of Varus in AD 9, and later to the four Rhineland legions which either surrendered to Civilis or lost their eagles in the revolt of AD 69–70.[422] The rule may not, however, have been invariable. Velleius reports that a *legio* V lost its eagle during the fighting in Germany under Lollius in 16 BC.[423] This legion has been identified by some scholars as V *Alaudae*: if the identification is correct, the loss of the eagle did not necessitate the disbandment of the legion.[424] Again, XII *Fulminata*, according to Suetonius, lost its eagle in AD 66 when fighting under Cestius Gallus in the Jewish War:[425] it certainly continued to exist. Either of these losses may, of course, have been only temporary, but it does not appear that the loss of the eagle led to inevitable disbandment.

The *aquila* first became the legionary emblem as part of the reforms of Marius. The responsibility for guarding it, at least during the Empire, rested with the first cohort, and ultimately devolved upon the *primus pilus*; the actual care of the eagle was the duty of the *aquilifer*.[426] The eagle was in Republican times of silver; with increasing prestige it became more precious, and Dio tells us that some of the eagles of Pompey's legions in 45 BC carried in their talons thunderbolts of gold.[427] By the time of the Empire the entire eagle was of gold or, more probably, silver-gilt.[428] A special chapel was built in each legionary headquarters to house the eagle and the other legionary standards, *signa*, of which there was probably one for each cohort.[429] An innovation of the Empire was the addition of *imagines*, which were standards containing medallions with the portraits of the emperors. Dio gives a short account of the eagle:[430] 'There is a small shrine, and in this there is an eagle of gold. Every legion in the army list has an eagle, and it never leaves the winter quarters unless the entire legion sets out. It is mounted on a large pole, which is tapered to a sharp point so that it may be fixed firmly in the ground, and it is carried by one man.' The veneration felt for the eagle caused it on occasion to be used for the purpose of sanctuary. Tacitus relates an incident of the mutiny of AD 14, which almost brought about the murder of L. Munatius Plancus, the leader of a senatorial delegation:[431] 'The men heaped insults upon them and were on the point of killing them, Plancus above all. His rank made it impossible for him to withdraw, and in this crisis his only hope of refuge was the camp of the First Legion. There he sought sanctuary by clasping the eagle and the standards. But if the *aquilifer*, Calpurnius, had not prevented his assassination, there would have occurred an event which is uncommon even among our enemies: a legate of the Roman people, in a Roman camp, would have stained with his own blood the altars of the gods.'

*Festivals*

Since the *signa* had such a prominent position in the religious life of the army, it was only natural that festivals should be attached to them. Of these the most important in a legion was the *natalis aquilae*, which celebrated the anniversary of the legion's foundation. This is attested, for instance, in an inscription from Emporiae in Spain, in which a vexillation of *legio* VII *Gemina felix* makes a dedication to Iuppiter Optimus Maximus in honour of the *natalis aquilae*.[432] Another festival is that of the *rosaliae signorum*, which in the *Feriale Duranum* occurs on two separate days, (10?)th and 31st May.[433] Hoey, however, sees the *rosaliae* rather as the military form of a festival taken over from civil life than as a military festival proper.[434] He rightly points out that the standards had a prominent place at and were assigned a significant part in military ceremonies of all kinds. For this reason he considers that the rose festival was attached to the *signa* simply in order to make it an integral part of the army's religion. Be that as it may, it is worthy of notice that the dedication in honour of the *natalis aquilae* was made not to the *signa* as such, but to Iuppiter Optimus Maximus, the chief deity in the Capitoline triad, and regarded as the chief protector of the Roman state. Dedications to him and to his partners in the triad were common in the army, though individual dedications to Iuno Regina appear less common than those to Iuppiter himself and to Minerva.[435] Dedications were, however, sometimes made to the *signa* themselves, though even then usually in association with other gods.[436] No doubt the reason for dedications to a multiplicity of gods is to be found in the religious outlook of the average soldier. His real faith probably rested in the Genius of his unit alone, but doubtful of the efficacy of an unsupported prayer, he strengthened it by the inclusion of as many compatible deities as he could manage. This attitude was assisted by the prevalent Roman habit of assimilating one god to another, or *interpretatio Romana*, by which a minor provincial deity, such as Cocidius, could be endowed with the attributes of a major Roman one, such as Mars, and both be worshipped together as Mars Cocidius.[437]

It was undoubtedly the religious aspect of the *signa* which led
to the siting of the regimental bank with the standards and under
the care of the *signiferi*.[438] This normally meant in practice that
the rooms on each side of the shrine of the standards, or *sacellum*,
were offices for regimental records and for pay, and that beneath
the latter was the underground strongroom.[439]

## Official cults

The deities worshipped by soldiers may be divided for convenience into two main groups. The first group comprises the gods of
the established state religions, whose worship was regulated by
official calendars such as the *Feriale Duranum*, and also personified
virtues such as *Disciplina* and *Virtus*, which are obviously desirable
in military life. The second group includes other cults, mainly
non-Roman, which were adopted and encouraged by military
units, but which were not included in the official calendars.[440]

The official gods, some of whom had their statues in the
regimental chapel, were essentially the Capitoline triad of
*Iuppiter Optimus Maximus*, *Iuno Regina* and *Minerva*, besides the
war god of the Roman army, *Mars*, and the personified goddess of
victory, *Victoria*.[441] Other personifications which might be so
honoured included *Urbs Roma*, whose cult was instituted by
Hadrian, *Disciplina*, *Fortuna*, *Honos*, *Pietas*, *Virtus*, and *Bonus
Eventus*.[442] In the third century *Hercules*, who had for long been
the protecting deity of the *equites singulares*, tended to supplant
*Mars* among the units stationed along the Rhine and Danube.[443]
This was probably assisted by the transference of the attributes of
the German god *Donar* to the Roman *Hercules*.[444] It is small
wonder, therefore, that Maximian elected to take the name
*Herculius* in counterbalance to Diocletian's *Jovius*. Finally,
amongst the statues of the gods and next to the standards in the
regimental chapel a place of honour was reserved for the statue
of the reigning emperor.[445]

## Unofficial cults

Much more interesting individually are the unofficial cults. But
here it must be realized that very few of these are primarily

military. Men from all over the Empire took with them their own beliefs, and because this was so there is at times an exotic flowering of out-of-the-way cults in the most apparently unpromising neighbourhood. So, for instance, the *cohors I Hamiorum* took their goddess *Hammia* to Carvoran, besides the *dea Syria*, the Germans from Twenthe in Over-Yssel, Holland, established *Mars Thincsus* and the two *Alaisiagae*, *Beda* and *Fimmilena*, at Housesteads, the Tungrians brought the goddess *Viradecthis* to Birrens, while the sailors of the Misene fleet, who came mainly from the hellenized East, had a special regard for *Serapis*.[446] Besides the imported deities, however, the soldiers, who were nothing if not eclectic in their religious views, took enthusiastically to such local cults as that of the goddess *Coventina* at Carrawburgh, whose well provides evidence of offerings late into the fourth century.[447] Other local deities in Britain are *Belatucadrus* and *Cocidius* in the Western region of Hadrian's Wall, and *Maponus*, whose name may still survive in the modern Lochmaben.[448]

## Iuppiter Dolichenus

There were, however, two cults which were both widespread and mainly military. The first of these is that of *Iuppiter Dolichenus*, named after Doliche, a hill in Commagene which is still known as Tell Dülük, and worshipped there apparently since Hittite times. Just as *Dolichenus* was equated with *Iuppiter*, so his consort was addressed as *Iuno*.[449] His appeal to the army was no doubt due to his close association with iron, since in dedications he is described as 'born where the iron is born'.[450] His worship in the West reached its peak in the third century, thanks to a deliberate policy on the part of its priesthood of popularizing the cult by associating it with other deities.[451] It was to share in their decline.

## Mithras

The second cult is that of Mithras. Although his worship reached the Roman world as early as the first century BC, brought by the Cilician pirates suppressed by Pompey, it was not until the second century AD that Mithraism really began to take a firm hold in the West.[452] It was in the third century that it reached its peak.

Its appeal was to both the army and the merchant class, but its attraction, though powerful, was nevertheless restricted. Firstly, there was no room in Mithraism for women, and secondly, its members formed a secret society. Its exclusive nature appealed particularly to the officer class, and it is perhaps significant that the Mithraic temples are all small and that the dedications are generally made by officers. Thus, of the ten dedicators of Mithraic inscriptions on Hadrian's Wall at least five, and perhaps six, are prefects; two were centurions, one a *beneficiarius consularis*, who doubtless thought of himself as well on the way to the centurionate, and the other had an Eastern name.[453]

## Christianity

Finally, there is the question of Christianity. This religion was never at all prominent in military circles during the first three centuries, though no doubt there always were some Christians. Even with the coming of the Christian Empire, the expected instant conversion of the army did not take place; instead, the army remained the last refuge of paganism, and it was not until the second half of the century after the passing of Julian the Apostate that the turning-point came. For the first half of the century the lower ranks of the army, doubtless because of their recruitment from the rural areas, remained obstinately pagan. It is noticeable that the traces of Christianity found on military sites in Roman Britain are very few indeed.[454]

### MARRIAGE AND DISCHARGE

Theoretically, an army may be more efficient if its members are celibate and wedded only to the idea of discipline. There is then no heart-searching when a unit is suddenly posted from one end of the empire to another, there is no attached civilian population to defend and to take into account in the siting and construction of camps and forts, and the soldier's only ties are to the army in which he serves. Such a theory probably inspired the legal position of the soldier at the beginning of the Empire. At that date and for long afterwards soldiers were incapable of contracting a legal marriage during the entire extent of their service.[455] Even marriages which were already in existence when the men enlisted were broken off.[456] This ban covered all ranks up to the centurionate. Equestrian officers, who were members of the army only for the duration of their appointments, and who could not therefore be considered professional soldiers in the fullest sense, were naturally exempt from the ban. Yet even they were forbidden to marry women from the provinces in which they were serving.[457] Augustus attempted to extend the ban to the highest level, by forbidding senatorial officers to take their wives with them to their provinces.[458] But the example of members of the imperial house, such as Germanicus, whose son Gaius got the nickname 'Caligula' from being brought up among the troops, made it difficult to enforce this.[459] These measures were, however, all in harmony with the firm intention of creating a celibate army, wedded only to the service.

### Unofficial unions

Difficulties arose at once. It might have been possible in a short-service army to keep the men unattached until their period of service was over, but the Roman army was not of that model. It was a long-service army in which the average recruit was eighteen or nineteen, an age when very few were already married and with children. The men served for at least twenty-five years, and often for a great deal longer, and though many did have children after they had retired, the best years of their lives in that respect were far behind them. The soldier's answer was obvious. If he could not be married officially, he would be married unofficially. The men's intentions, therefore, were working against the official policy.

The long-term interest of the government was that there should be a constant succession of recruits from the right background, who were imbued with the military spirit and accustomed to the rigours of military life. On the one hand, therefore, the Roman state wanted to keep the men from marrying, in case the presence of family ties should impede the mobility of the army and endanger its morale; on the other hand, they wanted the men to have children, in order that there might be a plentiful supply of potential recruits. The natural conclusion, then, was to enforce the ban on legal marriage, but at the same time to encourage unofficial marriage. The unfortunate legal consequences of this policy were to some extent ameliorated by a succession of *ad hoc* measures. It is noticeable that though the interests of the fathers were usually considered, and the interests of the children were protected more and more, the mothers appear to have been looked upon merely as an unavoidable necessity.

The local women with whom the soldiers formed more or less permanent associations were usually of peregrine status, at least in the frontier areas where most of the soldiers were stationed. Many of them formed lifelong partnerships with their husbands, and their marriages became regularized after the husband's retirement from service. The inscriptions on tombstones set up by adoring husbands naturally make no distinction between wives who were legally married, and therefore *coniuges* in the strict sense, and the others, who would be in common usage *focariae*.[460] In the same way, the wives make affectionate dedications in honour of their husbands.

The first problem to be dealt with was that although the men were unofficially married and were raising families, they were still apparently liable to the legal penalties of the unmarried. Claudius, therefore, granted soldiers the privileges of married men, that is to say, he exempted them from the provisions of the *Lex Iulia de maritandis ordinibus* of 18 BC, as revised by the *Lex Papia Poppaea* of AD 9.[461] This was no more than fair: it is surprising that soldiers had ever been considered to be affected by these acts.

*Inheritance*

Rather more serious was the position of their children in regard to the inheritance of the parental estate. Since the children were technically illegitimate, they were debarred from inheriting in the usual way. It was still possible, of course, for the father to treat them like strangers and make them his heirs by testamentary deposition: one consequence of this action was that they then became liable to the 5 per cent tax on inheritance, usually known as the *vicesima hereditatum*.[462] Close relatives were exempt from this tax. It was left to Hadrian, in AD 119, to alleviate the situation by granting the (illegitimate) children of soldiers the right of inheriting their fathers' possessions.[463] The bulk of these estates would no doubt consist of *deposita* in the unit savings-bank.[464]

The ban on marriage with *conubium* did not immediately affect peregrines, who at this date still constituted the bulk of the auxiliary forces. But the right of *matrimonium ex iure gentium*, which otherwise would have been open to them, was equally denied them.[465]

### The legal position after service

So much for marriage during service. What is perhaps a more important topic is what were the consequences after the man's service was over. The position of each branch of the services differs in some material aspect. The situation is clearest in the case of the auxiliary soldiers, who, in common with the praetorians and the marines, were entitled to receive so-called *diplomata militaria* (the term is modern), i.e. a pair of bronze plates containing the documentary evidence of their status.[466] The diplomas furnished proof of the man's service and honourable discharge, and recorded the grant of citizenship and *conubium* where this was appropriate. If an auxiliary was already a Roman citizen he still required a grant of *conubium* before he could have a *matrimonium iustum*, unless his wife happened to have the citizenship also. The wife was not granted citizenship by virtue of her husband's service. Even in cases where the wife held the citizenship the diploma was still of advantage to the husband, at any rate until the year AD 140 or thereabouts; the diplomas up to that date granted the citizenship to the man's children already born, including the daughters.[467] From the time of Antoninus Pius onwards, however, the diplomas no longer had retrospective force, and existing children ceased to receive the citizenship.[468] The immediate effect of the change must have been a considerable reduction in the number of women of marriageable age who were in possession of the citizenship. This must have had its influence on the matrimonial chances of soldiers, especially in the frontier areas. The percentage of men with the citizenship, however, was continually increasing. The combination of these factors would suggest that it was women who were the chief beneficiaries of the *constitutio Antoniniana* of AD 212. The change in the privileges granted by the diplomas was undoubtedly intended to stimulate recruiting. The sons who were now left without the citizenship still had the possibility of acquiring it by military service. This tended to create a hereditary military caste.

## Septimius Severus' concession

In about the year AD 197 Septimius Severus as a concession allowed soldiers to live with their 'wives'.[469] It was for long debated whether this meant any more than that the state had at last recognized what had been happening for a long time, which would have meant that there was no real change and that the 'wives' were still concubines in law, or whether Severus was making a genuine concession and allowing the men to make a proper marriage.[470] The evidence, mainly indirect and implicit, from the legal codes and the *Digest*, supports the view that it was a genuine marriage which was intended.[471] The position, however, was complicated by differences in legal status. A soldier with the citizenship who married a woman with the citizenship would make a *matrimonium iustum*. If, however, either party or both parties lacked the citizenship, the only form of marriage possible would be a *matrimonium ex iure gentium*, except in the special case, as in the diplomas, where a husband with citizenship receives a grant of *conubium* to enable him to marry a peregrine wife. It cannot be assumed that the concession made by Severus included a grant of *conubium*. The probabilities, therefore, are that the immediate effect of Severus's concession was to make a great many couples married *ex iure gentium*. This was an important step forward, in so far as it made questions of inheritance, both for wives and children, very much easier, but it did no more for the men in the army than had probably been done by the year AD 166 by Marcus Aurelius for the fleet.[472] The final solution to the whole question of marriage in the armed forces was made by Caracalla, who in AD 212 granted the citizenship to all free people in the Empire: this step eliminated nearly all the legal complications which had arisen.

## The 'permitted custom'

In the fleets the situation had become liberalized at an earlier date. The sailors of the praetorian fleets of Misenum and Ravenna— the position of the provincial fleets is obscure—had not been affected by the change in style of auxiliary diplomas after AD 140, and for some years they continued to receive diplomas with the old formula.[473] Then in about 166 a change was made. The diplomas now gave the citizenship to the sailors and to those (male?) children whose mothers the men could prove to have lived with them in accordance with 'the permitted custom', besides conubium with the wives they had at the time the citizenship was granted with the usual limitation to prevent polygamy.[474] What was meant by 'the permitted custom'? It has commonly been taken to mean the official recognition of concubinage, but the requirement of proof demanded seems to militate against this interpretation, and Starr believes that it was matrimonium which was intended. Sander with more precision has declared this to be matrimonium ex iure gentium, since the fathers were generally of Latin rights.[475] If this is the correct view, the marital position of the sailors after AD 166 will have anticipated the situation of the rest of the armed services after 197. As Starr writes, 'With the navy, indeed, concessions might be made more easily; while engaged on active service the sailor could not hope to have his wife present or near by, and during the stops in port he had little to do of a military nature.'[476] We may take the view that it was as a result of the experience of the praetorian fleets over a generation that Septimius Severus found it possible to break with long-standing army tradition and make it legal for the men to be officially married.

## The continuance of diplomas

An indirect result of the concession made by Septimius Severus is that auxiliary units ceased apparently to be issued with diplomas, which were confined in future to the praetorian guard, the urban cohorts, the equites singulares (whose only surviving diplomas are of this period), and the praetorian fleets.[477] Apart from one diploma, which was issued to a member of the cohors XIII urbana at

Lugdunum, all the diplomas of this period are concerned with units which were stationed in Italy.[478] The single exception is the one which proves the rule, for one urban cohort could hardly have been treated differently from the others. The question which we have to answer, therefore, is why the Italian units, with the noticeable exception of *legio II Parthica*, which as the emperor's personal legion was based at Albanum near Rome from AD 202, were still issued with diplomas at a time when all other forces had ceased to require them.[479] The legionaries, of course, with the exception of some who had previously served as marines, had never received diplomas; presumably the levelling-up process had by now proceeded so far that the auxiliary units were being treated in the same way. Durry believed that the praetorians still required diplomas to regularize their marriages, and that the general permission for soldiers to marry which had been granted by Severus did not apply to the élite corps at Rome.[480] This would have been a sufficient explanation had it not been for the fact that the sailors too still had diplomas, and Durry himself admits that they could marry. The most convincing answer is given by Starr, who believes that the diplomas were still issued after the time of Severus to members of the Italian units, and only to these, not because they might still be peregrines or could not legally marry, but solely *honoris causa* and as the traditional evidence of their service.[481] It may be added that this argument would apply with the greatest force to members of the praetorian guard, and that if diplomas were issued to them *honoris causa*, it would be not unreasonable to extend the privilege to all troops serving under the general surveillance of the *praefectus praetorio*.[482]

The wording of the diplomas in the third century shows no material change from that employed in the second half of the second century, except that those diplomas which were issued to members of the praetorian fleets require a minimum period of service of twenty-eight years in place of the previous twenty-six.[483] Yet even this change may not necessarily be of Severan date or later. The earliest diploma to contain the new term of service is Dipl. 138 of AD 213/17. The latest diploma to give positive evidence of the old term is Dipl. 100 of AD 152. In the interesting diploma which first introduces the phrase *concessa consuetudine* ('in accordance with the permitted custom') the length of service has had to be restored, since in the text only the word *viginti* survives.[484] The spacing would allow either *sex*, which has been accepted by the editors, or *octo*. Starr, assuming the orthodox reading *sex*, suggests that the change to a term of twenty-eight years could have been made either by Marcus Aurelius in his later years, or else by Septimius Severus to offset difficulty in naval recruiting.[485] Against this interpretation it may be argued that it would appear to have been a good deal easier to carry through what must surely have been an unpopular measure by making it part of a package deal with a much more popular one. In this case the extension of the term of service by two years would have been made much more acceptable by the linking with it of the introduction of permission to marry. This would appear to be a sound reason for bringing forward the date of this change to the early years of Marcus Aurelius before AD 166, and for associating with it the recognition of marriage in the navy.

*Civil settlements*
The lifting of the general ban on marriage about 197 can have had very little immediate effect upon the way of life of the serving soldier in the frontier areas. There is no evidence that at this date the men's families began to live inside the forts, and it is both premature and an exaggeration to describe the change as 'the introduction of a form of married quarters'.[486] That was to come later, in the fourth century, and was a sign of the weakening in security of the frontier.[487] What did take place at this period was an increase in the size of the *vici*, or civil settlements in the immediate neighbourhood of the forts, and of the *canabae*, or civil towns beside the legionary fortresses.[488] These had been gradually increasing in size and importance during the second century, but their rate of increase must have been considerably accelerated by the reforms of Severus. Many more soldiers would now have permanent rather than transient relationships, and this must have encouraged the growth of considerable communities. Apart from the wives and families of serving soldiers, these

communities would include retired veterans and their families, traders, and presumably many of the local native population. Formal recognition was given to some of these communities, and the largest of them achieved a degree of self-government. In northern Britain, for example, some of the *vicani* had developed a communal organization by the middle of the third century.[489] The largest communities fared even better, and at York the *canabae* of the legionary fortress rose to the rank of a *colonia* and became the administrative capital of the province of Britannia Inferior.[490]

## The immobility of the frontier forces

If the short-term effect of the change was beneficial, the long-term effect was perhaps not quite so fortunate. The almost complete identification of the outlook of the men of the frontier forces with the feelings and aspirations of the areas in which they lived and worked meant that the men became reluctant to be posted elsewhere, and the mobility of the army was impaired. This left the Roman government with little option but to create a separate, more mobile force, the field-army, which could be used as a strategic reserve. Even in this it was sometimes found necessary to make arrangements for the transportation of families, which must have severely handicapped the conduct of operations.[491]

## The limitanei

The original frontier forces thus became, by the pressure of events, the collection of static units which comprised the *limitanei*.[492] This was the probably unforeseen final development of the Roman policy towards marriage in the army. The desire to make the army self-perpetuating had led first to the connivance of the authorities in the creation of unofficial domestic establishments, and then progressively to the recognition of these establishments as part of the military organization. The ultimate effect was to create an army, based largely on the frontiers, which was too immobile to make large troop movements practicable. The creation of the strategic reserve which was shown to be necessary by the crises of the third century, required the founding of a field-army, which quickly became an élite corps. Thereby the comparative importance of the frontier forces, now known as the *limitanei*, was still further depressed, though they continued to be the prime defence against barbarian invasions, and are by no means to be dismissed as a mere peasant militia.

The gradual assimilation of the frontier soldiers with the people amongst whom they served had one other unfortunate effect upon discipline. In times of crisis soldiers, especially recruits, tended to slip away from their posts and to disappear into the background of the civilian population. Desertion became most serious in the later fourth century; in the East it was most marked after the battle of Adrianople, in Britain after the 'barbarian conspiracy' of AD 367–9.[493]

# CHAPTER VI

# THE SOLDIER IN SOCIETY

## THE SOLDIER IN PEACETIME

Once the soldier had been trained, he could look forward to a life which would be spent mainly in conditions of peace. Although there was at most periods considerable military activity in various parts of the Empire, it was unusual for a large part of the army to be involved, and many soldiers may never have been called upon to take part in a campaign. As Ramsay MacMullen has put it, 'Many a recruit need never have struck a blow in anger, outside of a tavern.'[494] It was therefore highly desirable that the trained soldiers be found something to do, since an unoccupied army may soon become demoralized or dangerous.

This same problem of finding employment for soldiers in barracks can arise in modern armies. In these the usual answer is to invent tasks which have little or no practical value, such as the whitewashing of walls or the polishing of buckets. For the futility of much of this the commanders themselves are perhaps not entirely to blame. Army establishments are nowadays not so static as in Roman times, garrisons are more frequently changed, armaments become rapidly obsolete and retraining is made more necessary. There is not the same expectation, therefore, of a long period of underemployment, which could profitably be used for the teaching of non-military skills. Moreover, in many countries there would be objections from civilians, especially from trade unions, if military forces were regularly used on non-military duties.

The relationship of the Roman soldier to the civilian was very different. For the most part the armies were stationed in the less developed regions of the Empire, and to some degree they could legitimately be considered to be the torchbearers of civilization. Certainly they were a key factor in the Romanization of the Empire. Further, they were to a large extent in possession of skills and technical expertise which were uncommon in the surrounding population, and the application of which in civilian contexts aroused admiration even more than resentment. It was therefore comparatively easy for them to carry out tasks which would be of immediate practical value to the local community as well as to the Empire as a whole. The most obvious of these tasks is road-building. We have seen already how Julius Apollinaris congratulated himself on his promotion, which freed him from the painful necessity of stone-breaking.[495] He was serving in the then newly-conquered province of Arabia, and his unit was working in the quarries. The stone was probably intended for road-making. Apart from road-building, which was an obvious military requirement, soldiers were frequently employed in the construction and repair of canals, water-cisterns, aqueducts and public works generally.[496]

In the early Empire, however, the building works carried out by the army were normally intended for military purposes, at least in the first instance. Gradually, for various reasons, there came about a change of outlook towards civilian building. The first reason was that the army had by now come to contain a large number of the most highly-trained architects and surveyors in the Empire: these men had their training in the legions and were attached to the staffs of provincial governors or posted to the Praetorian Guard in Rome.[497] For technology, therefore, the provinces came to depend upon the army. So, for instance, when Pliny wrote to Trajan for a *librator* (surveyor) to inquire into the feasibility of joining the lake near Nicomedia in Bithynia to the sea by means of a canal, Trajan referred him to Calpurnius Macer, who was governor of Lower Moesia, the nearest province to Bithynia which contained legionary troops.[498] A second reason was that with the accession of Hadrian the army had become more static, and this encouraged the building of permanent camps and fortifications. When these were completed it was a natural step for the men to turn their building skills upon the cities of the provinces within which they were stationed, both to embellish them with fine buildings and to protect them with fortifications. The major reason, however, for the changeover to military building in civilian areas is to be found in the decline of civilian resources brought about by the loss of manpower due to plagues and the financial instability resulting from inflation which accompanied the wars of Marcus Aurelius and became endemic under his successors. The concern of the central government that building work should continue meant that an increasing percentage of the work necessarily fell to the army. So during the third century the army was called upon more and more to carry out tasks which should really have been done by civilians. What this could lead to is shown by the description in the *Historia Augusta* of the labours of the army in Egypt under the emperor Probus: 'The works which he made his soldiers carry out can still be seen in very many cities in Egypt. He did so much on the Nile that his works by themselves increased the amount of grain brought in as tribute. He had bridges, temples, colonnades and public buildings built by army labour, many river mouths opened up, many marshes drained, and fields of corn and farms created in place of them.'[499] No wonder his biographer says that Probus never allowed his soldiers to be idle![500] Disputes about the authenticity of much of the evidence of the *Historia Augusta* should not affect the value of such a general description as this, the truth or falsehood of most of which would have been obvious to an eyewitness even over a century later.[501]

### THE CENTURION IN PEACETIME

The trained soldier could be found employment in civilian or semi-civilian building work. For the centurion there were many more military, or paramilitary duties available, quite apart from the general oversight over building works carried out by military units.[502] He could be given a paramilitary role as *praepositus* (chief of detachment) in a police or security function.[503] He could be posted to duty in the mines or quarries in one of several capacities, either as a technical expert, or in charge of operations, or simply as the commander of a security guard.[504] If a community showed undue reluctance to pay its taxes he might be posted there as an *exactor tributorum* (special collector of taxes).[505] A more glamorous form of employment for some centurions was to be appointed as umpires (*iudices dati*) in boundary disputes between communities within a province. To this and similar duties they were seconded by the provincial governor.[506] Centurions were also regularly used as diplomatic envoys, both between emperor and provincial governor and even between emperor and internal dependent princeling or external dependent prince.[507] Finally, of course, centurions were widely used as security police.[508]

## THE PRINCIPALIS IN PEACETIME

Unlike the centurion, the *principalis* rarely exercised an independent command, except occasionally as *beneficiarius* in charge of some minor police post.[509] Usually, the ambitious *principalis* sought employment on the staff of the provincial governor or else on the considerably smaller staff of the procurator, who was directly responsible to the emperor for the finances of the province. The governor's staff, as we have seen, formed quite an elaborate hierarchy.[510]

In a special position were the *frumentarii*, who are attested from the early second century onwards as a kind of imperial secret service.[511] They not only formed part of the staff of the governor of the province in which they were stationed, but they also had a headquarters at Rome, the *castra peregrinorum*, where they were under the command of the *princeps peregrinorum*.[512] Their title implies that in origin at least they were somehow connected with *frumentum* (grain). Thus their basic functions were probably concerned with the administration of the military grain supply, the *annona militaris*, over the supply-routes of the Empire, and it may have been the ubiquitous nature of their employment that enabled them to act as confidential couriers. Once they had adopted this task, so indispensable did they become to the imperial administration that they continued to function until the Late Empire, when they were transformed into a civilian secret service and renamed as the *agentes in rebus*.[513]

## THE SOLDIER IN RETIREMENT

From the very foundation of the professional army the Roman administration recognized in some measure its responsibility for making financial provision for its veterans. In the beginning, the simplest possible course was adopted: soldiers were settled in colonies and given land. Augustus himself planted no less than 28 colonies in Italy, mainly to provide for veterans of the Civil Wars, but later colonies were founded mainly in the provinces.[514] After 13 BC payments gradually came to be made in money instead of in land, and finally in AD 6 the *aerarium militare* was established, and with it the institution of the *praemia militiae*.[515] This measure was fundamental, in that at last provision for soldiers on retirement was settled on a fixed basis as a right and no longer as a privilege. This decision to accept responsibility for the whole of the soldier's professional life was, of course, not the final stage of a far-reaching plan, but simply the solution forced upon the emperor by the pressure of events. The men were now in a state of unrest, they were bitter about their financial position, and they were unwilling to continue their service for longer than the regular period. Augustus, therefore, fixed a scale of gratuities for time-expired soldiers. This scale gave the praetorians 5000 *denarii* after sixteen years' service, and the legionaries 3000 *denarii* after twenty years' service.[516]

Unfortunately for the men the new system was not strictly adhered to. Already by AD 14 the soldiers were complaining that they were being allotted marshland or uncultivatable hillsides as the reward for their service.[517] Presumably the land was allotted as being the equivalent in value of the *praemia militiae*. It is clear, however, that the men felt they were being unfairly treated. The expedient of awarding land in lieu of money seems to have been adopted fairly frequently throughout the first century AD, sometimes with obviously unsatisfactory results. Tacitus tells us that the towns of Tarentum and Antium were sent veteran settlers by Nero; 'but this measure did not arrest the depopulation of these districts. Most of the settlers returned to the provinces in which they had spent their years of service; they were unaccustomed to marrying and bringing up children, and they left their new homes without a generation to succeed them.'[518] Tacitus puts the blame for this on a lack of *esprit de corps*: 'in former times, colonies had consisted of entire legions with their tribunes, their centurions and soldiers of every rank, and so they formed a community based on common consent and mutual affection. These colonists did not know one another, they came from different units, they had no leader, no common loyalties, they were a random selection of human beings suddenly collected into one place, a crowd rather than a colony.' To some extent this criticism may have been justified: now that with a fully professional army it was convenient that a proportion of the troops in each unit should be discharged every year, it would be unusual for there to be a sufficient number of settlers from any one unit to give a colony a feeling of solidarity.[519]

With Hadrian the situation changed: colonies of veterans ceased to be founded. This may have been simply a matter of economy: land-values may have risen and outstripped the *praemia militiae*, which some scholars believe remained unchanged till the time of Caracalla.[520] A more likely explanation is that the change was in harmony with the general trend of Hadrian's measures for the defence of the Empire. Local recruitment now became standard practice; in a period when a considerable proportion of recruits were born within the province or even near the camp (*castris*), it is natural to expect as a corollary local discharge and resettlement.

Surprisingly, there is no evidence for the regular payment of the *praemia militiae* or the granting of land in lieu either to the auxiliary forces or to the fleets.[521] Vespasian provides an exception. He settled veterans from the Misene fleet at Paestum, and others from the Ravennate fleet in Pannonia.[522] It has been pointed out that the settlement at Paestum has produced only one inscription, a circumstance which hardly suggests that the colony was entirely satisfactory.[523] Vespasian's apparent liberality is matched by his grant of *honesta missio*, not *missio causaria*, to disabled veterans of *legio* II *Adiutrix*, who were themselves ex-sailors, and also by his grant to certain sailors of *honesta missio* before the due date as a reward for bravery.[524] But Vespasian was unusual in that he owed a great deal to his naval forces. Most scholars have accepted the conclusion that the *auxilia*, as non-citizens, were not entitled to the *praemia militiae*.[525] P. A. Brunt, however, found it hard to believe that the *auxilia*, who frequently served side by side with the legions, did not share in the benefits which they must have known the legionaries enjoyed.[526] Yet the privileges granted to the auxiliary veterans by the diplomas, as we have seen, were rewards not shared by the legionaries.[527] It may well be that both parties were not unduly dissatisfied with their own benefits and found them reasonably comparable.

To the general principle that men of the *auxilia* did not receive gratuities there may have been a specific exception. The members of the *cohortes civium Romanorum* were granted by the will of Augustus the same legacies as legionaries, and it is not an unreasonable inference that they received the same pay and gratuities.[528] This favour, however, may not have been long-lasting: originally, as Cheesman says, they were practically on a level with legionaries, but later only their title distinguished them from the ordinary run of the *auxilia*. When exactly the change took place, or whether their benefits were merely gradually eroded, is not clear.[529]

The *praemia militiae* formed the Roman equivalent of a system of military superannuation. Before we can decide whether this system was fair or unfair, adequate or inadequate, there are certain points which we must consider. We must take into account the opportunities available for the men to make personal savings for retirement from their pay and donatives during service, the value of the *praemia militiae* or a grant of land to those who were eligible for such on the completion of their service, and the men's probable expectation of life in retirement. To object that these factors must have varied enormously in particular cases is beside the point. Even today, when superannuation generally has a firm actuarial basis, there can often be serious differences in adequacy of provision in individual instances. Such answers as are possible can be expressed only in the most general terms.

In the first place, we know of the existence of the regimental savings banks.[530] By the time of Domitian these contained so much money that in AD 89 the combined savings of two legions deposited in the camp at Mainz were sufficient to finance the revolution of Antonius Saturninus.[531] Domitian found it necessary, not only to abandon the practice of brigading legions in double camps, but also to restrict the size of deposits to 250 *denarii* a man. The implication is that many men must have had over a year's pay saved; the basic rate had formerly been 225 and now was 300 *denarii*. Domitian's restriction may have been only temporary, for the system of enforced savings described by Vegetius, in which each man was required to make a compulsory deposit with the regimental bank to the amount of one half of each donative, is hardly compatible with the 250 *denarii* limit.[532] In any case it seems clear that the legionaries were able to make some savings from their pay. The praetorians, who received higher pay and much higher donatives, would presumably have been able to save even more, even though the cost of living was probably somewhat higher for them at their headquarters in Rome.[533]

The much lower rate of pay of the auxiliary forces would lead us to expect that their chances of making personal savings would be negligible. The evidence which there is would bear this out. The majority of the auxiliary infantrymen whose accounts are given in the Berlin papyrus had exactly 100 *denarii* on deposit and 75 *denarii* held in *viatico*.[534] The former amount is very probably the half of a donative; the latter sum simply represents the regular *viaticum* which in this unit at least would appear to have been retained as a compulsory saving.[535] Only three men in these accounts had more on deposit, the amounts ranging from 187½ *denarii* to 206 *denarii*, and the conclusion must be that for the average auxiliary infantryman there was very little chance indeed of making any savings at all in the normal way. In the cavalry regiments, which enjoyed higher pay as well as higher status, the position was somewhat different. A certain Dionysius, of the *ala veterana Gallica*, about the year AD 175 had no less than 1,562 *denarii* to his credit.[536] This man was, of course, exceptional, since the grand total of deposits in this unit came to no more than 16,172 *denarii* 6½ obols, of which 11,129 *denarii* 10½ obols represented *deposita* proper, 3,626 *denarii* 3 obols *seposita* (enforced savings), and 1,416 *denarii* 21 obols *viatica*.[537] Dionysius had apparently saved the equivalent of more than seven years' pay. It is hardly likely that many men were able to do this. The implication remains, however, even if this sum was partly achieved at the expense of his comrades, by gambling or other means, the members of the *alae* had at least the possibility of saving. Taken together, these slight pieces of evidence suggest that the opportunities for saving varied directly in proportion to the pay received, which is hardly a surprising conclusion. We may assume, therefore, that the differences of social and financial status which divided the praetorians, the legionaries, the cavalrymen of the *alae* and the soldiers in the auxiliary cohorts, were intensified, rather than diminished, in retirement. Since it is probable as well that the auxiliary forces were not eligible for gratuities on retirement, the financial position of the ex-auxiliaries may have been hardly comparable with that of the praetorians and legionaries.

To estimate the value of the gratuity itself is comparatively simple. In the period before Domitian the legionary received an annual income of 225 *denarii* during service, and on retirement received a gratuity of 3,000 *denarii* if it was paid in cash. To achieve with this gratuity an annual return equal to his previous pay he would have had to invest it, in a farm or a business, to secure a return of 7½ per cent. At most times this should have been not impossible with reasonably hard work.[538] Those who received a grant of land in lieu would be in a much less certain position, and the instances of dissatisfaction that are recorded are from this category.

The problem of the expectation of life of the veteran on retirement is rather more complicated. The general question has been studied by A. R. Burn in relation to two particular areas, Roman Africa and the Danubian provinces.[539] His conclusion is that soldiers at Lambaesis in Africa had, up to about the age of 42, a slightly better expectation of life than the local civilians.[540]

But after the age of 42 the situation changed, and the survival rate for soldiers and veterans sank slowly but steadily below the civilian rate. In a further comparison between the death-rates of slaves, including freedmen, soldiers, including veterans, and the general male population of Roman Africa, Burn found that from about the age of 42 the line of the graph for soldiers took a course midway between that for civilians above, and that for slaves and freedmen below.[541] The figures for the Danubian provinces are even more startling: the survival rate for soldiers begins to be worse than that for civilians at about the age 30. The civilian figures for this area, however, also compare unfavourably with those from Roman Africa.[542] Local conditions obviously counted for a great deal. If we allow for individual variations, the general conclusion would appear to be that the soldier's expectation of life deteriorated from about the age of retirement. For this Burn blames the after-effects of wounds and injuries, and expresses the opinion that the Roman army had considerable success in getting the best out of its men before getting rid of them. This may well have been true in particular instances, but it hardly seems sufficient as a general explanation. It would appear more likely that the differences revealed in expectation of life directly reflected living standards, and that the social and financial position of the soldier tended to decline on his retirement in comparison with that of the civilian population as a whole. This would seem to suggest that although the *praemia militiae* may not appear unreasonable from an actuarial point of view, there was in practice a considerable difference between the standard of living possible during service on a soldier's pay and that on a veteran's income during retirement.

This gloomy picture of ex-servicemen living at some sub-standard level midway between that of free citizens and slaves, in a twilight zone of second-class citizenry, can by no means have been universal. True perhaps in some more prosperous areas, where the status even of the serving soldier remained low, it was almost certainly the reverse of the truth in remoter provinces such as Britain and the Germanies, where the army formed a considerable proportion of the population. Here, where the local civilians were more appreciative of their presence, the veterans were able to keep up their status and prestige, especially in the military areas, where regimental traditions and enthusiasms remained strong. So retired soldiers naturally gravitated towards the frontier zones and the legionary fortresses, where, as we have seen, the *vici* and the *canabae* grew in size and importance during the second and third centuries, and most vigorously after the lifting of the general ban on marriage by Septimius Severus.[543] Surprisingly, however, comparatively few veterans are recorded on the British frontier. Salway suggests that the conditions and the climate were too grim to encourage residence in retirement, despite the draws of friendship and familiarity.[544] Alternatively, the discrepancy may simply be due to chance in the discovery of inscriptions. In contrast, in the Rhineland there appear to have been organized bodies of veterans right from the Julio-Claudian period.[545] These were associations of veterans under a *curator veteranorum*. As ex-service associations, these are the Roman equivalent of the British Legion. It was in the *canabae* that these associations flourished, where there were not only large concentrations of veterans but many civilians also. In the *vici* beside the auxiliary forts there was little need for ex-service associations because the ex-auxiliaries themselves, their wives and families, there formed the bulk of the population.[546]

We have now traced the soldier's career from the prospect of enlistment to retirement. Our hypothetical volunteer has by now disappeared into the maze of ranks and units that formed the Roman army: once past the stage of initial training, it was hardly possible to concentrate on one career in isolation. We have seen also how it verges upon the absurd to make broad generalizations about the Roman army, since the several sections of the armed services were so different from one another, and even within the same service the opportunities available for promotion, especially within the legions and the Guard, led to widely different careers. The legionary recruit of ability could hope to rise at least to the ranks of the *principales*, and quite often to the centurionate. The recruit to the Guard, who started at a higher social level, generally maintained his superiority, and after *evocatio* might be promoted to a centurionate in a legion or in the *vigiles*, with a good chance of further promotion. For the auxiliary recruit the avenue of promotion was not so wide and did not lead so far; the goal of his ambition was the auxiliary centurionate, but the majority remained content with less. Even after retirement these differences of treatment remained, and they were perhaps even intensified, as financial pressures were added to social ones. On the other hand, it is probable that the great majority were content with their lot. The direction of social mobility for the soldier was normally upward; even the unpromoted auxiliary infantryman advanced in status, for the grant of *civitas* and *conubium* made to him on his discharge meant that he had climbed a step up the ladder of society.

# NOTES

| | |
|---|---|
| Domaszewski, *Truppensold* | A. von Domaszewski, 'Der Truppensold der Kaiserzeit', *Neue Heidelberger Jahrbücher* X (1900), 225 ff. |
| *Diz. epigr.* | *Dizionario epigrafico di antichità romane*, ed. E. de Ruggiero and others, 1886– . |
| *Dura* V | *The Excavations at Dura-Europos, Final Report V, Part 1, The Parchments and Papyri*, ed. C. B. Welles, R. O. Fink and J. F. Gilliam (New Haven 1959). |
| *Ecriture latine* | J. Mallon, R. Marichal and Ch. Perrat, *L'écriture latine de la capitale romaine à la minuscule* (Paris 1939). |
| *EE* | *Ephemeris Epigraphica* |
| Ehrenberg-Jones | V. Ehrenberg and A. H. M. Jones, *Documents illustrating the Reigns of Augustus and Tiberius* (Cambridge 1949). |
| *Etud. Pap.* | *Etudes de Papyrologie* |
| *Ges. Schr.* | Th. Mommsen, *Gesammelte Schriften* |
| Girard | P. F. Girard, *Textes du Droit Romain*, 5th edn. (Paris 1923); 6th edn. rev. by F. Senn (Girard-Senn), 1937. |
| *HThR* | *The Harvard Theological Review* |
| *IG* | *Inscriptiones Graecae* |
| *IGRR* | *Inscriptiones Graecae ad Res Romanas pertinentes* |
| *ILS* | *Inscriptiones Latinae Selectae*, ed. H. Dessau, 1892–1916. |
| *JEA* | *Journal of Egyptian Archaeology* |
| *JRS* | *Journal of Roman Studies* |
| *Jur. Pap.* | P. M. Meyer, *Juristische Papyri* (Berlin 1920). |
| Kromayer-Veith, *Heerwesen* | J. Kromayer and G. Veith, with contributions by A. Köster, E. von Nischer and E. Schramm, *Heerwesen und Kriegführung der Griechen und Romer* (Munich 1928). |
| *Leges* | *Fontes Iuris Romani Antejustiniani, Pars prima, Leges*, ed. S. Riccobono (Florence 1941). |
| Marichal, *La Solde* | R. Marichal, 'La solde des armées romaines d'Auguste à Septime-Sévère d'apres les P. Gen. lat. 1 et le P. Berlin 6.866', *Mélanges Isidore Lévy* (Brussels 1955). |
| McCrum and Woodhead | M. McCrum and A. G. Woodhead, *Select Documents of the Principates of the Flavian Emperors, AD 68–96* (Cambridge 1961). |
| Mitteis | L. Mitteis and U. Wilcken, *Grundzüge und Chrestomathie der Papyruskunde*, Vol. II, *Juristischer Teil* (Mitteis) (Berlin 1912). |
| *Negotia* | *Fontes Iuris Romani Antejustiniani, Pars tertia, Negotia*, ed. V. Arangio-Ruiz (Florence 1943). |
| *NRHD* | *Nouvelle Revue Historique de Droit français et étranger* |
| *Num. Chron.* | *Numismatic Chronicle* |
| *OCD* | *The Oxford Classical Dictionary* (Oxford 1949). |
| *OCT* | *Oxford Classical Texts* |

| | |
|---|---|
| O. Strassb. | *Griechische und griechisch-demotische Ostraka der Universitäts-und Landesbibliothek zu Strassburg im Elsass*, ed. P. Viereck (Berlin 1923). |
| O. Tait | *Greek Ostraca in the Bodleian Library at Oxford*, ed. J. G. Tait and Cl. Préaux (London 1930–    ). |
| O. Wilcken | *Griechische Ostraka aus Aegypten und Nubien*, ed. U. Wilcken (Leipzig-Berlin 1899). |
| P. Aberd. | *Catalogue of the Greek and Latin Papyri and Ostraca in the possession of the University of Aberdeen*, ed. E. G. Turner (Aberdeen 1939). |
| Pal. Soc. | *The Palaeographical Society* and *The New Palaeographical Society, Facsimiles of Ancient Manuscripts* (London 1873–  ). |
| P. Amherst | *The Amherst Papyri*, ed. B. P. Grenfell and A. S. Hunt (London 1900–  ). |
| P. Antinoopolis | *The Antinoopolis Papyri*, ed. C. H. Roberts, J. W. Barns and H. Zilliacus (London 1950–  ). |
| Par. d. Pass. | *Parola del Passato* |
| Parker, *RL* | H. M. D. Parker, *The Roman Legions*, reprint 1958 (1928) |
| *PBSR* | *Papers of the British School at Rome* |
| P. Dura | *The Excavations at Dura-Europos, Final Report V, Part I, The Parchments and Papyri*, ed. C. G. Welles, R. O. Fink and J. F. Gilliam (New Haven 1959). |
| P. Fay. | *Fayûm Towns and their Papyri*, ed. B. P. Grenfell, A. S. Hunt and D. G. Hogarth (London 1900). |
| P. Fayum Barns | J. Barns, 'Three Fayum Papyri', *Chronique d'Egypte* 24 (1949), 295–304. |
| P. Flor. | *Papiri Fiorentini*, ed. D. Comparetti and G. Vitelli (Milan 1906–1915). |
| P. Fouad | *Les Papyrus Fouad I*, ed. A. Bataille and others (Cairo 1939). |
| P. Gen. | *Les Papyrus de Genève*, ed. J. Nicole (Geneva 1896–1906). |
| P. Grenf. I | *An Alexandrian Erotic Fragment and other Greek Papyri chiefly Ptolemaic*, ed. B. P. Grenfell (Oxford 1896). |
| P. Grenf. II | *New Classical Fragments and other Greek and Latin Papyri*, ed. B. P. Grenfell and A. S. Hunt (Oxford 1897). |
| P. Hamb. | *Griechische Papyrusurkunden der Hamburger Staats-und Universitätsbibliothek*, ed. P. M. Meyer and others (Leipzig-Berlin 1911–  ). |
| *PIR²* | *Prosopographia Imperii Romani*, ed. altera, E. Groag, A. Stein and others, 1933–  . |

| | |
|---|---|
| P. Lond. | Greek Papyri in the British Museum, ed. F. G. Kenyon and H. I. Bell (London 1893– ). |
| P. Mich. | Papyri in the University of Michigan Collection, ed. C. C. Edgar, A. E. R. Boak, J. G. Winter and others (Ann Arbor 1931– ). |
| P. Oxy. | The Oxyrhynchus Papyri, ed. B. P. Grenfell, A. S. Hunt, H. I. Bell and others (London 1898– ). |
| P. Princeton | Papyri in the Princeton University Collections, ed. A. C. Johnson, H. B. van Hoesen and others (Baltimore-Princeton 1931– ). |
| P. Ryl. | Catalogue of the Greek Papyri in the John Rylands Library at Manchester, ed. J. de M. Johnson, V. Martin, A. S. Hunt, C. H. Roberts and E. G. Turner, 1911– . |
| PSI | Papiri Greci e Latini (Pubblicazioni della Societa Italiana per la ricerca dei papiri greci e latini in Egitto), G. Vitelli, M. Norsa and others (Florence 1912– ). |
| P. Tebt. | The Tebtunis Papyri, ed. B. P. Grenfell A. S. Hunt, J. G. Smyly and others (London 1902– ). |
| RCHM | The Royal Commission on Historical Monuments |
| RE | Pauly-Wissowa, Real-Encyclopädie der klassischen Altertumswissenschaft, 1893– . |
| Rev. Arch. | Revue Archéologique |
| RhM | Rheinisches Museum |
| RIB | R. G. Collingwood and R. P. Wright, The Roman Inscriptions of Britain, I, Inscriptions on Stone (Oxford 1965). |
| RSt. | J. Marquardt, Römische Staatsverwaltung,[2] 1881–5. |
| SB | Sammelbuch griechischer Urkunden aus Aegypten, ed. F. Preisigke, F. Bilabel and E. Kiessling, 1915. |
| Schenk, Vegetius | Dankfrid Schenk, 'Flavius Vegetius Renatus, die Quellen der Epitoma rei militaris', Klio, Beiheft, 1920. |
| Schrifttafeln | C. Wessely, Schrifttafeln zur älteren lateinischen Palaeographie (Leipzig 1898). |
| Sel. Pap. | C. C. Edgar and A. S. Hunt, Select Papyri, I (1932), II (1934), Loeb. |
| SHA | Scriptores Historiae Augustae |
| Smallwood, Gaius | E. Mary Smallwood, Documents illustrating the Principates of Gaius, Claudius and Nero (Cambridge 1967). |
| Smallwood, Nerva | E. Mary Smallwood, Documents illustrating the Principates of Nerva, Trajan and Hadrian (Cambridge 1966). |
| Stud. Pal. | Studien zur Paläographie und Papyrusurkunde ed. C. Wessely (Leipzig 1901– ). |
| TAPhA | Transactions of the American Philological Association |

Wilcken, *Chrestomathie*  L. Mitteis and U. Wilcken, *Grundzüge und Chresto-mathie der Papyruskunde*, Vol. I, *Historischer Teil* (Wilcken) (Berlin 1912).

*YCS*  *Yale Classical Studies*

# INTRODUCTION

1 Cf. E. Gabba, 'Le origini dell'esercito professionale in Roma: i proletari e la riforma di Mario', *Athenaeum* 1949, 173–209; also 'Richerche sull'esercito professionale romano da Mario ad Augusto', *Athenaeum* 1951, 171–272. Cf. also R. E. Smith, *Service in the Post-Marian Roman Army* (Manchester 1958), and J. Harmand, *L'armée et le soldat à Rome de 107 à 50 avant notre ère* (Paris 1967).

2 Dio LIV 25, 6.

3 Dio LV 23, 1.

4 The work of Grosse and Van Berchem has shown that the army of the fourth century had its origin in the experiments of the third. Grosse has traced the roots of the military system of Diocletian and Constantine to the reforms of Septimius Severus, Gallienus and Aurelian; Van Berchem finds the origin of the *annona militaris* in the attempt of Septimius Severus to offset the effects of the late second century inflation. Cf. R. Grosse, *Römische Militärgeschichte von Gallienus bis zum Beginn der byzantinischen Themenverfassung* (Berlin 1920); Denis Van Berchem, 'L'annone militaire dans l'empire romain au IIIe siècle', *Mémoires de la Société Nationale des Antiquaires des France* 1937, 118ff.

5 *Bonner Jahrbücher* 117, 1908 (new edition, revised by Brian Dobson, Cologne 1967). Hereafter referred to as Domaszewski-Dobson.

6 To take but one instance, on pp. 43 f. he writes: 'Nach C.III 8047 scheint es, dass unter den Philippi der tesserarius nicht mehr bestand. Die schriftliche Ausgabe der Befehle war für ein Heer, in dem Offiziere wie Soldaten gleichmässig Analphabeten waren und die Kenntnis der lateinischen Dienstsprache ganz erlosch, bedeutungslos geworden. Das barbarische Heer war auf den Standpunkt der numeri herabgesunken.' But *AE* 1936, 55 (age of Gallienus) disproves this statement about the *tesserarius*, and with this the rest of Domaszewski's case. Cf. Passerini in De Ruggiero, *Diz. epigr.* IV (1949), 607, and now Domaszewski-Dobson, IV f., XIV.

7 Hyginus, *de mun. castr.* 3, gives 480 men for cohorts II to X, and 960 for cohort I. This gives a grand total of 5,280. Other writers seem less precise: Vegetius (I 17: nam in Illyrico dudum duae legiones fuerunt, quae sena milia militum habuerunt, quae, quod his telis scienter utebantur et fortiter, Mattiobarbuli vocabantur), Lydus, *de magistr.* I 46, and Isidore (*Etym.* IX 3, 46: legio sex milium armatorum est, ab electo vocata, quasi lecti, id est

armis electi) tend to give the round number of 6,000. Of some significance may be the remark made by one of his associates to Septimius Severus at the siege of Hatra, as reported in Dio 66, 12, 5, when he promised that he would take the city if he gave him only 550 of the European troops. This may have been the number of men in a normal legionary cohort at the time; on the other hand, he may merely have meant an auxiliary cohort.

8 Tac., *Ann.* I 17: an praetorias cohortis, quae binos denarios acceperint, quae post sedecim annos penatibus suis reddantur, plus periculorum suscipere? non obtrectari a se urbanas excubias: sibi tamen apud horridas gentis e contuberniis hostem aspici.

9 Tac., *Ann.* IV 5: Italiam utroque mari duae classes, Misenum apud et Ravennam, proximumque Galliae litus rostratae naves praesidebant, quas Actiaca victoria captas Augustus in oppidum Foroiuliense miserat valido cum remige. sed praecipuum robur Rhenum iuxta, commune in Germanos Gallosque subsidium, octo legiones erant. Hispaniae recens perdomitae tribus habebantur. Mauros Iuba rex acceperat donum populi Romani. cetera Africae per duas legiones parique numero Aegyptus, dehinc initio ab Syriae usque ad flumen Euphraten, quantum ingenti terrarum sinu ambitur, quattuor legionibus coercita, accolis Hibero Albanoque et aliis regibus qui magnitudine nostra proteguntur adversum externa imperia. et Thraeciam Rhoemetalces ac liberi Cotyis, ripamque Danuvii legionum duae in Pannonia, duae in Moesia attinebant, totidem apud Delmatiam locatis, quae positu regionis a tergo illis, ac si repentinum auxilium Italia posceret, haud procul accirentur, quamquam insideret urbem proprius miles, tres urbanae, novem praetoriae cohortes, Etruria ferme Umbriaque delectae aut vetere Latio et coloniis antiquitus Romanis. at apud idonea provinciarum sociae triremes alaeque et auxilia cohortium, neque multo secus in iis virium: sed persequi incertum fuit, cum ex usu temporis huc illuc mearent, gliscerent numero et aliquando minuerentur.

10 *ILS* 2288 Rome (= *CIL* VI 3492):

|  |  |  |
|---|---|---|
| | nomina leg. | |
| II Aug. | II Adiut. | IIII Scyth. |
| VI Victr. | IIII Flav. | XVI Flav. |
| XX Victr. | VII Claud. | VI Ferrat. |
| VIII Aug. | I Italic. | X Frete. |
| XXII Prim. | V Maced. | III Cyren. |
| I Miner. | XI Claud. | II Traian. |
| XXX Vlp. | XIII Gem. | III Aug. |
| I Adiut. | XII Fulm. | VII Gem. |
| X Gem. | XV Apol. | II Italic. |
| XIIII Gem. | III Gallic. | III Italic. |
| I Parth. | II Parth. | III Parth. |

The columns should be read downwards, beginning on the left. The legions are then listed by provinces, in the order Britain, Upper Germany, Lower

Germany, Upper Pannonia, Lower Pannonia, Upper Moesia, Lower Moesia, Dacia, Cappadocia, Syria, Judaea, Arabia, Egypt, Numidia and Spain. The legions thus unaccounted for, II and III *Italica*, stationed in Noricum and Raetia respectively, and the three Parthian legions, of which the first and third were stationed in Mesopotamia, the second in Italy, have been added at the end.

11 Even III *Augusta* was to be off the army list for fifteen years in the third century: it suffered *damnatio memoriae* in AD 238, but was restored by Valerian in 253.

12 Cf. *ILS* 2487 (= Smallwood, *Nerva* 328), Hadrian's address to the troops at Lambaesis in AD 128: difficile est cohortales equites etiam per se placere, difficilius post alarem exercitationem non displicere; alia spatia campi, alius iaculantium numerus, frequens dextrator, Cantabricus densus, equorum forma armorum cultus pro stipendi modo. They were worse paid, worse armed, and worse mounted than their cavalry opposite numbers.

13 The special position of the *cohortes civium Romanorum* in the time of Augustus is shown by the fact that by his will they were granted the same legacies as legionaries. Cf. Tac., *Ann.* I 8: legionariis aut cohortibus civium Romanorum trecenos nummos viritim dedit. For the later position, when the citizenship is more widespread, cf. the new formula for military diplomas adopted in AD 140: (dimissis) civitatem Romanam, qui eorum non haberent, dedit.

14 Cf. Cheesman, *Auxilia*, 86.

15 Cf. M. Durry, *Les cohortes prétoriennes* (Paris 1938), 81 ff. and in *RE s.v.* 'Praetoriae Cohortes' (1934).

16 Cf. Domaszewski-Dobson, XXVI f. and 99 ff.

17 Yet this advantage must not be overstated. Cf. the conclusions of Eric Birley, *Britain and the Roman Army*, 119: 'In other words, the reputed predominance of ex-praetorians resolves itself, after scrutiny of the material in this third category, into the following facts: out of twenty-nine praetorian centurions who became *primi ordines* or *primi pili*, eleven were promoted beyond the rank of *primus pilus* and two of these eleven entered the procuratorial career; and out of thirty-six praetorian other ranks who became legionary centurions, fifteen reached the rank of *primus pilus*, and six received further promotion. These statistics are sufficient to show that the praetorian had a good chance of promotion once he had been selected for the centurionate; but they are insufficient to support such sweeping assertions as have been made by Domaszewski and Durry.' These conclusions are supported by Brian Dobson, cf. Domaszewski-Dobson, XXVII: 'In meiner unveröffentlichten Dissertation über die primipilares ergab die Untersuchung der Fälle, in denen die Rangstufen vor dem Primipilat nicht angegeben werden, ein ähnliches Verhältnis wie es Birley feststellte (ca. 64%), obgleich ich etwa doppelt soviel Laufbahnen untersuchte, da Birley sich absichtlich auf die in Domaszewskis "Epigraphischer

Anhang" enthaltenen Beispiele beschränkt hat. Durrys These, dass die ehemalig praetorianischen primipilares, die "chevaliers-prétoriens", die höchsten Procuratoren und Praefecturen erhalten hätten, ist daher in zwei Punkten angreifbar: sowohl wegen der Voraussetzung, dass alle Beteiligten ehemalige Praetorianer gewesen seien, als auch wegen der Annahme, dass sie die Mehrzahl solcher Stellungen erhalten hätten.' For praetorian pay and donatives, see below pp. 97 ff. and 108 ff.

18 For an example of a fully documented career see *ILS* 2080 (= *CIL* III 7334) from Serrhae: – – – us D.f. Octavius Se[c]undus Curib(us) Sab(inis) mil(es) coh(ortis) X urb(anae), trans[l]at(us) in coh(ortem) VI pr(aetoriam), [s]ing(ularis) trib(uni) benef(iciarius) trib(uni), sing(ularis) pr(aefecti) [pr]aet(orio), optio in centur(ia), sign(ifer), [f]is[c]o curat(or), cornicu[l-(arius)] trib(uni), ev(ocatus) Aug(usti), [(centurio) l]eg(ionis) X [F]retensis, donis don(atus) ab divo Hadrian(o) ob bellum Iudaicum corona aurea tor[q]uib(us), armillis, p[h]aler(is) et ab eodem promotus succes(sione) in leg(ionem) prim[a]m [I]ta[l]ic(am), [p]rimipil(us) leg(ionis) eiusdem –.

19 One of the best-known instances is that of Vettius Valens: *ILS* 2648 (= *CIL* XI 395) from Ariminum: M. Vettio M.f. Ani(ensi) Valenti mil(iti) coh(ortis) VIII pr(aetoriae), benef(iciario) praef(ecti) pr(aetorio), donis donato bello Britan(nico) torquibus armillis phaleris, evoc(ato) Aug(usti), corona aurea donat(o), (centurioni) coh(ortis) VI vig(ilum), (centurioni) stat(orum), (centurioni) coh(ortis) XVI urb(anae), (centurioni) c(o)ho(rtis) II pr(aetoriae), exercitatori equit(um) speculatorum, princip(i) praetori leg(ionis) XIII Gem(inae) ex trec(enario), [p(rimo)p(ilo)] leg(ionis) VI Victr(icis), donis donato ob res prosper(e) gest(as) contra Astures torq(uibus) phaler(is) arm(illis), trib(uno) coh(ortis) V vig(ilum), trib(uno) coh(ortis) XII urb(anae), trib(uno) coh(ortis) III pr(aetoriae), [pr(imo)p(ilo)] leg(ionis) XIIII Gem(inae) Mart(iae) Victr(icis), proc(uratori) imp(eratoris) [[Neronis]] Caes(aris) Aug(usti) prov(inciae) Lusitan(iae) — AD 66.

20 Cf. the dedication to a remarkable number of deities in *CIL* VI 31174: I(ovi) O(ptimo) M(aximo), Iunoni, Minervae, Marti, Victoriae, Hercul(i), Mercurio, Felicitati, Saluti, Fatis, Campestribus, Silvano, [A]pollini, Deanae, Eponae, Matribus, Suleis, et Genio sing(ularium) Aug(usti), M. Ulpius Festus dec(urio) prin(ceps) eq(uitum) sing(ularium) Aug(usti) v(otum) s(olvit) l(ibens) m(erito). This group of deities is commonly associated with dedications of the *equites singulares*, cf. *ILS* 2180, 2181, 4832 (= *CIL* VI 31171), and 4833 (= *CIL* VI 31149).

21 Cf. Tac., *Ann.* VI 10–11, and E. Groag in *PIR²* C 289, who concludes that Piso was *praefectus urbi* from c. AD 13. Cf. also my comments in *Neue Beiträge zur Geschichte der alten Welt. Band II. Römisches Reich* (Berlin 1965) 148, n. 10.

22 For the urban cohorts now see H. Freis, *Die cohortes urbanae, Beiheft Nr. 16 der Bonner Jahrbücher*, and *RE* Suppl. X *s.v.* 'urbanae cohortes'. Domaszewski maintained (Domaszewski-Dobson 16) that command of the

urban cohorts was exercised in the second century by the *praefectus praetorio*. In this he was followed by Durry but is now refuted by Freis.

23 *Ann.* IV 5, cf. n. 9 above.

24 The suggestion was made by Domaszewski, cf. Domaszewski-Dobson 6: 'Aber schon in der Gliederung der 7 Cohorten in je 7 Centuriae ist es ausgesprochen, dass die Pompiers keine Soldaten sind, für welche die gerade Zahl der Centuriae als Vorbedingung der Kampfweise nach Manipeln notwendig war.' But the tactical use of the maniple was already obsolescent, if not actually obsolete at the time of the formation of the Vigiles.

25 Gaius I 32b; Ulpian III 5.

26 Ulpian III 5.

27 Ulpian *apud Dig.*, XXXVII 13: item vigiles milites sunt et iure militari eos testari posse nulla dubitatio est.

28 Cf. A. M. Duff, *Freedmen in the Early Roman Empire* (repr. 1958), 140 f., and P. K. Baillie Reynolds, *The Vigiles of Imperial Rome* (1926) 67 f.

29 For the events of AD 31 cf. Dio LVIII 9, 6 and 12, 2.

30 For the fleets in general see C. G. Starr, *The Roman Imperial Navy* (2nd edn., 1960).

31 Cf. Starr, *ibid.*, 13.

32 *ibid.*, 16 f.

33 *ibid.*, 32.

34 *ibid.*, 37 f.

35 Cf. *ILS* 2914 (= *CIL* VIII 21025), Caesarea in Mauretania: Ti. Claudio Aug. lib. Eroti, trierarcho liburnae Nili exacto classis Aug. Alexandrinae, L. Iulius C.f. Fab. Saturninus et M. Antonius Heraclea trier., heredes eius fecerunt. For the earlier title cf. *ILS* 2816 (= *CIL* VI 32775; Smallwood, *Gaius* 182), Rome: Ti. Iulio Aug. lib. Xantho, tractatori Ti. Caesaris et divi Claudi et sub praef. classis Alexandriae, Atellia Prisca uxor et Lamyrus l. heredes. V(ixit) a(nnis) LXXXX.

36 Cf. Starr, *op. cit.*, 114 ff.

37 VI, 19 ff.

38 Cf. Parker, *RL*, 26 ff. and M. Marin y Peña, *Instituciones militares romanas* (Madrid 1956), paras. 95–102.

39 For the period up to 50 BC cf. J. Harmand, *op. cit.* in n. 26 ff. Veith in Kromayer-Veith, *Heerwesen*, 388, comes to much the same conclusion for Caesar's legions during the Civil Wars: 'Caesar scheint relativ kleine Truppenkörper bevorzugt zu haben, vielleicht war 4000 oder 4200 "seine" Sollstärke, d.h. das Mass, über das er auch bei unbeschränkter Ergänzungsmöglichkeit nicht hinausgegangen ist; selbst 3600 ist nicht ganz abzuweisen. Eine Eigentümlichkeit Caesars ist es, dass er seine Veteranenlegionen, auch wenn sie tief unter dem Sollstand waren, nicht ergänzt hat, offenbar um ihre Qualität nicht zu verwässern, und lieber neue Legionen aufstellte.'

40 Cf. n. 7 above.

41  See now Eric Birley, 'Promotions and Transfers in the Roman Army, II: The Centurionate', *Carnuntum Jahrbuch* 1963-4, 21 ff.

42  Cf. Parker, *RL*, 140 ff., and A. Passerini *s.v.* 'Legio' in *Diz. epigr.* IV 556 f.

43  The order of the disappearance of these two legions is still a vexed question. The problem is linked with the order of creation of II *Traiana* and XXX *Ulpia* in the reign of Trajan. It is obvious that the naming of XXX *Ulpia* implies that there were 29 other legions in existence at the time, for had Trajan merely wanted to use an unoccupied number he could have called this legion XXIII. Parker, *RL*, 109 ff., would go further and hold that II *Traiana* was so named because it was Trajan's second legionary creation. This would then imply that there were 29 legions in existence at the accession of Trajan, which would leave room for only one to be lost in the reign of Domitian. This Parker believes to have been V *Alaudae* in AD 92; XXI *Rapax* he maintains to have been lost early in the reign of Trajan, but subsequently to the creation of XXX *Ulpia*. XXI *Rapax* was then replaced by II *Traiana*. The view followed in the text is that of Ritterling, who maintained that II *Traiana* was not named to mark Trajan's second legionary creation, but that the number reflected honour on a legion numbered I, perhaps I *Adiutrix* or I *Minervia*. A simpler explanation would be that the last new legion to be created before II *Traiana* was a legion numbered I, that is, I *Minervia*, and that II *Traiana* was so numbered, not to honour I *Minervia*, but just to carry on the numeration. Cf. also Sir Ronald Syme, *JRS* XVIII (1928) 46, *CAH* IX 171 n. 1, *Laureae Aquincenses* I (1938) 269 f., and A. Passerini, *op. cit.*, 557.

44  Cf. Cheesman, *Auxilia*, 49 ff., for the relation of the *auxilia* to the legions, and Eric Birley, *Archaeologia Cambrensis* (1952), 17 ff., for a discussion of how the legionary command structure worked in Britain.

45  For the *militia equestris* in general see Eric Birley, 'The Equestrian Officers of the Roman Army', *Roman Britain and the Roman Army* (1953), 133 ff. The sequence of the *tres militiae* is well-established from the time of Nero onwards; before the reign of Claudius the order was by no means settled, and for a short time in Claudius' reign the *praefectura equitum* actually preceded the legionary tribunate. (Suet., *Claudius* 25: equestris militias ita ordinavit, ut post cohortem alam, post alam tribunatum legionis daret.) Birley also suggests (*op. cit.*, 149) that in the second and third centuries, possibly as an innovation of Hadrian, the command of an *ala miliaria* became established as a *militia quarta*, to be held after the normal *praefectura alae*. Since there were only about a dozen units of this type in the Roman Army, their commanders might well, as Birley remarks, be regarded as the cream of the equestrian military service.

46  Hyginus, *de mun. castr.* 16: nunc, ut suo referam loco, ad alam miliariam. turmas habet XXIIII . . . ala quingenaria turmas habet XVI.

47  Cf. *ILS* 2525 (= *CIL* III 5938), Untersaal: M. Vir(ius) Marcellus dec(urio) (princeps) al(ae) I F(laviae) s(ingularium) A(ntoninianae) . . .

48 Cf. Cheesman, *Auxilia*, 28 ff.

49 Hyginus, 26–7: habet itaque cohors equitata miliaria equites CCXL . . . cohors equitata quingenaria in dimidio eandem rationem continet quam cohors miliaria. habet itaque cohors equitata miliaria centurias X, turmas X; omnes tendunt papilionibus CXXXVI, ex eis centuriones et decuriones singulis papilionibus utuntur. cohors equitata quingenaria habet centurias VI, turmas VI, reliqua pro parte dimidia.

50 Cf. Robert O. Fink in *The Excavations at Dura-Europos, Final Report V, Part I* (1959), 28 ff.

51 Cf. Birley, *loc. cit.*

52 Cf. Schenk, *Vegetius*, 3 n. 2; O. Seeck, *Hermes* 1876, 68 ff.; V. A. Sirago, *Galla Placidia e la transformazione politica dell'occidente*, App. 2, 'Vegezio ed il dedicatario del suo Trattato Militare' (1961).

53 I 8: haec necessitas conpulit evolutis auctoribus ea me in hoc opusculo fidelissime dicere, quae Cato ille Censorius de disciplina militari scripsit, quae Cornelius Celsus, quae Frontinus perstringenda duxerunt, quae Paternus diligentissimus iuris militaris adsertor in libros redegit, quae Augusti et Traiani Hadrianique constitutionibus cauta sunt. nihil enim mihi auctoritatis adsumo, sed horum, quos supra rettuli, quae dispersa sunt, velut in ordinem epitomata conscribo.

54 Schenk, *Vegetius*, 8 n. 1: 'Da Paternus († 183) die letzte Quelle des Vegetius ist, gehen alle Einrichtungen, die einer späteren Periode angehören, auf den Verfasser selbst zurück.'

55 H. M. D. Parker, 'The *antiqua legio* of Vegetius', *CQ* 1932, 137–49. Schenk followed Lange and Förster in ascribing the *antiqua legio* to the age of Hadrian. The majority of modern scholars, though differing considerably in details, have concurred in placing the *antiqua legio* in the third century. Cf. E. Nischer in Kromayer-Veith, *Heerwesen*, 493 f.; E. Sander, 'Die *antiqua ordinatio legionis* des Vegetius', *Klio* 1939, 382–391; Eric Birley, *Actes du deuxième Congrès international d'épigraphie grecque et latine*, Paris 1952 (1953), 234. Parker and Sander agree on the period from Gallienus to Diocletian, Nischer seems to assume the age of Diocletian, while Birley, arguing from Cassius Dio LXXV, 12, prefers the age of Severus. A convenient résumé of the views of Nischer, Parker and Sander may be found in M. Marin y Peña, *Instituciones militares romanas* (1956), paras. 385 ff.

56 Lydus, *De mag.* I 47.

57 Cf. *JRS* 1952, 60 f.

58 Edited by Lange, 1848; Gemoll, 1879; A. von Domaszewski, 1887. Cf. also F. Stolle, *Das Lager und Heer der Römer* (1912). The work is dated to the first half of the second century by Domaszewski, 'frühestens kurz vor Hadrian' by Stolle, to the middle years of Marcus Aurelius by Birley (*op. cit.* in n. 55, 234), and to the beginning of the third century by Marquardt (*R. St.* V II³ 600).

59 For the jurists see W. Kunkel, *Herkunft und soziale Stellung der römische Juristen* (1952), esp. 219 ff.

60 See below, p. 39.

61 Polybius in Book VI gives a detailed description of the Roman Army. Cf. F. W. Walbank, *A Historical Commentary on Polybius*, I (1957). In Book III of the *Wars of the Jews* and also in Book V (III 6, 2 and V 2, 1) Josephus describes the order of march of the Roman Army.

62 Cheesman, *Auxilia*, 102 n. 2. He cites Herodian II 15, 6 and Lucian, *de hist. conscrib.*

63 *Ann.* I 65: per quae egeritur humus aut exciditur caespes.

64 For the material from Trajan's Column, see I. A. Richmond, 'Trajan's Army on Trajan's Column', *PBSR* 1935, 1–40. For the column of Marcus Aurelius, see the work of C. Caprino, A. M. Colini, G. Gatti, M. Pallottino, P. Romanelli, *La Colonna di Marco Aurelio* (1955).

65 *CIL* XVI ed. H. Nesselhauf, 1936; Suppl. 1955.

66 The ostraca listed in Appendix C include: *CR* XXXIII (1923), O. Fay., O. Milne, O. Strassb., O. Tait II, O. Tell Edfou, O. Wâdi Fawâkhir, O. Wâdi Hammamat, O. Wilb.-Brk., O. Wilcken, O. Würzburg, *SB* III 6957, 6961, 6963, 6967, VI 9118.

67 Those listed in Appendix C are P. Dura 94, 109, 110, 112 and 119.

68 R. Cavenaile, *Corpus Papyrorum Latinarum* (Wiesbaden 1958); hereafter referred to as *CPL*.

69 S. Daris, *Documenti per la storia dell'esercito romano in Egitto* (Milan 1964). Hereafter referred to as *Documenti*. Reviewed by R. W. Davis, *JRS* 1966, 242 f.

# THE RECRUIT

70 Cf. Parker, *RL*, 185. Eric Birley points out ('The Epigraphy of the Roman Army', *Actes du deuxième congrès international d'épigraphie grecque et latine*, Paris 1952 (1953), 235): 'Mommsen's *Conscriptionsordnung*, I think, assumes too readily that the *dilectus* was normal and voluntary enlistment of little significance; yet the implication of Vegetius (*epit. rei milit.*, II 3) is surely that there were plenty of volunteers in "the good old days", and we have the specific testimony of Arrius Menander (*Digest* XLIX 16, 4) to show that, at least in the early years of the third century, the bulk of recruits to the Roman army were in fact volunteers and not conscripts.' Cf. also J. C. Mann, 'The Role of the Frontier Zones in Army Recruitment', *V Congressus Internationalis Limitis Romani Studiorum* (Zagreb 1963), 145–50.

71 Pliny, *epp.* III 8 and VII 22.

72 For the technical term see Cicero, *Ad Fam.* V, 5, 1: etsi statueram nullas ad te litteras mittere nisi commendaticias (non quo eas intellegerem satis apud te valere, sed ne iis qui me rogarent, aliquid de nostra coniunctione imminutum esse ostenderem), tamen, etc. Book XIII of the *Ad Familiares* is almost entirely composed of *litterae commendaticiae*. Cf. also *Digest* XLI, I, 65.

73 *P. Mich.* VIII 468 (= *CPL* 251, *Documenti* 7), 35 ff. et si deus volueret spero me frugaliter [v]iciturum et in cohortem [tra]nsferri. hic a[ut]em sene aer[e] [ni]hil fiet neque epistulae commandaticiae nihil val⟨eb⟩unt nesi si qui sibi aiutaveret.

74 *P. Oxy* I 32 (= *CPL* 249): I[u]lio Domitio tribuno mil(itum) leg(ionis) ab Aurel(io) Archelao benef(iciario) suo salutem. Iam tibi et pristine commendaveram Theonem amicum meum et mod[o qu]oque peto domine ut eum ant⟨e⟩ oculos habeas tanquam me. est enim tales omo ut ametur a te. reliquit enim su[o]s [e]t rem suam et actum et me secutus est, et per omnia me secu[r]um fecit. et ideo peto a te ut habeat intr[o]itum at te. et omnia tibi referere potest de actu[m] nostrum . . . . . . . hanc epistulam ant⟨e⟩ oculos habeto, domine. puta[t]o me tecum loqui. vale.

75 *P. Berlin* 11649 (= *CPL* 257): Priscus Petronio patri suo salutem. Apri duplicari Carum duplicarium, hominem probum, commendo tib[i], qui si qu[i]d eguerit auxili tui, rogo in meum honorem adiuves eum salvo pudore tu[o]. opto bene valeas. Salutem dic nostris omnibus, salutem tibi dicunt nostri omnes. vale.

76 *P. Fayum Barns* 2 (= *CPL* 102, *Documenti* 2) is a declaration by an *optio* of *legio III Cyrenaica* in AD 92 that he is of free birth, a Roman citizen, and has the right to serve in a legion. Presumably his eligibility had been contested.

77 As in *P. Gen. lat.* 1, iii 4: C. Valerius C.f. Pol. Bassus castr(is). For the matrimonial status of the parents of such recruits, see below pp. 134 ff. In cases where the *praenomen* is Sp(urius) cf. Eric Birley, *Roman Britain and the Roman Army* (1953), 161: 'Spurius was an old and, in its day, distinguished *praenomen*—witness the Spurius Lartius of the *Lays of Ancient Rome*; but the Roman army assigned it in their filiation to the men born out of wedlock in the cantonments, on their entry to service in the legions and the receipt of Roman citizenship (which was a prerequisite for such service); and it seems clear that the origin of the use of Spurius for such cases was in Roman military book-keeping. Such men had no father, legally speaking, and the original entry was *s.p.* for *sine patre*; and *Sp.* was the standard abbreviation for Spurius.'

78 Cf. the *Gnomon of the Idios Logos* (*BGU* V 1210 = *Documenti* 1), para. 55.

79 Vegetius, *epit. rei milit.*, I 5: proceritatem tironum ad incommam scio semper exactam, ita ut VI pedum vel certe V et X unciarum inter alares equites vel in primis legionum cohortibus probarentur. sed tunc erat amplior multitudo, et plures militiam sequebantur armatam; necdum enim civilis pars florentiorem abducebat iuventutem. si ergo necessitas exigit, non tam staturae rationem convenit habere quam virium.

80 *Cod. Theod.* VII 13, 3 (27 April 367): Idem AA. ad Magnum vic(arium) urbis Rom(ae). In quinque pedibus et septem unciis usualibus delectus habeatur. Dat. V Kal. Mai. Lupicino et Iovino conss.

81 *Cod. Theod.* VII 13, 4 (27 April 367): Idem AA. ad Magnum vic(arium) urb(is) Rom(ae). Eos, qui amputatione digitorum castra fugiunt, secundum

divi Constantini decretum tua sinceritas non sinat manus deformatione defendi, si quidem possint in quacumque rei publicae parte prodesse qui se sponte truncaverunt. Dat. V Kal. Mai. Lupicino et Iovino conss.

82 *Cod. Theod.* VII 13, 10: Idem AAA. Eutropio p(raefecto) p(raetori)o. Qui spurca amputatione digiti usum declinat armorum, non evadat illa quae vitat, sed insignitus macula ferat inpositum militiae laborem qui declinaverit dignitatem. ipsis quin etiam provincialibus, qui ex horum ausis iuniorum saepe patiuntur penuriam praebendorum, haec optio inmobilis decernatur, ut tempore dilectus agitandi, ubi commune coeperint conveniri, duos mutilos iuniores pro uno integro eminentiae tuae dispositionibus offerant. Dat. Non. Sept. Hadrianopoli Eucherio et Syagrio conss. (5 Sept. 381.)

83 Suetonius, *Div. Aug.*, 24: equitem R., quod duobus filiis adulescentibus causa detrectandi sacramenti pollices amputasset, ipsum bonaque subiecit hastae; quem tamen, quod inminere emptioni publicanos videbat, liberto suo addixit, ut relegatum in agros pro libero esse sineret.

84 *P. Oxy.* I 39, with corrections in *Oxy. Pap.* II, 319, and further comments in *Oxy. Pap.* XII, 152. Repr. by Wilcken, *Chrestomathie*, 456.

85 Vegetius, *epit. rei milit.*, I 7: sequitur ut, cuius artis vel eligendi vel penitus repudiandi sint milites, indagemus. piscatores aucupes dulciarios linteones omnesque, qui aliquid tractasse videbuntur ad gynaecea pertinens, longe arbitror pellendos a castris; fabros ferrarios carpentarios, macellarios et cervorum aprorumque venatores convenit sociare militiae.

86 *Cod. Theod.* VII, 13, 8 (29 January 380): Imppp. Gratianus, Valentinianus et Theodosius AAA. edictum ad provinciales. Inter optimas lectissimorum militum turmas neminem e numero servorum dandum esse decernimus neve ex caupona ductum vel ex famosarum ministeriis tabernarum aut ex cocorum aut pistorum numero vel etiam eo, quem obsequii deformitas militia secernit, nec tracta de ergastulis nomina. poenam etenim gravis dispendii nulla excusatione fugituri sunt, si hoc cuiusdam indicio inlustribus viris magistris equitum peditum fuerit intimatum. sed cum illum animadversio dura damnavit offerentem, tum triplicata nobilioris tironis fatigabit inlatio. Dat. IIII Kal. Feb. Const(antino)p(oli) Gratiano A. V et Theodosio A. I conss.

87 *P. Oxy.* VII 1022 (= *CPL* 111, *Documenti* 4): e(xemplum e(pistulae). [C.] Minicius Italu[s C]elsiano suo sal[u]tem. Tirones sexs probatos a me in coh(orte) cui praees in numeros referri iube ex XI Kalendas Martias: nomina eorum et icon[i]smos huic epistulae subieci. Vale frater karissim[e]. C. Veturium Gemellum annor(um) XXI sine i(conismo), C. Longinum Priscum annor(um) XXII, i(conismus) supercil(io) sinistr(o), C. Iulium Maximum ann(orum) XXV sine i(conismo), [.] Lucium Secundum annor(um) XX sine i(conismo), C. Iulium Saturninum annor(um) XXIII, i(conismus) manu sinistr(a), M. Antonium Valentem ann(orum) XXII, i(conismus) frontis parte dextr(a).

$m^2$ Accepta VI K(alendas) Martias ann(o) VI Imp(eratoris) Traiani n(ostri) per Priscum singul(arem). Avidius Arrianus cornicular(ius) coh(ortis) III Ituraeorum scripsi authenticam epistulam in tabulario cohortis esse.

88 *Digest* XXIX 1, 42 (Ulpian): Ex eo tempore quis iure militari incipit posse testari, ex quo in numeros relatus est, ante non: proinde qui nondum in numeris sunt, licet etiam lecti tirones sint et publicis expensis iter faciunt, nondum milites sunt: debent enim in numeros referri. For a discussion of this point and the meaning of the phrase *in numeros referri* see J. F. Gilliam, 'Enrollment in the Roman Imperial Army', *Eos* XLVIII (1957) 207 ff. Cf. also W. G. Sinnigen, *Classical Philology* (1967), 108 ff.

89 Pliny, *epp.* X 29 and 30.

90 *BGU* II 423, 8–10 (= Wilcken, *Chrestomathie*, 480).

91 For *P. Berlin* 6866 (= *CPL* 122, *Documenti* 35) cf. R. Marichal, *L'Occupation romaine de la Basse Egypte* (Paris 1945), and 'La solde des armées romaines d'Auguste à Septime-Sévère d'après les P. Gen. lat. 1 et le P. Berlin 6.866', *Mélanges Isidore Lévy* (Brussels 1955), 399 ff. (hereafter referred to as Marichal, *La Solde*). Marichal dates the document to the years AD 192–6; Fink, *Synteleia Vincenzo Arangio-Ruiz* (Naples 1964), 233, more precisely to the year AD 192.

92 For the amount of the *stipendium* see below, pp. 91 ff.

93 Polybius VI 21, 1–3; Paulus, *epit. Festi* 250 L. For the oath in Republican times see now S. Tondo, 'Il "sacramento militiae" nell'ambiente culturale romano-italico', *Studia et Documenta Historiae et Iuris* XXIX (1963), 1–123, esp. 11 f., and J. Harmand, *L'armée et le soldat à Rome de 107 à 50 avant notre ère* (Paris 1967), 299–302.

94 R. O. Fink, *Yale Classical Studies* VII 51, argues for 3 January. On the other hand A. von Premerstein, *Vom Werden und Wesen des Prinzipats* (1937), 73–99 adopts what is perhaps a legalistic view, and maintains that the *sacramentum* was sworn once for all, at the time of attestation; the annual oath he considers to be a *Gefolgschaftseid* only. While it is true that the *sacramentum* was binding without renewal, it is doubtful whether in the eyes of the troops the annual renewal of the oath could be considered to be anything other than the renewal of the *sacramentum*.

95 Dion. Hal. X 18, 2; XI 43. Servius *ad Aen.* VIII 614: sacramentum, in quo iurat unusquisque miles se non recedere nisi praecepto consulis post completa stipendia, id est militiae tempora. VIII 1: legitima erat militia eorum, qui singuli iurabant pro re publica se esse facturos, nec discedebant nisi completis stipendiis, id est militiae temporibus. Vegetius, *epit. rei milit.*, II 5: iurant autem per Deum et Christum et Sanctum Spiritum et per maiestatem imperatoris, quae secundum Deum generi humano diligenda est et colenda. . . . iurant autem milites omnia se strenue facturos quae praeceperit imperator, nunquam deserturos militiam nec mortem recusaturos pro Romana republica. Isidore, *etym.* IX 3, 53:

sacramentum, in quo post electionem iurat unusquisque miles se non recedere a militia, nisi post completa stipendia, id est, militiae tempora; et hi sunt qui habent plenam militiam. nam viginti et quinque annis tenentur.

96 Livy XXII 38: dilectu perfecto consules paucos morati dies dum ab sociis ac nomine Latino venirent milites. tum, quod nunquam antea factum erat, iure iurando ab tribunis militum adacti milites; nam ad eam diem nihil praeter sacramentum fuerat iussu consulum conventuros neque iniussu abituros; et ubi ad decuriandum aut centuriandum convenissent, sua voluntate ipsi inter sese decuriati equites, centuriati pedites coniurabant sese fugae atque formidinis ergo non abituros neque ex ordine recessuros nisi teli sumendi aut petendi et aut hostis feriendi aut civis servandi causa. id ex voluntario inter ipsos foedere ad tribunos ac legitimam iuris iurandi adactionem translatum.

97 Polybius VI 33, 1; Cincius Alimentus *apud* Gell. XVI 4, 2.

98 Vegetius, *epit rei milit.*, I 8: sed non statim punctis signorum scribendus est tiro dilectus, verum ante exercitio pertemptandus ut utrum vere tanto operi aptus sit possit agnosci. II 5: nam victuris in cute punctis milites scripti, cum matriculis inseruntur, iurare solent.

99 *Cod. Theod.* X 22, 4 (15 Dec. 398 = *Cod. Iust.* XI 10, 3): stigmata, hoc est nota publica, fabricensium bracchiis ad imitationem tironum infligatur, ut hoc modo saltem possint latitantes agnosci.

100 PSI IX 1063 (= *Documenti* 33). See now J. F. Gilliam, *Bonner Historia-Augusta/Colloquium* 1964/5 (1966), 91 ff.

101 The deposits amount to a total of 1,726 *denarii* 22 obols, an average of 13 *denarii* 20 obols a man.

102 Vegetius, *epit. rei milit.*, II 19: sed quoniam in legionibus plures scholae sunt, quae litteratos milites quaerunt, ab his, qui tirones probant, in omnibus quidem staturae magnitudinem, corporis robur, alacritatem animi convenit explorari, sed in quibusdam notarum peritia, calculandi computandique usus eligitur. totius enim legionis ratio, sive obsequiorum sive militarium munerum sive pecuniae, cotidie adscribitur actis maiore prope diligentia, quam res annonaria vel civilis polyptychis adnotatur.

103 For *matricula* see my note in *JRS* 1952, 59 ff., and the remarks of R. O. Fink, *The Excavations at Dura-Europos. Final Report V. Part I. The Parchments and Papyri* (1959), 45 f. For *numeri* see Gilliam, *op. cit.* in n. 88.

104 *P. Dura* 89 (= *CPL* 331) i 15: tirones duos quorum nomi[na                    ] item staturas subici pr[a]ecepi ar . . . sagitare . . e . to [.] . probatos . . . in c[o]h(ortem) XX Palm(yrenorum) Gor[d]ianam.

# THE SOLDIER

105 Cf. Schenk, *Vegetius*, 26 ff.

106 Vegetius, *epit. rei milit.* I 9: primis ergo meditationum auspiciis tirones

militarem edocendi sunt gradum. nihil enim magis in itinere vel in acie custodiendum est, quam ut omnes milites incedendi ordinem servent. quod aliter non potest fieri, nisi assiduo exercitio ambulare celeriter et aequaliter discant. periculum enim ab hostibus semper gravissimum sustinet divisus et inordinatus exercitus. militari ergo gradu XX milia passuum quinque horis dumtaxat aestivis conficienda sunt. pleno autem gradu, qui citatior est, totidem horis XXIIII milia peragenda sunt. quicquid addideris, iam cursus est, cuius spatium non potest definiri.

107 Twenty Roman miles are approximately equal to 18.4 statute miles.

108 For running and jumping cf. I 9: sed et cursu praecipue adsuefaciendi sunt iuniores, ut maiore impetu in hostem procurrant, ut loca opportuna celeriter, cum usus advenerit, occupent vel adversariis idem facere volentibus praeoccupent, ut ad explorandum alacriter peragant, alacrius redeant, ut fugientium facilius terga comprehendant. ad saltum etiam, quo vel fossae transiliuntur vel impediens aliqua altitudo superatur, exercendus est miles ut, cum eiusmodi difficultates evenerint, possint sine labore transire. For swimming and carrying loads see below, nn. 109 ff. and 138 ff. For a consideration of these passages see A. R. Neumann, 'Römische Rekrutenausbildung im Lichte der Disziplin', *Class. Phil.* 1948, 157 ff. See esp. 158.

109 Vegetius I 10: natandi usum aestivis mensibus omnis aequaliter debet tiro condiscere.

110 Vegetius III 4: seu mare sive fluvius vicinus est sedibus, aestivo tempore ad natandum cogendi sunt omnes.

111 Cf. in general E. Mehl *s.v.* 'Schwimmen' in *RE* Suppl. V 847–64. For the Batavians see the famous Soranus inscription (*ILS* 2558 = *CIL* III 3676) and Dio LXIX 9; Tac., *Hist.* IV 12; *Ann.* II 8. In Tac., *Agric.* 18 the phrase *lectissimos auxiliarium, quibus nota vada et patrius nandi usus* probably refers to Batavians (cf. 36, 1), though some (e.g. Gudeman) have thought that British auxiliaries are meant. This is most unlikely.

112 Vegetius I 11: antiqui, sicut invenitur in libris, hoc genere exercuere tirones. scuta de vimine in modum cratium conrotundata texebant, ita ut duplum pondus cratis haberet quam scutum publicum habere consuevit. idemque clavas ligneas dupli aeque ponderis pro gladiis tironibus dabant. eoque modo non tantum mane sed etiam post meridiem exercebantur ad palos. palorum enim usus non solum militibus sed etiam gladiatoribus plurimum prodest. nec umquam aut harena aut campus invictum armis virum probavit, nisi qui diligenter exercitatus docebatur ad palum. For a recent discussion of these practice weapons see R. W. Davies, 'Fronto, Hadrian and the Roman Army', *Latomus* XXVII (1968), 75 ff.

113 Valerius Maximus II 3, 2: armorum tractandorum meditatio a P. Rutilio consule Cn. Mallii collega militibus est tradita: is enim nullius ante se imperatoris exemplum secutus ex ludo C. Aureli Scauri doctoribus gladiatorum arcessitis vitandi atque inferendi ictus subtiliorem rationem

legionibus ingeneravit virtutemque arti et rursus artem virtuti miscuit, ut illa impetu huius fortior, haec illius scientia cautior fieret.

Frontinus, *Strat.* IV 2, 2: C. Marius, cum facultatem eligendi exercitus haberet ex duobus, qui sub Rutilio et qui sub Metello ac postea sub se ipso meruerant, Rutilianum quamquam minorem, quia certioris disciplinae arbitrabatur, praeoptavit.

114 Pliny, *Panegyricus* 13, 4: hac mihi admiratione dignus imperator non videretur, si inter Fabricios et Scipiones et Camillos talis esset; tunc enim illum imitationis ardor semperque melior aliquis accenderet. postquam vero studium armorum a manibus ad oculos, ad voluptatem a labore translatum est, postquam exercitationibus nostris non veteranorum aliquis, cui decus muralis aut civica, sed Graeculus magister adsistit, quam magnum est unum ex omnibus patrio more, patria virtute laetari et sine aemulo ac sine exemplo secum certare, secum contendere ac, sicut imperare solum, solum ita esse, qui debeat imperare! It is not necessary, of course, to suppose that the *Graeculus magister* was inevitably a Greek. For another view see E. Sander, 'Die Kleidung des römischen Soldaten', *Historia* XII (1963), 146.

115 Fronto, *princ. hist.*, 8–9. Cf. R. W. Davies, *Latomus* XXVII (1968), 75 ff.

116 Vegetius I 11: a singulis autem tironibus singuli pali defigebantur in terram, ita ut nutare non possent et sex pedibus eminerent. contra illum palum tamquam contra adversarium tiro cum crate illa et clava velut cum gladio se exercebat et scuto, ut nunc quasi caput aut faciem peteret, nunc a lateribus minaretur, interdum contenderet poplites et crura succidere, recederet adsultaret insiliret, quasi praesentem adversarium, sic palum omni impetu, omni bellandi arte temptaret. in qua meditatione servabatur illa cautela, ut ita tiro ad inferendum vulnus insurgeret, ne qua parte ipse pateret ad plagam. praeterea non caesim sed punctim ferire discebant. nam caesim pugnantes non solum facile vicere sed etiam derisere Romani.

117 Vegetius I 13: praeterea illo exercitii genere, quod armaturam vocant et a campidoctoribus traditur, imbuendus est tiro; qui usus vel ex parte servatur. constat enim etiam nunc in omnibus proeliis armaturas melius pugnare quam ceteros. ex quo intellegi debet, quantum exercitatus miles inexercitato sit melior, cum armaturae utcumque eruditi reliquos contubernales suos bellandi arte praecedant. ita autem severe apud maiores exercitii disciplina servata est, ut et doctores armorum duplis remunerarentur annonis et milites, qui parum in illa prolusione profecerant, pro frumento hordeum cogerentur accipere, nec ante eis in tritico redderetur annona, quam sub praesentia praefecti legionis, tribunorum vel principiorum experimentis datis ostendisset se omnia quae erant in militari arte complere.

118 Polybius X 20, 3–4; Livy XXVI, 51, 4 gives the training programme under Scipio at New Carthage: primo die legiones in armis quattuor milium spatio decurrerunt; secundo die arma curare et tergere ante tentoria iussi; tertio die rudibus inter se in modum iustae pugnae concurrerunt praepilatisque missilibus iaculati sunt; quarto die quies data; quinto iterum in

armis decursum est. hunc ordinem laboris quietisque quoad Carthagine morati sunt servarunt. For the *praepilata missilia* see R. W. Davies, *op. cit.*, 86 ff.

119 Vegetius I 14: tiro, qui cum clava exercetur ad palum, hastilia quoque ponderis gravioris quam vera futura sunt iacula, adversum illum palum tamquam adversum hominem iactare compellitur. *ibid.*: eo enim exercitio et lacertis robur adcrescit et iaculandi peritia atque usus adquiritur. II 23: missilibus etiam palos ipsos procul ferire meditentur, ut et ars dirigendi et dexterae virtus possit adcrescere.

120 For details see P. Couissin, *Les armes romaines* (Paris 1926), esp. 195 ff., and A. Schulten in *RE s.v.* 'pilum'.

121 Cf. A. Schulten, *loc. cit.* Cf. also F. W. Walbank, *A Historical Commentary on Polybius*, Vol. I (1957), 705.

122 Plutarch, *Marius* 25. Cf. T. F. Carney, *CQ* 1955, 203 f.

123 Caesar, *BG* I 25: Gallis magno ad pugnam erat impedimento quod pluribus eorum scutis uno ictu pilorum transfixis et colligatis, cum ferrum se inflexisset, neque evellere neque sinistra impedita satis commode pugnare poterant; multi ut diu iactato bracchio praeoptarent scutum manu emittere et nudo corpore pugnare.

124 See notes 112, 115 and 118 above.

125 Tac., *Ann.* XII 35: et si auxiliaribus resisterent, gladiis ac pilis legionariorum, si huc verterent, spathis et hastis auxiliarium sternebantur.

126 Cf. Cichorius in *RE* IV 234 *s.v.* 'cohors': 'Benennung nach besonderer Bewaffnung oder Ausrüstung findet sich bei den Cohorten sowohl als Haupt- wie als Beiname, jedoch nicht sehr häufig. Es sind hier auzuführen die Namen *Gaesatorum, Sagittariorum, Scutata* und vielleicht *Expedita*.'

127 e.g. Caesar, *BG* II 7: Numidas et Cretas sagittarios et funditores Balearis subsidio oppidanis mittit.

128 Hadrian's *adlocutio* (in this instance addressed to the *equites* of *cohors VI Commagenorum*) is contained in *ILS* 2487 (= *CIL* VIII 18042 and Smallwood, *Nerva* 328): verum vos fastidium calore vitastis, strenue faciendo quae fieri debebant; addidistis ut et lapides fundis mitteretis et missilibus confligeretis; saluistis ubique expedite. Cf. Cheesman, *Auxilia*, 131 f.

129 Vegetius I 15: sed prope tertia vel quarta pars iuniorum, quae aptior potuerit reperiri, arcubus ligneis sagittisque lusoriis illos ipsos exercenda est semper ad palos. et doctores ad hanc rem artifices eligendi, et maior adhibenda sollertia, ut arcum scienter teneant, ut fortiter impleant, ut sinistra fixa sit, ut dextra cum ratione ducatur, ut ad illud quod feriundum est oculus pariter animusque consentiat, ut sive in equo sive in terra rectum sagittare doceantur. quam artem et disci opus est diligenter et cotidiano usu exercitioque servari.

130 Vegetius II 23: sagittarii vero vel funditores scopas, hoc est fruticum vel straminum fasces, pro signo ponebant, ita ut sexcentis pedibus removerentur a signo, ut sagittis vel certe lapidibus ex fustibalo destinatis signum

saepius tangerent. propterea sine trepidatione in acie faciebant quod ludentes in campo fecerant semper. adsuescendum est etiam, ut semel tantum funda circa caput rotetur cum ex ea emittitur saxum. sed et manu sola omnes milites meditabantur libralia saxa iactare, qui usus paratior creditur quia non desiderat fundam. missibilia quoque vel plumbatas iugi perpetuoque exercitio dirigere cogebantur usque adeo, ut tempore hiemis de tegulis vel scindulis, quae si deessent, certe de cannis, ulva vel culmo et porticus tegerentur ad equites et quaedam velut basilicae ad pedites, in quibus tempestate vel ventis aëre turbato sub tecto armis erudiebatur exercitus. ceteris autem etiam hibernis diebus, si nives tantum pluviaque cessarent, exerceri cogebantur in campo, ne intermissa consuetudo et animos militum debilitaret et corpora.

131 Apparently here a technical term, explained by the gloss 'hoc est, fruticum vel straminum fasces'. *Scopae* means literally 'brush' or 'broom', and presumably the target was first so called in the *sermo castrensis* because of its likeness to a brush with the bristles projecting horizontally (like some present-day forms of targets and dart-boards).

132 'Loaded javelins', or *plumbatae*, were weapons of the late third and fourth centuries. Cf. Vegetius I 17: plumbatarum quoque exercitatio, quos mattiobarbulos vocant, est tradenda iunioribus. nam in Illyrico dudum duae legiones fuerunt, quae sena milia militum habuerunt, quae quod his telis scienter utebantur et fortiter Mattiobarbuli vocabantur. per hos longo tempore strenuissime constat omnia bella confecta, usque eo ut Diocletianus et Maximianus, cum ad imperium pervenissent, pro merito virtutis hos Mattiobarbulos Iovianos atque Herculianos censuerint appellandos eosque cunctis legionibus praetulisse doceantur. quinos autem mattiobarbulos insertos scutis portare consuerunt, quos si opportune milites iactent, prope sagittariorum scutati imitari videntur officium. nam hostes equosque consauciant, priusquam non modo ad manum sed ad ictum missibilium potuerit perveniri. Cf. also E. A. Thompson, *A Roman Reformer and Inventor* (1952), 67 f.

133 For an example of such a *basilica exercitatoria* cf. the drill-hall found at Inchtuthill (*JRS* 1960, 213), 'an elaborate building with porch, nave, aisles, and ranges of rooms at side and back, set at the back of a small forecourt and bounded on the E. by the *scamnum tribunorum*'.

134 Cf. Liebenam in *RE s.vv.* 'funditores' and 'glans'. In the latter article he writes: 'In der Kaiserzeit ist der Brauch aufgegeben . . . nur Steine werden noch geschleudert.' This is the traditional view. I am reminded, however, by R. W. Davies that the only evidence for legionaries throwing stones from slings during the Principate is from Vegetius. It was a band of civilians that threw stones in Liguria (though the wording of Tacitus' description—*etiam* paganorum manus—suggests that the ability to do so was not confined to civilians). Tac., *Hist.* 2, 14: Trevirorum turmae obtulere se hosti incaute, cum exciperet contra veteranorum miles, simul

a latere saxis urgeret apta ad iaciendum etiam paganorum manus, qui sparsi inter milites, strenui ignavique, in victoria idem audebant. Lead sling bullets have been discovered in quantity only at Burnswark, though if they had been standard equipment they would surely have been found in some of the Wall forts or on the German *limes*. Cf. now R. W. Davies, 'The Romans at Burnswark', *Trans. of the Dumfries and Galloway Nat. Hist. and Antiqu. Society*, forthcoming (XLV, 1968). He believes that Burnswark was a Roman artillery range and that the lead sling bullets were the equivalent of shrapnel. He would conclude that Vegetius II 23 does not refer to the use of slings by regular soldiers in the Principate. A smaller quantity of lead sling bullets has been discovered at Birrens in a second century level by Miss A. S. Robertson in 1967.

135 Vegetius I 18: non tantum autem a tironibus sed etiam ab stipendiosis militibus salitio equorum districte est semper exacta. quem usum usque ad hanc aetatem, licet cum dissimulatione, pervenisse manifestum est. equi lignei hieme sub tecto, aestate ponebantur in campo; supra hos iuniores primo inermes, dum consuetudo proficeret, deinde armati cogebantur ascendere. tantaque cura erat, ut non solum a dextris sed etiam a sinistris partibus et insilire et desilire condiscerent, evaginatos etiam gladios vel contos tenentes.

136 Neumann, *op. cit.*, in n. 108, 167, believes that all legionaries were so trained. He cites as evidence Caesar, *BG* I 42, 5: commodissimum esse statuit, omnibus equis Gallis equitibus detractis, eo legionarios milites legionis decimae, cui quam maxime confidebat, imponere, ut praesidium quam amicissimum, si quid opus facto esset, haberet.

137 One hundred and twenty men to each legion in the Flavian period. Cf. Josephus, *BJ* III 6, 2.

138 For accounts of the origin of the name cf. Frontinus, *Strat.* IV 1, 7; Plutarch, *Marius* 13; Festus 121 L and 267 L.

139 F. Stolle, *Der römische Legionär und sein Gepäck (mulus Marianus): eine Abhandlung über den Mondvorrat, die Gepäcklast und den Tornister des römischen Legionärs und im Anhang Erklärung der Apokalypse 6.6* (Strassburg 1914), 52.

140 Neumann, however (*op. cit.*, 169), points out that in the closing decades of the nineteenth century these amounts were sometimes exceeded, e.g. the Swiss carried about 35 kg., and the Russians almost 38 kg. J. Sulser, *Disciplina: Beiträge zur inneren Geschichte des römischen Heeres von Augustus bis Vespasian* (Basel 1923), 33 n. 2, adds that *Gebirgsmitrailleure* carry as much as 50 kg. In the parachute landings of 6 June 1944, no man was carrying less than 85 lb., some more than 100 lb.; in addition, each man had strapped to his leg a 60 lb. kitbag. Cf. Chester Wilmot, *The Struggle for Europe* (1952), 233 and 239. These amounts are all, in one way or another, abnormal. J. Harmand, *L'armée et le soldat à Rome de 107 à 50 avant notre ère* (1967), p. 162, lists the conclusions of other modern scholars about the

weight of the load which the Roman soldier had to carry. These range from 60 Roman pounds (about 19 kg.)—cf. Masquelez, *Etude sur la castraméation des Romains et sur leurs institutions militaires* (1864), 125, and R. Schneider, *Jahresber. d. Philol. Vereins in Berlin*, XIX (1893), 284 f.—through 15 to 22½ kg. without arms—cf. Rüstow, *Heerwesen und Kriegsführung C. Julius Caesars* (2nd edn., Nordhausen 1862), 14—and 20 to 30 kg. without arms— cf. F. Marstrander, *Symbolae Osloenses* XXXII (1956), 41—or about 30 kg. without arms—cf. G. Veith in Kromayer-Veith, *Heerwesen*, 425—to at least 50 kg., including arms—cf. Moineville, *Deux campagnes de César* (Paris 1900), 13.

141 Cicero, *Tusc.* II 37: ferre plus dimidiati mensis cibaria. SHA, *Alex.*, 47, 1: nec portarent cibaria decem et septem, ut solent, dierum. Amm. Marc. XVII 9, 2: ex annona decem dierum et septem, quam in expeditionem pergens vehebat cervicibus miles.

142 A. Momigliano, *Secondo Contributo alla Storia degli Studi Classici* (Rome 1960), 105–43, argues with great force for the conclusion that the problem of the date of the *Historia Augusta* has not yet been solved. It is no part of the scope of this work to attempt to solve it. For what it is worth, however, the habit of carrying seventeen days' ration on a campaign, which appears to be envisaged by the writer of the life of Severus Alexander as normal in his own day, would seem to be consistent with the standard practice in the time of Ammianus Marcellinus. Cf. now Sir Ronald Syme, *Ammianus and the Historia Augusta* (Oxford 1968).

143 For the *lancea* as a legionary weapon in the first and second centuries see Parker, *RL* 251. Arrian, *Exped. contra Alanos*, 14–16, shows the legions adopting a phalanx formation eight deep, with the first four ranks armed with the *pilum* and the rear four with the *lancea*.

144 Josephus, *BJ* III 95.

145 Kromayer-Veith, *Heerwesen*, 423 ff.

146 Caesar, *BC* III 53, 5: cohortemque postea duplici stipendio, frumento, veste, cibariis militaribusque donis amplissime donavit. It must be added, however, that the MSS reading is *vespeciariis*, which is retained by Du Pontet in the OCT, or *vespetiariis*, and that *veste, cibariis* is merely a conjecture of Cuiacius. Another suggestion is *congiariis*, 'bounties'.

147 Caesar, *BC* I 78: premebantur Afraniani pabulatione, aquabantur aegre. frumenti copiam legionarii non nullam habebant, quod dierum XXII ab Ilerda frumentum iussi erant efferre, caetrati auxiliaresque nullam, quorum erant et facultates ad parandum exiguae et corpora insueta ad onera portanda. XXII *codd.*, VII *Menzel*, VIII *Von Göler*, IX *Stolle*, XII *vel* XVII *alii*.

148 T. Rice Holmes, *Caesar's Conquest of Gaul* (2nd edn., Oxford 1911), 585.

149 Vegetius I 19: pondus quoque baiulare usque ad LX libras et iter facere gradu militari frequentissime cogendi sunt iuniores, quibus in arduis expeditionibus necessitas imminet annonam pariter et arma portandi. nec

hoc credatur esse difficile, si usus accesserit; nihil enim est quod non adsidua meditatio facillimum reddat.

150 The Roman pound weighed 327.45 grammes, and was equivalent to 0.721 lb. avoirdupois. Sixty Roman pounds, therefore, which was the maximum additional load, represented an extra burden of just over three stones (43.26 lb.) in weight, or about 20 kg. (precisely 19.647 kg.) .

151 Polybius VI 39, 12–15, allows ⅔ of a *medimnus* of wheat per month to an infantryman. If we assume 4½ *modii* to the *medimnus* (cf. Walbank, *A Historical Commentary on Polybius* I (1957), *ad. loc.*), the infantryman had 3 *modii* per month, or approximately 25.7 litres. On the basis of a thirty-day month this works out at about 0.86 litres a day. Since the specific gravity of corn is close to unity this is near enough to Stolle's figure of 0.845 kg.

152 Cf. n. 58 above. Cf. also I. A. Richmond, 'Roman Britain and Roman Military Antiquities', *Proceedings of the British Academy* 1955, 298 ff. He called for a series of selective excavations with a view to illustrating the field-work of the Roman Army. He expected that the result would be a modern *de munitionibus castrorum* which would be based throughout upon contact with reality, and which would make 'some striking contributions to the study of Imperial castrametation, a question concerning which there has been so much conjecture to so little profit that this most interesting subject of inquiry has fallen into positive disrepute.'

153 Vegetius I 21: castrorum quoque munitionem debet tiro condiscere; nihil enim neque tam salutare neque tam necessarium invenitur in bello; quippe, si recte constituta sunt castra, ita intra vallum securi milites dies noctesque peragunt, etiam si hostis obsideat, quasi muratam civitatem videantur secum ubique portare. sed huius rei scientia prorsus intercidit; nemo enim iam diu ductis fossis praefixisque sudibus castra contituit. sic diurno vel nocturno superventu equitum barbarorum multos exercitus scimus frequenter adflictos.

154 Cf. E. A. Thompson, *A Roman Reformer and Inventor* (1952), 79, who contrasts Vegetius with the *Anonymus* in this connection. All but one of the new or modified weapons proposed by the *Anonymus* are weapons of attack.

155 Vegetius I 24 f.: castrorum autem diversa triplexque munitio est. nam si nimia necessitas non premit, caespites circumciduntur e terra et ex his velut murus instruitur, altus tribus pedibus supra terram, ita ut in ante sit fossa, de qua levati sunt caespites; deinde tumultuaria fossa fit lata pedes novem et alta pedes VII. sed ubi vis acrior imminet hostium, tunc legitima fossa ambitum convenit munire castrorum, ita ut XII pedes lata sit et alta sub linea, sicut appellant, pedes novem. supra autem saepibus hinc inde factis quae de fossa levata fuerit terra congeritur et crescit in altum IIII pedes. sic fit ut sit XIII alta et XII lata; supra quam sudes de lignis fortissimis, quas milites portare consueverunt, praefiguntur. ad quod opus ligones rastra

qualos aliaque utensilium genera habere convenit semper in promptu.
25. sed facile est absentibus adversariis castra munire, verum si hostis
incumbat, tunc omnes equites et media pars peditum ad propulsandum
impetum ordinantur in acie, reliqui post ipsos ductis fossis muniunt castra,
et per praeconem indicatur, quae centuria prima, quae secunda, quae tertia
opus omne compleverit. post hoc a centurionibus fossa inspicitur ac
mensuratur et vindicatur in eos qui neglegentius fuerint operati. ad hunc
ergo usum instituendus est tiro, ut, cum necessitas postulaverit, sine
perturbatione et celeriter et caute castra possit munire.

156  *ILS* 2487 (AD 128, cf. *ILS* 9133–5 = Smallwood, *Nerva* 328): (*in latere
    dextro*) [munitiones quas] alii [per] plures dies divisis[sent, e]as uno die per-
    egistis; murum lo[ngi] operis et qualis mansuris hibernaculis fieri solet non
    [mul]to diutius exstrucxistis quam caespite exstruitur, qui m[o]dulo pari
    caesus et vehitur facile et tractatur et sine mo[les]tia struitur, ut mollis et
    planus pro natura sua: vos lapi[dibus] grandibus gravibus inaequalibus,
    quos neque vehere n[e]que attollere neque locare quis possit, nisi ut inaequa-
    [lita]tes inter se conpareant. fossam glaria duram scabram[que] recte
    percussistis et radendo levem reddidistis.

157  Cf. I. A. Richmond, *op. cit.* 302 f. For Haltwhistle Common see R. G.
    Collingwood, *Roman Britain* (1923), map on end-paper. Castle Collen:
    Eric Birley, 'Three notes on Roman Wales', *Arch. Cambr.* 1936, 58 ff., esp.
    69 ff. Cf. also *JRS* 1958, 96 f. Ten practice camps have been identified on
    the ground out of the eighteen seen by the Rev. Thomas Price in 1811.
    Cawthorn: I. A. Richmond, *Arch. Journ.* 1933, 17 ff.; for air photograph
    cf. *JRS* 1949, 100 and pl. xiv. Woden Law: cf. *JRS* 1951, 122.

158  Appian, *Roman History* VI 14, 85.

159  Tacitus, *Ann.* XIII 35: sed Corbuloni plus molis adversus ignaviam militum
    quam contra perfidiam hostium erat: quippe Syria transmotae legiones,
    pace longa segnes, munia castrorum aegerrime tolerabant. satis constitit
    fuisse in eo exercitu veteranos qui non stationem, non vigilias inissent,
    vallum fossamque quasi nova et mira viserent, sine galeis, sine loricis,
    nitidi et quaestuosi, militia per oppida expleta. igitur dimissis quibus
    senectus aut valetudo adversa erat supplementum petivit. et habiti per
    Galatiam Cappadociamque dilectus, adiectaque ex Germania legio cum
    equitibus alariis et peditatu cohortium. retentusque omnis exercitus sub
    pellibus, quamvis hieme saeva adeo ut obducta glacie nisi effossa humus
    tentoriis locum non praeberet. ambusti multorum artus vi frigoris et
    quidam inter excubias exanimati sunt. adnotatusque miles qui fascem
    lignorum gestabat ita praeriguisse manus, ut oneri adhaerentes truncis
    brachiis deciderent. ipse cultu levi, capite intecto, in agmine, in laboribus
    frequens adesse, laudem strenuis, solacium invalidis, exemplum omnibus
    ostendere. dehinc quia duritia caeli militiaeque multi abnuebant desere-
    bantque, remedium severitate quaesitum est. nec enim, ut in aliis exercitibus,
    primum alterumque delictum venia prosequebatur, sed qui signa reliquerat,

statim capite poenas luebat. idque usu salubre et misericordia melius
adparuit: quippe pauciores illa castra deseruere quam ea in quibus
ignoscebatur.

160 The legion was probably IV *Scythica*, though this had been stationed in
Moesia, not Germany. Tacitus may have confused it with IV *Macedonica*
which was in Upper Germany. Cf. Parker, *RL*, 135.

161 Vegetius I 26: nihil magis prodesse constat in pugna, quam ut adsiduo
exercitio milites in acie dispositos ordines servent necubi contra quam
expedit aut conglobent agmen aut laxent. nam et constipati perdunt
spatia pugnandi et sibi invicem impedimenta sunt, et rariores atque
interlucentes aditum perrumpendi hostibus praestant. necesse est autem
statim metu universa confundi, si intercisa acie ad dimicantium terga hostis
accesserit. producendi ergo tirones sunt semper ad campum et secundum
matriculae ordinem in aciem dirigendi, ita ut primo simplex et extenta sit
acies, ne quos sinus, ne quas habeat curvaturas, ut aequali legitimoque
spatio miles distet a milite. tunc praecipiendum, ut subito duplicent aciem,
ita ut in ipso impetu is, ad quem respondere solent, ordo servetur. tertio
praecipiendum, ut quadratam aciem repente constituant, quo facto in
trigonum, quem cuneum vocant, acies ipsa mutanda est. quae ordinatio
plurimum prodesse consuevit in bello. iubetur etiam, ut instruant orbes,
quo genere, cum vis hostium interruperit aciem, resisti ab exercitatis
militibus consuevit, ne omnis multitudo fundatur in fugam et grave
discrimen immineat. haec si iuniores adsidua meditatione perceperint,
facilius in ipsa dimicatione servabunt.

162 It would appear to be a point of purely technical interest whether we
consider the *ambulatura* (as in the text) as the main exercise of the trained
soldier, or follow Neumann (*op. cit.*, 171) in describing it as the fourth or
final stage of recruit training. The former seems more in line with
Vegetius' account, and intrinsically more likely, since the exercise would
surely be more successful if performed by a majority of trained soldiers
with a leavening of recruits than by the recruits alone, and the men would
learn more quickly. If, however, the majority of those taking part were
already experienced, it can hardly be described as a kind of passing-out
parade.

163 Onasander X 1-6 deals with the need for drilling the army in time of
peace. He recommends first, that the general should drill the army in
adopting different formations, and secondly, that he should divide the
army into two parts and conduct a sham battle, with the men armed with
sticks or the shafts of javelins. He even suggests that the men throw clods
of earth at one another. Similar exercises are envisaged for the cavalry.

164 Cf. the comments of W. A. Oldfather in the Loeb edition of Aeneas
Tacticus, Asclepiodotus and Onasander by the Illinois Greek Club, 394 f.

165 Cf. Schenk, *Vegetius*, 81 ff.

166 Cf. *ibid.*, 24 and Anhang.

167 Vegetius I 27: praeterea et vetus consuetudo permansit et divi Augusti atque Hadriani constituitonibus praecavetur, ut ter in mense tam equites quam pedites educantur ambulatum; hoc enim verbo hoc exercitii genus nominant. decem milia passuum armati instructique omnibus telis pedites militari gradu ire ac redire iubebantur in castra, ita ut aliquam itineris partem cursu alacriore conficerent. equites quoque divisi per turmas armatique similiter tantum itineris peragebant, ita ut ad equestrem meditationem interdum sequantur interdum cedant et recursu quodam impetus reparent. non solum autem in campis, sed etiam in clivosis et arduis locis et descendere et ascendere utraque acies cogebatur, ut nulla res vel casu prorsus pugnantibus posset accidere, quam non ante boni milites adsidua exercitatione didicissent.

168 This duty-roster is *P. Gen. lat.* 1, v. *verso*; first published with facsimile by J. Nicole and Ch. Morel, *Archives militaires du Ier siècle* (Geneva 1900). It has frequently been republished in whole or part, notably by A. von Premerstein, 'Die Buchführung einer ägyptischen Legionsabteilung', *Klio* 1903, 1–46; J. Lesquier, *L'armée romaine d'Egypte d'Auguste à Dioclétien* (Cairo 1918), 141; and with photograph by R. Marichal, *Chartae latinae antiquiores* I, no. 7. Texts are available also in McCrum and Woodhead, *Select Documents of the Principates of the Flavian Emperors* (1961), 114 and in *CPL* 106 and *Documenti* 10. The document was dated to AD 90 by Premerstein, but to AD 87 by Marichal, *Ann. de l'Inst. de Phil. et d'Hist. Orient. et Slaves* XIII (*Mélanges Isidore Lévy*) 409 and *ChLA* I p. 18. See Appendix B.

169 Suetonius, *Dom.* 13, 3: post autem duos triumphos Germanici cognomine assumpto Septembrem mensem et Octobrem ex appellationibus suis Germanicum Domitianumque transnominavit, quod altero suscepisset imperium, altero natus est.

170 *P. Gen. lat.* 1 iv b *verso*:

|  | RELIQVI | XXXX |
|---|---|---|
|  | ex eis |  |
|  | opera vacantes |  |
| 5 | armorum custos | [I] |
|  | conductor Porcius | I |
|  | carrarius Plotinus | I |
|  | secutor tri[b(uni)] . . tius Severus | I |
|  | custos domi Coti . r . . . . Staur | I |
| 10 | librarius et ce[r]a⟨r⟩i[u]s | II |
|  | Curiati . . . . |  |
|  | Aurel . . . . . . |  |
|  | supranumerar[ius] | I |
|  | Do[mitius] |  |
|  | stationem a[ge]ns | I |
|  | Domitius |  |
|  | F[iunt IX] |  |

Reliqui                                    XXXI
8 tri[b(uni)]  *Gilliam*      9 domi ... iti .... Staius *Nicole* domi iti
Sallusti Staius *Premerstein*

171 The previous list is *P. Gen. lat.* 1 iv a *verso*, which is almost completely destroyed. It occupied the extreme left part of the sheet and only the right-hand edge of its text survives.

172 A. von Premerstein, *op. cit.*, 25, reckoned the total strength of the century at about 58 men. This is very conjectural.

173 Cf. A. von Premerstein, *op. cit.*, 23 and 36.

## CONDITIONS OF SERVICE

174 Erich Sander, 'Zur Rangordnung des römischen Heeres: die gradus ex caliga', *Historia* III (1954/5), 87–105. See esp. p. 89: 'Im Anfang der Kaiserzeit gelten die später als principales bez. immunes bezeichneten Chargen nicht als militärische Dienstgrade, sondern nur als eine Funktion, ein munus des miles gregarius.'

175 Caesar, *BC* III 74, 1: nonnullos signiferos ignominia notavit ac loco movit.

176 See p. 92.

177 See p. 121.

178 *Dig.*, 50, 6, 7: quibusdam aliquam vacationem munerum graviorum condicio tribuit, ut sunt mensores, optio valetudinarii, medici, capsarii, et artifices qui fossam faciunt, veterinarii, architectus, gubernatores, naupegi, ballistrarii, specularii, fabri, sagittarii, aerarii, bucularum structores, carpentarii, scandularii, gladiatores, aquilices, tubarii, cornuarii, arcuarii, plumbarii, ferrarii, lapidarii, et qui calcem cocunt, et qui silvam infindunt, qui carbonem caedunt ac torrent. in eodem numero haberi solent lani, venatores, victimarii, et optio fabricae, et qui aegris praesto sunt, librarii quoque qui docere possint, et horreorum librarii, et librarii depositorum, et librarii caducorum et adiutores corniculariorum, et stratores, et polliones, et custodes armorum, et praeco, et bucinator. hi igitur omnes inter immunes habentur.

The significance of some of these terms is doubtful. For *capsarii*, translated here as 'dressers', cf. Liebenam, *RE* VI 1649, who held that the *discentes capsario[rum]* of *ILS* 2438 (= *CIL* VIII 2553) were clerks, and so called from their practice of keeping their books in a *capsa*. On the other hand Passerini, *Diz. epigr.* IV 608, connected them with the medical services on the evidence of *ILS* 9182 (= *CIL* XIII 11979). Cf. Domaszewski-Dobson 45: '*capsarii* vielleicht Lazarettgehilfen, von der capsa mit Verbandzeug so genannt.' The position of the term in this passage (immediately after *medici*) seems conclusive in favour of the latter explanation.

The phrase 'qui aegris praesto sunt' is obscure. It is taken here to mean 'sick-bay attendants', but it could represent almost any function of the medical services.

*pollio* is described as of uncertain meaning by Domaszewski-Dobson 47. From *CIL* III 14507 b 51 we learn that a *pollio* may also be an *eques*. This seems significant when we remember that in Paternus's list *polliones* are next to *stratores* ('grooms'). 'Horse-trainers' is therefore suggested as a possible translation. Du Cange's definition, 'qui arma polit', though supported by the proximity in this passage of the words 'polliones et custodes armorum', seems on balance less probable.

179 Cf. E. Sander, *op. cit.*, 92 f., and my article 'Immunis librarius' in *Britain and Rome: Essays presented to Eric Birley*, ed. Michael G. Jarrett and Brian Dobson (1965), 45–55, esp. p. 51. Sander cites Aurelius Victor 14, 11: officia sane publica et palatina nec non militiae in eam formam statuit, quae paucis per Constantinum immutatis hodie perseverant. This shows that fourth-century tradition recognized Hadrian as an innovator in military administration whose work remained almost unchanged. Add Dio 69, 9, where Hadrian's reorganization of the army is shown to be still effective in Dio's own time, the third century. Cf. also *SHA, Hadr.*, 10, 3. The military writings of Tarruntenus (or Tarrutenius, cf. *JRS* 1952, 60, n. 32) Paternus are known to be based largely on Hadrian's *constitutiones*. Cf. Schenk, *Vegetius*, 8–26. Schenk's conclusion (p. 26) is: 'Die im zweiten Buch der epit. rei milit. des Veg. dargestellte ordinatio antiqua gibt die Verhältnisse der hadrianische Epoche wieder und ist vollständig aus der Schrift des Paternus "de re militari" geschöpft, der seinerseits die Konstitutionen des Augustus, Trajan und Hadrian verwertete.' Though we need not accept Schenk's attribution of the *ordinatio antiqua* to the time of Hadrian, his general verdict about Paternus will stand.

180 p. 74.

181 See p. 52.

182 *P. Mich.* VIII 466, 18 ff.

183 *P. Mich.* VIII 465, 13 ff. Mr R. W. Davies points out in a letter that this papyrus does not have the year marked on it; consequently 465 could be eleven months later than 466, not one month earlier.

184 Vegetius II 7: hi sunt milites principales, qui privilegiis muniuntur. The posts common to both lists are *librarii, bucinatores* and *mensores*.

185 Cf. Sander, *op. cit.* 92, and *Klio* XXXII (1939), 386. Vegetius says explicitly: principalium militum et, ut proprio verbo utar, principiorum nomina et dignitates *secundum praesentes matriculas* indicabo. *matricula* is itself a technical term of the Late Empire and is not clearly attested before the middle of the fourth century. Cf. *JRS* 1952, 60. Yet the sentence 'signiferi, qui signa portant: quos nunc draconarios vocant' implies an earlier source in which the term *signiferi* appeared. Cf. Schenk, *Vegetius*, 9.

186 Cf. E. Sander, *op. cit.*, 92: 'Demgegenüber trennt Paternus die immunes von den principales (Dig. 50, 6, 7). Der Jurist befindet sich also im Widerspruch mit dem soldatischen Sprachgebrauch und ist in seiner Formulierung wesentlich genauer (*CIL* VI 229). Die Verschiedenheit des militärischen

und juristischen Sprachgebrauches ist wohl zu erklären, dass das Heer die immunes als notwendige Vorstufe betrachtete und die dadurch bedingte Zusammengehörigkeit betonte, den Trennungsstrich zwischen der grossen Masse und den irgendwie Herausgehobenen zog, während der Rechtsgelehrte den gesetzlich festgelegten Zustand anerkennt. Daraus ergibt sich einmal, dass die immunes keine Vorgesetzten-Eigenschaften hatten, sondern auch nach der trajanischen Reform nur eine Funktion des miles blieben, und dass sie demzufolge unter einander rangleich waren (Rangordnung S. 13).'

J. E. Dunlap, who edited *P. Mich.* VII 447 (= *CPL* 121; *Documenti* 26), described it as 'a list of soldiers recommended for special recognition or promotion'. Each man, he believed, was 'designated an *immunis* and the abbreviation *im* was placed before his name to indicate this fact.' Doubt was expressed of this interpretation by J. F. Gilliam in *AJP* 1950, 432–8, and R. O. Fink in *AJA* 1964, 297–9, not only read the notation as *iussi*, but also suggested that the document was not military at all, but should probably be viewed as a record of police action or other civil action in which centurions were employed. R. Marichal in *ChLA* III 218 reads *iusi*.

187 The inscription, which refers to the *vigiles* and therefore is not necessarily indicative of standard procedure throughout the army, is *ILS* 2160 (= *CIL* VI 221): principales infra scripti aediculam et Genium Centuriae d(ono) d(ederunt). b(eneficiarius) s(ub)pr(aefecti) ... vex(illarius) ... optio ... tess-(erarius) ... b(eneficiarius) trib(uni) ... lib(rarius) ur(banus ?) s(ub)pr(aefecti) ... lib(rarius) coh(ortis).

188 E. Sander, *op. cit.* 92 f.: 'Wenn wir dieser Notiz (Aurelius Victor ep. 14, 11) Glauben schenken können, so müsste das Auftauchen der Bezeichnung principalis in *CIL* VI 221 unter Trajan so erklärt werden, dass diese Titulatur zwar schon unter Trajan erscheint, aber gleichsam nur inoffiziell, während die amtliche Einführung erst unter Hadrian erfolgte. Ein Gedanke, der viel für sich hat, denn auch die anderen Grade tauchen früher auf, ehe sie amtlichen Charakter bekamen.' Presumably the same explanation would be given of the use in *P. Mich.* VIII 466, which he does not mention.

189 The earliest dated instance of *principalis* in an inscription is *CIL* VI 221 (AD 113). The next appears to be *CIL* XIII 6728—[factus principali]s Eru[cio Claro II et Cl. Seve]ro cos (146)—but the inscription itself is of AD 192. For *immunis* the earliest dated inscriptional evidence is in a pair of inscriptions from Troesmis of about AD 134—*CIL* III 6178, i, 9 and 6179, i, 11—which contain the expression *ex imm(uni)*, thus implying that the term had already been in existence for some time. The next instance, however, is not till AD 155 (*CIL* III 7449), which also mentions *principales*.

190 See n. 170.

191 Of the inscriptions used by Domaszewski to determine the establishment of the 'Officium des Statthalters' (Domaszewski-Dobson 29 ff.), the following bear some indication of Severan or post-Severan dating: *CIL*

II 4122, 4154 (= *ILS* 2369), III 138, p. 970 (= *ILS* 4283), 3021, 3327, 3524 (= *ILS* 2375), 4030, 4452 (= *ILS* 2382), 4800 (= *ILS* 4198), 4803, 6754, 7794, 8173 (= *ILS* 2377), 10060, 10360, 10403, 10568, 13719, 14068, 14479, 14507, VIII 217 (= *ILS* 2658), 702 (= 12128), 2564, 2586 (= *ILS* 2381), 2751 (= *ILS* 1162), 4332 (= *ILS* 2448), 17625 (= *ILS* 2399), XIII 1732, 2596, 5170, 6738 (= *ILS* 3156), 6803, 7335 (= *ILS* 7096), XIV 2255; *ILS* 484, 8847, 8880; *IGRR* I 134 (= *ILS* 8837), III 1008; *AE* 1898 n. 108 (= *ILS* 9100); 1902 n. 138; 1905 n. 68; and perhaps *CIL* III 93, 9996, 10315, 10437 (= *ILS* 2390), 10505, V 8275 (= *ILS* 2408), VI 2977 (= *ILS* 2173), VII 1038 (= *RIB* 1271), VIII 21000, XIII 1860; *AE* 1902 n. 73, 135. Not before the second half of the second century may be dated *CIL* III 5812 (= *ILS* 2386), 7394 (= *ILS* 1093), VIII 17626 (= 10718), 21567, XIII 6542, 6543, 6598, 7277. Earlier may be some of these: *CIL* III 5211 (= *ILS* 1362), 6627 (= *ILS* 2482), 7542 (= 767, *ILS* 1074), 14137[1] (= *ILS* 8997), 14349[2] (= McCrum & Woodhead 370), 14387 (= *ILS* 9199, McCrum & Woodhead 355), V 8660, VIII 2746, XI 390 (= McCrum & Woodhead 356), 395 (= *ILS* 2648), XII 2602 (= *ILS* 2118, McCrum & Woodhead 361), XIII 6884 (= *ILS* 2261), 7709 (= *ILS* 3456), 8203, XIV 3472, and possibly III 2035, 14349[9], VIII 17631 (= 10720), XIII 7556 (= *ILS* 2649), 11990.

Uncertain are *CIL* II 4145, 4179 (= *ILS* 2384), 6111, III 433 (= *ILS* 2368), 894 (= *ILS* 3035), 1106, 1471, 1650 p. 1021 (= *ILS* 2378), 1783, 1907, 2013, 2015 (= *ILS* 2379), 2052 (= *ILS* 2586), 2063 (= *ILS* 2370), 3020 (= 10057), 3306, 3543 (= *ILS* 2391), 3634, 4311 (= *ILS* 2388), 4412, 6760, 7395, 8750, 8752, 9908, 10842, 12659 (= *ILS* 7173), 12679 (= *ILS* 4837), V 6867, 7004, VI 3358 (= *ILS* 2372), VIII 1875, 9763, 17619 (= 2226), 17627, 17634 (= 10723), 17635 (= 10724), 18025, 18276, 20251 (= *ILS* 4496), 21056, XIII 1869, 1903 (= *ILS* 2407), 6429a, 6575, 6721, 7299, 8282, 8292; *IGRR* III 394; *AE* 1902 n. 41 (= *ILS* 9090); 1904 n. 10 (= *ILS* 9170), 128.

192 Domaszewski-Dobson 43: 'Die drei Chargen werden geschlossen hinter-einander bekleidet und bilden die notwendige Zwischenstufe für die Beförderung von den Immunes zu den Beneficiarchargen der Stäbe.'

193 Vegetius II 20: haec ratio apud signiferos, ut nunc dicunt, in cofino servabatur. et ideo signiferi non solum fideles sed etiam litterati homines eligebantur, qui et servare deposita scirent et singulis reddere rationem. See also above, p. 52.

194 As by Parker, *RL*, 207: 'Next to him (*sc.* the centurion) was the *optio ad spem ordinis*. He was a specially qualified *optio*, because, whereas he was promoted directly to be centurion, the latter normally ranked as inferior to the *signifer*. Perhaps he may in some cases have been "seconded" from his century while holding the rank of *optio*, and on his "restoration to the establishment" have been promoted centurion.' *optio ad spem ordinis*, *CIL* III 12411 (= *ILS* 2666b), *ILS* 2441, *AE* 1937, 101. *optio spei*, *CIL* III 3445

(= *ILS* 2442), V 6423. *optio ad ordinem, CIL* V 7872 (= *ILS* 4823). *optio retentus ad spem, CIL* III 6180, 3, 1 (cf. Domaszewski-Dobson 41 n. 9). *optio retentus spe, CIL* VIII 18085, b, 2.

195 Cf. his article 'Legio' in *Diz. epigr.* IV, 595: 'Ma pare dubbio che sia esistita una speciale categoria di *optiones*: una qualche indicazione dovrebbe essere stata impiegata nel regolamento della *schola* degli *optiones* di *Lambaesis*, C. VIII 2554, dove pure si tratta di *optiones* ammessi normalmente alla promozione al centurionato, come risulta dalla disposizione *uti collega proficiscens ad spem suam confirmandam accipiat sestertium octo mil(ia) n(ummum).*'

196 Consider the order of posts in careers such as these: *CIL* III 12411: d.m. L. Val(erius) L.f. Proclus mil(es) leg(ionis) V M(acedonicae), b(eneficiarius) legat(i), opt(io) ad spe(m) ordin(is), 7 leg(ionis) eius(dem). V 7004: Peregrinus [mil(es)] legionis XXII Pr(imigeniae) p(iae) fid(elis), [b(ene)f-(iciarius)] legat(i), a comment(ariis) [leg(ati) pr(o) pr(aetore)], optio, centurio [leg]ionis eiusdem. Cf. *AE* 1937, 101; 1951, 194.

197 Vegetius II 7: tesserarii qui tesseram per contubernia militum nuntiant; tessera autem dicitur praeceptum ducis, quo vel ad aliquod opus vel ad bellum movetur exercitus. Domaszewski (Domaszewski-Dobson 43 f.) believed that by the time of Philip the Arab the rank of *tesserarius* had ceased to exist: 'Die schriftliche Ausgabe der Befehle war für ein Heer, in dem Offiziere wie Soldaten gleichmässig Analphabeten waren und die Kenntnis der lateinischen Dienstsprache ganz erlosch, bedeutungslos geworden. Das barbarische Heer war auf den Standpunkt der numeri herabgesunken.' This view has now been shown to be nonsense by an inscription from Poetovio of the age of Gallienus (*AE* 1936, 55): D(eo) S(oli) i(nvicto) M(ithrae) pro salute tesserarior(um) et custod(um) armor(um) leg(ionum) V M(acedonicae) et XIII Gemin(a)e Gallienarum. Cf. Passerini, *art. cit.*, 607, and Dobson in Domaszewski-Dobson xiv.

198 Vegetius II 21: nam quasi in orbem quemdam per diversas cohortes et diversas scholas milites promoventur, ita ut ex prima cohorte ad gradum quempiam promotus vadat ad decimam cohortem et rursus ab ea crescentibus stipendiis cum maiore gradu per alias recurrat ad primam. Domaszewski's rule, however, that the *optiones* of a cohort were promoted together to the next cohort above them (Domaszewski-Dobson 43), was never of universal application, as is shown by *CIL* VIII 2554 from Lambaesis, in which *optiones* from different cohorts are promoted to different grades and even to the centurionate. Cf. Passerini, *loc. cit.*, and Parker, *RL*, 208 ff.

199 They also took their titles from the rank of the officer under whom they served, as is shown by the descriptions *beneficiarius consularis, beneficiarius procuratoris, beneficiarius praesidis,* for those serving at a provincial headquarters, *beneficiarii legati legionis, beneficiarius tribuni,* for those serving on a legionary staff.

200 See further Domaszewski-Dobson 29 ff., and A. H. M. Jones, 'The Roman Civil Service (Clerical and Sub-Clerical Grades)', *JRS* XXXIX (1949), 44 ff.

201 Cf. Domaszewski-Dobson 31 n. 2, citing *CIL* XII 2602: M. Carantius Macrinus centurio coh(ortis) primae urbanae, factus miles in ead(em) cohorte Domitiano II cos (73), beneficiar(ius) Tettieni Sereni leg(ati) Aug(usti) Vespas(iano) X cos (77), cornicular(ius) Corneli Gallicani leg(ati) Aug(usti) equestrib(us) stipendis Domit(iano) VIIII cos (83), item Minici Rufi legati Aug(usti), evocatus Aug(usti) Domit(iano) XIIII cos (88), centurio imp(eratore) Nerva II cos (90).

202 *CIL* II 4179 (= *ILS* 2384), Tarraco: d.m. L. Gargilio Rufo com(mentari-ensi) ab actis civil(ibus) homini optimo et honestissimo. Cf. A. von Premerstein in *RE s.v.* 'a commentariis'.

203 *CIL* III 14137¹ (= *ILS* 8997), Alexandria: Q. Rammio Martiali praef(ecto) Aeg(ypti) A. Rutilius Cilo opt(io) specul(atorum) o(b) m(erita). Cf. Domaszewski-Dobson 32; 'Der Vorstand des sakralen Kollegiums führt den Tital optio.'

204 For the *frumentarii* see P. K. Baillie Reynolds, 'The Troops quartered in the Castra Peregrinorum', *JRS* XIII (1923), 168 ff., and W. G. Sinnigen, 'The origins of the *frumentarii*,' *Mem. Amer. Acad. Rome* XXVII (1962), 213 ff.

205 Cf. Ramsey MacMullen, *Soldier and Civilian in the Later Roman Empire* (1963), 66–70 and 157 f.

206 Cf. the curious career illustrated in *CIL* XII 2234 (Gratianopolis): Sex. Sammio Volt(inia) Severo 7 leg(ionis) prim(ae) Germanic(ae), qui [e]o-[d(em)] co(n)s(ule) quo militare coepit aquilifer factus est, anno[s] XIII aquili[f]er militavit, 7 factus C. Antistio Vetere II M. Suillio Nerullino co(n)s(ulibus) ex [te]sta[mento] (AD 50). After rapid promotion in his first year he had only a single further promotion after thirteen more years of service. A more normal career is attested in *CIL* XIII 6952 (Moguntiacum): .. P.f. [. . . . . Ae]quo Dal[matiae] aquilif(er) [leg(ionis) XXX VI]p(iae) Vict(ricis), [promot(us) 7 l]eg(ionis) XIIII Ge(minae) [M(artiae) V(ictricis), 7] leg(ionis) XIII Gem(inae), [7 leg(ionis) XX]II Prim(igeniae) p(iae) f(idelis), [qui me]r(uit) stip(endia) XLV, [vixit] an(nos) LXX.

207 Vegetius II 7: aquiliferi qui aquilam portant. imaginiferi qui imperatoris imagines ferunt. optiones ab adoptando appellati, quod antecedentibus aegritudine praepediti hi tamquam adoptati eorum atque vicarii solent universa curare. signiferi qui signa portant, quos nunc draconarios vocant. *CIL* II 2553 (= *ILS* 9127) places the *imaginifer* between the *beneficiarius procuratoris* and the *tesserarius*: .. [e]t Aeli Flavi b(eneficiarii) proc(uratoris) Augustorum et Lucretii Materni [i]mag(iniferi) leg(ionis) VII Ge(minae) f(elicis) et Iuli(i) Seduli tesserari(i) c(ohortis) I C(eltiberorum), posit(a) VI Idibus Octo(bribus) imp. Aurel. Vero III et Quadrato cos. (AD 167)

208 Cf. Eric Birley, 'Promotions and Transfers in the Roman Army, II: The Centurionate', *Carnuntum Jahrbuch* 1963-4, 21 ff.

209 Cf. Birley, *op. cit.*, and *Laureae Aquincenses* II (1941), 47–62 (reprinted in *Roman Britain and the Roman Army* (1953), 104–24.)

210 Juvenal, XIV 193.

211 Pliny, *epp.* VI 25, 2: suspicor enim tale nescio quid Robusto accidisse quale aliquando Metilio Crispo municipi meo. huic ego ordinem impetraveram atque etiam proficiscenti quadraginta milia nummum ad instruendum se ornandumque donaveram, nec postea aut epistulas eius aut aliquem de exitu nuntium accepi. A. N. Sherwin-White comments (*The Letters of Pliny: A Historical and Social Commentary*, Oxford 1966), 'Pliny's gift was probably to meet maximal requirements—compare his generosity in I.19.2.' He compares the much smaller amount allowed by the *schola* of *optiones* at Lambaesis; *CIL* VIII 2554: . . . ob quam sollemnitatem decreverunt, uti collega proficiscens ad spem suam confirmandam accipiat (sestertium) VIII mil(ia) n(ummum).

212 Tac., *Hist.* III 49: utque licentia militem imbueret interfectorum centurionum ordines legionibus offerebat. eo suffragio turbidissimus quisque delecti; nec miles in arbitrio ducum, sed duces militari violentia trahebantur.

213 *CIL* VIII 217 cf. p. 2353 [= *ILS* 2658 add.; *Inscr. latines de la Tunisie* 332; Domaszewski-Dobson 238; cf. Eric Birley, *Carnuntum Jahrbuch* 1963/4, 23 (1)]; . . . .] militavit L annis, IV in leg. I Ita[lica] librar(ius), tesser(arius), optio, signif(er), [7] factus ex suffragio leg(ionis) eiu[sdem,] militavit 7 leg. I Ital., 7 leg. VI [Ferratae?], 7 leg. I Min., 7 leg. X Gem., 7 leg. II A[ug.], 7 leg. III Aug., 7 leg. II[I] Gall., 7 leg. XXX U[l]p., 7 leg. VI Vic., 7 leg. III Cyr., 7 leg. XV Apol., 7 leg. II Par., 7 leg. I Adiutricis, consecutus ob virtutem in expeditionem Parthicam coronam muralem vallarem torques et phaleras, agit in diem operis perfecti annos LXXX, sibi et Claudiae Marciae Capitolinae koniugi karissimae, quae agit in diem operis perfecti annos LXV, et M. Petronio Fortunato filio, militavit ann. VI 7 leg. X[X]II Primig., 7 leg. II Aug., vixit ann. XXXV, cui Fortunatus et Marcia parentes karissimo memoriam fecerunt.

214 See now the discussion by Brian Dobson (Domaszewski-Dobson XX ff.) of Domaszewski's treatment of the centurionate (*ibid.*, 80–112), and his most useful summary and criticism of the findings of modern research.

215 This was the conclusion reached by Th. Wegeleben, *Die Rangordnung der römischen Centurionen* (Berlin 1913). It is supported by Eric Birley (*op. cit.*, 21); Brian Dobson, however, finds that 'über diese Frage gibt es noch immer keine einheitliche Meinung' (Domaszewski-Dobson XXIII).

216 Domaszewski-Dobson XXI.

217 Cf. the arguments of Eric Birley, *Roman Britain and the Roman Army* (1953), 122 f.

218 Diod. Sic. XIV 16, 5; Livy IV 59, 11.

219 VI 39.

220 Cf. G. Veith in Kromayer-Veith, *Heerwesen*, 329; Parker, *RL*, 214;

P. A. Brunt, *PBSR* 1950, 50 f.; M. Marin y Peña, *Instituciones militares romanas* (1956), 208; F. W. Walbank, *A Historical Commentary on Polybius,* I (1957), 722. Most recently, J. Harmand, *L'armée et le soldat à Rome de 107 à 50 avant notre ère* (Paris 1967), 263, declares for a daily rate of 5 *asses* and an annual rate of 114.06 *denarii.*

221  Cf. my remarks in *Historia* VII (1958), 113 ff.

222  Suetonius, *Div. Iul.,* 26: legionibus stipendium in perpetuum duplicavit. On Harmand's hypothesis the pay now became 228.12 *denarii* (*op. cit.,* 226).

223  Cf. H. Mattingly, *Num. Chron.* 1934, 81 ff.; *JRS* 1937, 101 f.; *OCD s.v.* 'Coinage, Roman, 10'.

224  Tacitus, *Ann.* I 17: denis in diem assibus animam et corpus aestimari. On a 360-day year this works out at exactly 225 *denarii.*

225  VI 39.

226  *RL,* 214.

227  Cf. W. S. Messer, 'Mutiny in the Roman Army. The Republic', *Class. Phil.* 1920, 158–75.

228  Plutarch, *C. Gracch.* 5.

229  Tacitus, *Ann.* i 17: hinc vestem arma tentoria, hinc saevitiam centurionum et vacationes munerum redimi.

230  Suetonius, *Dom.* 7, 3: addidit et quartum stipendium militi, aureos ternos. Cf. my remarks in *Historia* V (1956), 332 ff.

231  Domaszewski, *Truppensold,* 230, deduced an increase under Commodus from the price paid for the throne by Didius Iulianus. But the statement of Herodian (iii, 8), that Severus was the first to increase army pay, seems decisive. Cf. A. Passerini, *Athenaeum* XXIV, 155, and P. A. Brunt, *PBSR* 1950, 56.

232  *Contra* Domaszewski, *Truppensold,* 231, who argues for a total of 500 *denarii.* But, as R. Marichal points out (Marichal, *La Solde,* 418 n. 1), 'Le chiffre de 500 deniers, soit d'augmentation, est donc bizarre.' It is not payable in three *stipendia,* and Marichal would prefer a figure of 525 *denarii.* But 450 (cf. Delbrück, *Geschichte der Kriegskunst* II³, 240, and Nischer in Kromayer-Veith, *Heerwesen,* 525 f.) would represent a simpler, and therefore more probable increase (50 per cent as opposed to 75 per cent). It is perhaps not without significance that the next increase, which was made by Caracalla, was also of 50 per cent.

For the evidence for three pay periods in the third century cf. J. F. Gilliam, *HThR* XLVII (1954), 191 and *P. Dura* 95.

233  Herodian iv, 4, 7. The actual total is, of course, dependent upon the size of the pay under Severus: if Domaszewski's figure of 500 for Severus is correct, the amount under Caracalla would be 750; Marichal's 525 would give the odd result of 787½, a further reason for thinking it unlikely.

234  Cf. Denis van Berchem, 'L'annone militaire dans l'empire romain au IIIème siècle', *Mém. Soc. nat. des Ant. de France* (1936) 1937, 118 ff.

235  Varro, *De Lingua Lat.,* 5, 90: duplicarii, dicti quibus ob virtutem duplicaria

cibaria ut darentur institutum. Vegetius II, 7: duplares duas, sesquiplicares unam semis consequebantur annonam.

236 Erich Sander, 'Zur Rangordnung des römischen Heeres: der Duplicarius', *Historia* VIII (1959), 239–47, distinguishes between two different kinds of *duplicarii*, those who receive double pay and those whose reward is merely double rations. In the first group he places the *duplicarii* of the auxiliary cavalry and the *equites singulares*, in the second group the *duplicarii* of the legions. (Then what of the *duplicarii* and *sesquiplicarii* of the infantry portion of a *cohors equitata*, attested (e.g.) in Hunt's *pridianum*?) Sander's thesis presents us with a problem. We know that the men were subject to deductions from their pay to cover their rations. Did the *duplicarii* of the legions suffer double deductions? A more likely explanation would be that the term *duplicarius* denoted not a rank but a pay grade; the same term could then describe men in very different ranks, those in the higher class of *principales* (*beneficiarii* and the like), who were in receipt of double pay as the pay appropriate to their rank, and men in lower ranks who had been awarded the privilege of double pay as the reward for outstanding service. These are the men referred to in Varro (see previous note), and they are also mentioned by Vegetius, II 7: torquati duplares, torquati sesquiplares, quibus torqueus aureus solidus virtutis praemium fuit, quem qui meruisset, praeter laudem interdum duplas consequebatur annonas. duplares duas, sesquiplares unam semis consequebantur annonam. This explanation provides a more satisfactory account of *AE* 1895, n. 204 [d. n. Au]ggg. Arab. Adiab. [Parth. max. pro in]columitate domus [divinae scholam cum im]aginibus sacris fece[r. et ob eam] sollemnitat. [d]ec(reverunt), uti duplis stipend[is suis arca fiat, regressi] de exp(editione) fel(icissima) Mesopo[tamica] [mil(ites) duplari l]eg. III Aug. p.v., quoru[m nomina s]ubiecta sunt . . . . . . . Aemilius Cattianus corn(icularius) L . . . . . . . b(ene)f(iciarii) praef(ecti), T. Flavius Surus actar(ius) . . . A similar situation is revealed in *CIL* VIII 2564 (= *ILS* 470): duplari leg. III Aug. p.v. Antoninianae devoti numini maiestatique eorum regressi de expeditione felicissima orientali. (The nominal roll following includes 3 *tesserarii*, 4 *tubicines*, 2 *cornicines*, 5 *immunes*, 2 *beneficiarii tribuni*, 2 *bucinatores*, and individual *armorum custodes, mensores, librarii, polliones, marsi* and plain *duplarii*, making a grand total of 205 names.) Of *AE* 1895, n. 204 Sander writes (*op. cit.*, 243, n. 24): 'Aus duplis stipendiis zu entnehmen, dass die duplari milites doppelten Sold erhielten und der dritten Soldklasse der Beneficiarchargen angehörten, ist nicht abgängig. In diesem titulus heisst stipendium in Verbindung mit duplis zweifellos Sold. Doch handelt es nicht um eine dauernde Soldverdoppelung, sondern um eine einmalige Gratifikation anlässlich der Beendigung der mesopotamischen Expedition.' It would be a strange coincidence if *duplicarii* were so called because they received double rations permanently and double pay on a single occasion!

237 Cf. E. Sander, 'Zur Rangordnung des römischen Heeres: die gradus ex

caliga', *Historia* III (1954–5), 87 ff. He concludes that the appearance of *principalis* in *ILS* 2160 (AD 113) was unofficial, and that the official adoption of the term was due to Hadrian. But this is to ignore the papyrological evidence (*P. Mich.* VIII 465 of AD 107). The term *immunis* occurs in *CIL* III 7449 of AD 155 and *ex imm(uni)* in III 6178, i, 9 and 6179, i, 11 of AD 134. There is as yet no evidence of *immunis* for before the time of Hadrian. Perhaps under Trajan *principalis* was a comprehensive term embracing the later *immunes*, but under Hadrian a differentiation was imposed. See also p. 79 above, and n. 189.

238 Cf. Domaszewski-Dobson 71.

239 LIII, 11.

240 LV, 23.

241 As did the legacies of Augustus in AD 14. See n. 247.

242 249L.

243 Though these were not necessarily ever paid in *aurei*. But cf. the description of the 75 *denarii* of the *viaticum* in *BGU* II 423 as three gold pieces. The Thorngrafton hoard contained, besides a quantity of silver, three *aurei*. This may conceivably have been a single *stipendium*, or rather part of one, but it more probably represented the *viaticum*, which for reasons of tradition and prestige may have been paid in gold. Cf. *CW²* liv 65.

244 As by Domaszewski, *Truppensold*, 220 ff.; E. von Nischer in Kromayer-Veith, *Heerwesen*, 525–8; M. Durry, *Les cohortes prétoriennes*, (Paris 1938), 264 ff.; P. A. Brunt, *PBSR* XVIII (*NS* V) (1950), 55; G. R. Watson, *Neue Beiträge* II, 147. Contra A. Passerini, *Le coorti pretorie* (Rome 1939), 107, who accepts literally the *binos denarios* of Tacitus, *Ann.* I 17, and, working on a 360-day year, arrives at 720 *denarii* for the praetorians. This sum, of course, could not be paid in *aurei*. In view of the legacies of AD 14 (see n. 247), it seems certain that *binos denarios* was an approximation.

245 Tacitus, *Ann.* VI 11. Cf. Groag in *PIR²* C 289.

246 Sir Ronald Syme, *Tacitus* (1958), 369, sees 'the genuine inception of a new period' in AD 4, when Tiberius was designated the future ruler of Rome.

247 Dio LVI 32; Suetonius, *Div. Aug.*, 101; Tacitus, *Ann.* I 8.

248 Doubted in the case of the increase under Domitian by A. Passerini, *op. cit.*, 108, who writes: 'È strano però che almeno Dione, abbastanza particolareggiato, non ne dica verbo; e se pare naturale che Domiziano abbia finalmente dato ascolto ai desideri di tutte le lezioni, migliorandone la sorte, si comprenderebbe anche bene che non avesse fatto nulla di simile per i pretoriani, la cui condizione era già buona.' But now see C. M. Kraay, *Am. Numism. Soc. Museum Notes* IX (1960), 116.

249 Suetonius, *Claud.*, 10: armatos pro contione iurare in nomen suum passus est promisitque singulis quina dena sestertia, primus Caesarum fidem militis etiam praemio pigneratus. Tacitus, *Ann.* XII 69; inlatusque castris Nero et congruentia tempori praefatus, promisso donativo ad exemplum

paternae largitionis, imperator consalutatur. Cf. Josephus, *Ant. Iud.*, XIX, 247. For the donatives in general see pp. 108 ff. below.
250 Cf. P. K. Baillie Reynolds, *The Vigiles of Imperial Rome* (1926), 68 f.
251 Dio LIX 2.
252 For the regular sequence of city tribunates see Domaszewski-Dobson XXX and 115, and the inscriptions there cited.
253 Cf. for instance *ILS* 2648 (= *CIL* XI 395), 2742 (= *CIL* XIV 3626), and 2081.
254 They were granted by the will of Augustus the same legacies as the legionaries (Tac., *Ann.* I 8). Originally, as Cheesman says (*op. cit.*, 66 f.), they were practically on a level with legionaries, but later only their title distinguished them from the ordinary *auxilia.* Cf. also *Neue Beiträge* II (1965), 152 f.
255 *ILS* 2487 (= *CIL* VIII 18042; Smallwood, *Nerva*, 328): difficile est cohortales equites etiam per se placere, difficilius post alarem exercitationem non displicere: alia spatia campi, alius iaculantium numerus, . . . equorum forma armorum cultus pro stipendi modo.
256 *P. Berlin* 6866 A and B (= *CPL* 122, *Documenti* 35). Cf. R. Marichal, *L'Occupation romaine de la Basse Egypte* (1945), 9–22, with plates; and Marichal, *La Solde*, 399 ff.
257 Cf. n. 235 above.
258 Tacitus, *Hist.* IV 19: intumuere statim superbia ferociaque et pretium itineris donativum, duplex stipendium, augeri equitum numerum, promissa sane a Vitellio, postulabant, non ut adsequerentur, sed causam seditioni.
259 *Duplicarii*: *CIL* VI 3169, 32762, 32769 (= *ILS* 9222), 32771; X 3414 (= *ILS* 2871), 3416, 3422 (= *ILS* 2898), 3424 (= *ILS* 2870), 3424, 3425, 3426, 3438 (= *ILS* 2891), 3441, 3443 (= *ILS* 2899), 3444 (= *ILS* 2900), 3499 (= *ILS* 2878), 3500 (= *ILS* 2879), 3503, 3504, 3506, 3507, 3882; XI 29, 56, 77 (= *ILS* 2892), 343.
       *Sesquiplicarius*: *CIL* XVI 154.
260 Cf. Chester G. Starr, *The Roman Imperial Navy* (2nd edn., Cambridge 1960), 66 ff.
261 Cf. Starr, *ibid.*, 77. See above p. 39, n. 78.
262 Starr points out (*ibid.*, 99 n. 38) that if the provisions of *Gnomon* 55 were strictly enforced, the Egyptians who served in the Syrian and Alexandrian fleets, both *remiges* and *nautae*, must have been *epikekrimenoi.*
263 See p. 12 above and Dio LV 23, 1. Cf. also Starr, *op. cit.*, 80 f. and n. 47.
264 Dipl. 100 (5 Sept. 152) shows 26 years. In Dipl. 122 (30 April 166) the number is conjectural. The earliest diploma which definitely attests 28 years is Dipl. 138, which falls within the period from October 213 to April 217. See below p. 139 f.
265 *op. cit.*, 81.
266 See above p. 44 f.
267 See above p. 91 f. and n. 230.

268 Erich Sander, 'Zur Rangordnung des römischen Heeres: Die Flotte', *Historia* VI (1957), 365, suggests that the basic rate for the sailors (and also for the *vigiles*) was 125 *denarii* yearly, and was doubled by Commodus to 250 *denarii*.

269 Tacitus, *Ann*. I 17: denis in diem assibus animam et corpus aestimari: hinc vestem arma tentoria, hinc saevitiam centurionum et vacationes munerum redimi.

270 Tacitus, *Hist*. I 46: sed Otho ne vulgi largitione centurionum animos averteret, fiscum suum vacationes annuas exsoluturum promisit, rem haud dubie utilem et a bonis postea principibus perpetuitate disciplinae firmatam. See also pp. 108, 110 below.

271 *P. Gen. lat*. 1 (= *CPL* 106, *Documenti* 10 and 30). See Appendix A.

272 Mommsen, *Hermes* 35 (1900), 451 (= *Ges. Schr*. VI 126), took *faenaria* as corresponding to *tentoria* in the list in *Annals* I 17, and therefore as equivalent to 'bedding'. He discounted the possibility of the hay's being fodder, since there was nothing to show that either soldier was mounted, and the amount in any case was far too small. Premerstein, *Klio* III (1903), 11, preferred to interpret *faenaria* as fodder, not for the horses of the *equites legionis* but for the pack-animals which carried the heavy baggage of each *contubernium*: 'In einer Zeit sinkender Heeredisziplin, wie das ausgehende erste Jahrhundert der Kaiserzeit war, muss sich namentlich bei den orientalischen Legionen der Train der Wagen (*vehicula*) und Lasttiere ausserordentlich vermehrt haben.' This seems exaggerated.

273 Mommsen, *op. cit.* 452 (127), supposed these 20 drachmas to be spending money given to the men on the occasion of the *Saturnalia*. Premerstein (*loc. cit.*) preferred to see in them a deduction made to cover the cost of the feast. The latter explanation seems to be the more likely.

274 In the original publication Morel (p. 18) understood *ad signa* to refer to the *saccus undecimus* mentioned in Vegetius II 20: addebatur etiam saccus undecimus, in quem tota legio particulam aliquam conferebat, sepulturae scilicet causa, ut, si quis ex contubernalibus defecisset, de illo undecimo sacco ad sepulturam ipsius promeretur expensa. Mommsen (*loc. cit.*) rejected this and thought rather of a contribution to the upkeep of the standards. Premerstein (*loc. cit.*) thought that this might take place on the *natalis aquilae* of the legion, if that fell within the right period. It might seem preferable to think of the *rosaliae signorum*, cf. Hoey, *HThR* XXX (1937) 14–35, and *YCS* VII (1940), 115–20. Cf. also Sir Ian Richmond, *AA*⁴ XXI (1943) 162–5.

275 See above p. 90 and n. 225.

276 See above p. 90 and n. 228.

277 See below p. 108 and n. 297.

278 *P. Fay*. 105 (= *CPL* 124, *Documenti* 34) ii 18 (44). Cf. R. Marichal, *L' occupation romaine de la Basse-Égypte* (1945), 44 ff.

279 II 20: illud vero ab antiquis divinitus institutum est, ut ex donativo, quod

milites consequuntur, dimidia pars sequestraretur apud signa et ibidem ipsis militibus servaretur, ne per luxum aut inanium rerum comparationem ab contubernalibus posset absumi.

280 Suetonius, *Dom.* 7: geminari legionum castra prohibuit nec plus quam mille nummos a quoquam ad signa deponi, quod L. Antonius apud duarum legionum hiberna res novas moliens fiduciam cepisse etiam ex depositorum summa videbatur.

281 That Titus gave a donative on his accession is implicit in Suetonius, *Dom.* 2: patre defuncto diu cunctatus an duplum donativum militi offerret, numquam iactare dubitavit relictum se participem imperii, sed fraudem testamento adhibitam; neque cessavit ex eo insidias struere fratri clam palamque, quoad correptum gravi valetudine, prius quam efflaret animam, pro mortuo deseri iussit.

282 Schenk, *Vegetius*, 8 ff., believes that Tarruntenus Paternus is the source for the passage in which Vegetius describes the system of enforced deposits. If so, the system could well be a second-century innovation. On the other hand, P. A. Brunt, 'Pay and Superannuation in the Roman Army', *PBSR* XVIII (NS V) (1950), 61, n. 78, would maintain that the rule was in force at a time when the troops were paid in kind and literate soldiers were exceptional, i.e. in the third century, if not later. But *P. Berlin* 6866 seems decisive against this theory.

283 = *CPL* 122, *Documenti* 35. Cf. R. Marichal, *op. cit.*, 9–22 and *La Solde*, 399–421. Cf. also my note in *Historia* VIII (1959), 372–8, and n. 256 above.

284 Severus is known to have given the legionaries a donative of 250 *denarii* (see p. 113 below); the auxiliaries presumably received less.

285 Cf. A. C. Johnson, *Roman Egypt*, 671; P. A. Brunt, *op. cit.*, 61.

286 Cf. Johnson, *loc. cit.*

287 In its most developed form this theory required the conversation of 75 *denarii* first into 300 drachmas and ultimately into 248 drachmas. The belief is that the 300 drachmas were deemed to be copper drachmas of 6 obols each, and therefore equivalent to 1,800 obols; these were then converted into billon tetradrachms at the special rate of 29 obols to the tetradrachm, i.e., into 62 tetradrachms 2 obols. The tetradrachms were then changed into drachmas, disregarding the 2 obols, and the soldier was paid the resulting 248 drachmas. Cf. my comments in 'The Pay of the Roman Army: Suetonius, Dio and the quartum stipendium', *Historia* V (1956), 332–40, esp. 336 f.

288 *P. Gen. lat.* 4 (= *CPL* 107, *Documenti* 31).

289 Suetonius, *Dom.* 7: addidit et quartum stipendium militi aureos ternos.

290 Cf. P. A. Brunt, *op. cit.*, 54, who interprets the language of Dio (lxvii 3, 5) to mean that Domitian did not increase the number of *stipendia* each year from three to four, but simply increased the amount of the individual *stipendium* from 75 *denarii*, or 3 *aurei*, to 100 *denarii*, or 4 *aurei*. But cf. my argument in *Historia* V (1956), 332 ff.

291 Even though Marichal writes in his commentary on line 29 in *ChLA* I, no. 9: 'Third hand. CCXCVII cannot be soldier's pay, there would have been in any case 4 *stipendia* during the year, the first, then, would be September to November, however, l. 6, 128 dr. = 100 dr. (cf. l. 15 and 24) + 28 dr. which equals the *saturnalicium*, cf. *P. I*, Ia, 8. Domitian having granted a *quartum stipendium*, at the end of 83, which could not be incorporated in the pay and had been considered as a *congiarium*, cf. *Fasti Ostienses*, A. Degrassi, *Inscriptiones Italiae*, XIII (1947), p. 193 (restored), which has been added, here, at the moment of establishing the pay credits.'

292 *P. Berlin* 6866 shows seven instances of men in debt to their units on current account—i 29; ii 29; iii 19; frag. A, i 14; i 25; ii 17; frag. F (186). It is true that in all these cases they have apparently an untouchable deposit of 100 *denarii*, which presumably represents the half of a donative, and that in a real sense, therefore, they can be said to be in credit, since only two of them owe as much as 23 *denarii* 19 obols.

293 *P. Gen. lat.* 4 shows 297 drachmas paid in place of 300. This may represent a commission of 1 per cent.

294 Ignatius to Polycarp, 6, 2: τὰ δεπόσιτα ὑμῶν τὰ ἔργα ὑμῶν, ἵνα τὰ ἄκκεπτα ὑμῶν ἄξια κομίσησθε.

295 Tacitus, *Hist.* III 50: et ipsos in regione bello attrita inopia et seditiosae militum voces terrebant, clavarium (donativi nomen est) flagitantium.

296 Suetonius, *Vesp.* 8, 3: classiarios vero, qui ab Ostia et Puteolis Romam pedibus per vices commeant, petentes constitui aliquid sibi calciarii nomine, quasi parum esset sine responso abegisse, iussit posthac excalciatos cursitare; et ex eo ita cursitant.

297 Tacitus, *Ann.* XV, 72: quibus perpetratis Nero et contione militum habita bina nummum milia viritim manipularibus divisit addiditque sine pretio frumentum, quo ante ex modo annonae utebantur.

298 Suetonius, *Nero* 10: item praetorianis cohortibus frumentum menstruum gratuitum.

299 Tacitus, *Hist.* i 46: flagitatum ut vacationes praestari centurionibus solitae remitterentur; namque gregarius miles ut tributum annuum pendebat. quarta pars manipuli sparsa per commeatus aut in ipsis castris vaga, dum mercedem centurioni exsolveret, neque modum oneris quisquam neque genus quaestus pensi habebat: per latrocinia et raptus aut servilibus ministeriis militare otium redimebant. tum locupletissimus quisque miles labore ac saevitia fatigari donec vacationem emeret. ubi sumptibus exhaustus socordia insuper elanguerat, inops pro locuplete et iners pro strenuo in manipulum redibat, ac rursus alius atque alius, eadem egestate ac licentia corrupti, ad seditiones et discordias et ad extremum bella civilia ruebant. sed Otho ne vulgi largitione centurionum animos averteret, fiscum suum vacationes annuas exsoluturum promisit, rem haud dubie utilem et a bonis postea principibus perpetuitate disciplinae firmatam.

300 Tacitus, *Hist.* I 58: igitur laudata militum alacritate Vitellius . . . vacationes centurionibus ex fisco numerat.

301 For donatives in general see Thedenat *s.v.* 'donativum' in *DA* III 385 ff.; Fiebiger in *RE* V (1905) 1542 ff.; J. Sulser, *Disciplina* 1920, 9 ff. and 66 ff.; Passerini, *Le coorti pretorie* (1939), 114 ff.; G. Forni, *Il reclutamento delle legioni da Augusto a Diocleziano* (1953), 35 f.

302 Dio LV, 6, 4.

303 Tacitus, *Ann.* I 8: praetoriarum cohortium militibus singula nummum milia, ⟨urbanis quingenos *add. Saupe,*⟩ legionariis aut cohortibus civium Romanorum trecenos nummos viritim dedit.

   Suetonius, *Augustus* 101: legavit . . . . . . praetorianis militibus singula milia nummorum, cohortibus urbanis quingenos, legionariis trecenos nummos.

   Cf. Dio LVI, 32.

304 Dio LIX, 2, 2.

305 Suetonius, *Tiberius* 48: militi post duplicata ex Augusti testamento legata nihil umquam largitus est, praeterquam singula milia denariorum praetorianis, quod Seiano se non accommodassent, et quaedam munera Syriacis legionibus, quod solae nullam Seiani imaginem inter signa coluissent.

306 Dio LVIII, 9, 6.

307 This is the figure given by Suetonius, *Claudius* 10: promisitque singulis quina dena sestertia, primus Caesarum fidem militis etiam praemio pigneratus. An even higher figure, 5,000 *denarii*, is stated by Josephus, *Ant. Iud.*, 19, 4, 2 (247). J. P. V. D. Balsdon, *The Emperor Gaius* (1934), 188, points out that even the Suetonian figure must have eaten up something near 135,000,000 sesterces.

308 Tacitus, *Ann.* XII, 41: additum nomine eius donativum militi, congiarium plebei.

   Suetonius, *Nero* 7: deductus in forum tiro populo congiarium, militi donativum proposuit.

309 Dio LX, 12, 4.

310 Tacitus, *Ann.* XII, 69: promisso donativo ad exemplum paternae largitionis. Cf. Dio LXI, 3, 1.

311 Dio LXI, 14, 3; Tacitus, *Ann.* XV ,72; Suetonius, *Nero,* 10.

312 Plutarch, *Galba* 2, 2.

313 Tacitus, *Hist.* 1, 5: miles urbanus . . . postquam neque dari donativum sub nomine Galbae promissum neque magnis meritis ac praemiis eundem in pace quem in bello locum praeventamque gratiam intellegit apud principem a legionibus factum, pronus ad novas res scelere insuper Nymphidii Sabini praefecti imperium sibi molientis agitatur.

   Suetonius, *Galba* 16: per haec prope universis ordinibus offensis vel praecipua flagrabat invidia apud milites. nam cum in verba eius absentis iurantibus donativum grandius solito praepositi pronuntiassent, neque ratam rem habuit et subinde iactavit legere se militem, non emere consuesse; atque eo quidem nomine omnis, qui ubique erant, exacerbavit. Cf. also Plutarch, *Galba* 18, and Dio LXIV, 3, 3.

314 Tacitus, *Hist.* 1, 82: finis sermonis in eo ut quina milia nummum singulis militibus numerarentur.

315 Cf. n. 299 above.

316 Cf. n. 300 above.

317 Tacitus, *Hist.* II, 82: donativum militi neque Mucianus prima contione nisi modice ostenderat, ne Vespasianus quidem plus civili bello obtulit quam alii in pace, egregie firmus adversus militarem largitionem eoque exercitu meliore. Fiebiger (*op. cit.*) believed that the 25 *denarii* given by Mucianus to the troops when he presented Domitian to them (Dio LXV, 22, 2) was Vespasian's accession donative. Passerini (*op. cit.*, 118 n. 5) rightly condemns this theory. It may be added that the real accession donative is apparently referred to in Dio LXVI, 10, 1a, in which Vespasian's actions on arrival in Rome are described, but the sum is not mentioned.

318 Dio LXVI, 26, 3.

319 Cf. n. 281 above.

320 Dio LXVII, 7, 3.

321 For Nerva's donative cf. H. Mattingly, *BMC Imp.* III p. xlvi: 'Adlocut. Aug. S.C. represents the harangue delivered by the Emperor to his troops— in this case, unquestionably, to the praetorian guard. The type does not recur under Nerva, and we may therefore apply it directly to the first appearance of Nerva before the guard, when he gave them their donative in honour of his accession.' For Trajan cf. Pliny, *Panegyr.* 25, 2: nisi vero leviter attingi placet locupletatas tribus datumque congiarium populo et datum totum, cum donativi partem milites accepissent. So the military donative required at least two instalments. For Hadrian cf. *SHA, Hadr.* 5, 7: militibus ob auspicia imperii duplicem largitionem dedit.

322 For L. Aelius cf. *SHA, Ael.* 3, 3: datum etiam populo congiarium causa eius adoptionis conlatumque militibus sestertium ter milies. Cf. also *SHA, Hadr.* 23, 12: ob cuius adoptationem ludos circenses dedit et donativum populo ac militibus expendit. For the donative on the accession of Pius cf. *SHA, Anton. Pius.* 8, 1: congiarium populo dedit, militibus donativum addidit. For the occasion of his daughter's marriage cf. *ibid.*, 10, 2: nuptias filiae suae Faustinae, cum Marco Antonino eam coniungeret, usque ad donativum militum celeberrimas fecit.

323 *SHA, M. Ant. Phil.* 7, 9: castra praetoria petiverunt et vicena milia nummum singulis ob participatum imperium militibus promiserunt et ceteris pro rata. Cf. Dio LXXIII, 8, 4.

324 After the increase under Domitian the praetorians probably received 1,000 *denarii* a year. See above p. 98.

325 *SHA, M. Ant. Phil.* 17, 4: cum autem ad hoc bellum omne aerarium exhausisset suum neque in animum induceret, ut extra ordinem provincialibus aliquid imperaret, in foro divi Traiani auctionem ornamen-

torum imperialium fecit vendiditque aurea pocula et cristallina et murrina, vasa etiam regia et vestem uxoriam sericam et auratam, gemmas quin etiam, quas multas in repositorio sanctiore Hadriani reppererat. Cf. Zonaras 12, 1 and Boissevain, *Dio* III, p. 281.

326 Dio LXXI, 3, 3.

327 *SHA, Comm. Ant.* 16, 8: congiarium dedit populo singulis denarios septingenos vicenos quinos. This sum seems high, and is in any case inconsistent with Dio (LXXII, 16, 2), who reports that Commodus frequently gave *congiaria* of up to 140 *denarii*. The 725 *denarii* here mentioned may, however, be the sum total of a number of smaller *congiaria*: the numismatic evidence would allow for eight such.

328 *SHA, Pertinax,* 7, 5: donativa et congiaria, quae Commodus promiserat, solvit. Passerini (*op. cit.,* 120) includes as a donative under Commodus an authorization given by Commodus to Clodius Albinus on the occasion of the latter's elevation to the rank of Caesar to pay up to 75 *denarii* a head. The evidence for this is a 'document' of the *Vita Albini* which must be dismissed as a forgery. Rather oddly, it speaks of a *stipendium*. (*SHA, Clod. Albin.* 2, 4: habebis praeterea, cum id feceris, dandi stipendi usque ad tres aureos liberam potestatem, quia et super hoc ad procuratores meos litteras misi, quas ipse signatas excipies signo Amazonio et, cum opus fuerit, rationalibus dabis, ne te non audiant, cum de aerario volueris imperare.)

329 *SHA, Pert.* 7, 8: auctionem rerum Commodi habuit, ita ut et pueros et concubinas vendi iuberet, exceptis his qui per vim Palatio videbantur inserti. . . . cuius nundinationis pecuniam, quae ingens fuit, militibus donativo dedit. Cf. Dio LXXIII, 50, 4.

330 Dio LXXIII, 1, 2; cf. also LXXIII, 8, 4.

331 *SHA, Pert.* 15, 7: congiarium dedit populo denarios centenos, praetorianis promisit duodena milia nummum, sed dedit sena. quod exercitibus promissum est, datum non est, quia mors eum praevenit.

332 Dio LXXIII, 11, 5.

333 For the distress caused by the wars and the great plague, note the significant remission of arrears of taxation towards the end of the reign of Marcus Aurelius, which is mentioned in Dio LXXI, 32, 2. It was left to Septimius Severus to increase the army pay.

334 *SHA, Did. Iul.* 3, 2: sane cum vicena quina milia militibus promisisset, tricena dedit.

335 Herodian II, 7, 1.

336 Herodian II, 11, 7–8.

337 *SHA, Sev.,* 7, 6: sed cum in senatu esset, milites per seditionem dena milia poposcerunt a senatu exemplo eorum, qui Augustum Octavianum Romam deduxerant tantumque acceperant. et cum eos voluisset comprimere Severus nec potuisset, tamen mitigatos addita liberalitate dimisit. From Dio XLVI, 46, 6–7 we learn that he actually paid 250 *denarii*.

338 Cf. Dio, *ibid.* For a modern comment cf. Domaszewski, *Truppensold*, 232: 'Unmöglich können sich die Provinzialsoldaten der Donauländer auf einen Vortrag berufen haben, der sich 250 Jahre früher zugetragen hatte und anders als in der gelehrten Erinnerung nicht fortlebte.' Cf. also Passerini, *Le coorti pretorie*, 120, n. 4.

339 Probably published about AD 160, cf. his preface, 7 and 9. For the amount of the donative paid by Octavian we have confirmation in Appian, *BC* III 94. A recent study of the march on Rome is by A. Alföldi, 'Der Einmarsch Octavians in Rom, August 43 v. Chr.', *Hermes* LXXXVI (1958), 480 ff. It is noteworthy that a fragment of Appian's *Bellum Mithridaticum* was found at Dura-Europos (*P. Dura* 2). This proves that Appian was read in the army, at least in the East.

340 Dio LXXIV, 2, 4–6.

341 Dio LXXVI, 1, 1.

342 *SHA, Sev.*, 16, 5: harum appellationum causa donativum militibus largissimum dedit concessa omni praeda oppidi Parthici, quod milites quaerebant. Dio LXXV, 9, 4 gives the name of the city as Ctesiphon, and adds that 100,000 prisoners were taken.

343 Herodian II 14, 5 and III 8, 4.

344 Herodian IV 4, 7.

345 Cf. A. H. M. Jones, *The Later Roman Empire*, 28.

346 *ibid.*, 27.

347 *ibid.*, 29 ff.

348 This view goes back to Domaszewski, cf. Domaszewski-Dobson 70. It is repeated in Kromayer-Veith, *Heerwesen*, 538, and in Marin y Peña, *Instituciones militares romanas* (Madrid 1956), 250 para. 553.

349 Cf. P. Steiner, 'Die dona militaria', *Bonner Jahrbücher*, 114–15, 1906, 1–98, esp. p. 79, in which he states the principle 'dass vornehmlich für die Charge des evocatus Augusti eine corona aurea als donum militare typisch war.'

350 *CIL* XI 395 (= *ILS* 2648): M. Vettio M.f. Ani. Valenti mil. coh. VIII pr., benef. praef. pr., donis donato bello Britan. torquibus armillis phaleris, evoc. Aug. corona aurea donat., 7 coh. VI vig., 7 stat., 7 coh. XVI urb., 7 coh. II pr., exercitatori equit. speculatorum, princip. praetori leg. XIII Gem. ex trec., [p.p.] leg. VI Victr., donis donato ob res prosper. gest. contra Astures torq. phaler. arm., trib. coh. V vig., trib. coh. XII urb., trib. coh. III pr., [p.p.] leg. XIIII Gem. Mart. Victr., proc. imp. Caes. Aug. prov. Lusitan., patron. coloniae, speculator. X. h. c. L. Luccio Telesino C. Suetonio Paulino cos (66).

351 Cf. Val. Max. III 2, 24; Pliny, *NH* VII 102, XXII 9; Gell. II 11, 2.

352 Cf. Steiner, *op. cit.*, 43; Domaszewski-Dobson XVIII and 69. *AE* 1900, 95: C. Didio C.f. Sab. Saturnino p.p. donato bello Parthico a divo Vero item bello Germanico a divo M. torq. et arm., item divis Seveo et Magno Antonino corona aurea civica et asta pura argent.

NOTES 199

353 Cf. for instance, *CIL* II 1086 (=*ILS* 2712); ... in Britan[nia praef. coh.] II Vasconum equit., [trib. mi]litum legionis II Aug., praef. alae I Asturum, donis donato corona murali et coronis aureis IIII, item vexillo et hastis puris V, honorato ab exercitibus in quibus militavit bigis auratis et statuis equestribus. Q. Fulvius Euchir IIIIvir Aug. amico bene merenti. *ILS* 2663: Sex. Vibio Gallo tr[e]cenario, primipilari, praef. kastror. leg. XIII Gem., donis donato ab imperatoribu[s] honoris virtutisq. causa torquib. armi[l]lis phaleris coronis muralibus III vallaribus II aurea I hastis puris V vexillis II, Sex. Vibius Cocceianus patrono bene merenti.

354 Cf. Steiner, *op. cit.*, 89 ff.

355 Cf. A. von Domaszewski, 'Die Fahnen im römischen Heere', *Abh. d. arch.-epigr. Sem. d. Univ. Wien* 1885, 67 and 51; Domaszewski-Dobson 118; Kromayer-Veith, *Heerwesen* 539.

356 *CIL* III 6748 and 11931–2. Other units so decorated include the *Ala Moesica felix torquata* (*ILS* 2729 = *CIL* VI 3538), the *Ala Augusta Gallorum Petriana bis torquata miliaria civium Romanorum* (*ILS* 2728 = *CIL* XI 5669), the *Ala Siliana bis torquata bis armillata c. R.* (*CIL* III 5775), and the *Cohors I Vlpia Brittonum miliaria torquata c. R.* For the practice see Zonaras 7, 21.

357 Cf. Dio LV, 24, 3 and for the title *ILS* 2279 ( = McCrum and Woodhead 387) from near Bonn: L. Magius L. Ouf. Dubius Mediolani mil. leg. I F(laviae) M(inerviae) p(iae) f(idelis) D(omitianae) armorum custos 7 Aufidi Martialis ann. XXXI stip. XIII h.f.c.

358 Since 1938, however, when G. Bendz published *Die Echtheitsfrage des vierten Buches der Frontinschen Strategemata*, Book IV has been generally believed to be by Frontinus.

359 VI 39, 11.

360 W. S. Messer, 'Mutiny in the Roman Army. The Republic', *Class. Phil.* XV (1920), 158–75.

361 *BJ* III 5, 7.

362 Cf. Tacitus, *Ann.* XIII 35 (n. 159 above). For an earlier experience of a similar lack of discipline, cf. Caesar, *BC* III 110, 2; milia enim XX in armis habebat. haec constabant ex Gabinianis militibus, qui iam in consuetudinem Alexandrinae vitae ac licentiae venerant et nomen discip- linamque populi Romani dedidicerant uxoresque duxerant, ex quibus plerique liberos habebant. A second-century example is contained in Fronto, *ad Verum* II, i, 22: exercitus tibi traditus erat luxuria et lascivia et otio diutino corruptus. milites Antiochiae adsidue plaudere histrionibus consueti, saepius in nemore vicinae ganeae quam sub signis habiti. equi incuria horridi, equites volsi; raro brachium aut crus militum hirsutum ... pauci militum equum sublimitus insilire, ceteri aegre calce genu poplite repere; haud multi vibrantis hastas, pars maior sine vi et vigore tamquam lanceas iacere. alea in castris frequens, somnus pernox aut in vino vigilia. Cf. also Fronto, *princ. hist.* 12: corruptissimi vero omnium Syriatici milites, seditiosi, contumaces, apud signa infrequentes, freti armis,

praesidiis vagi, exploratorum more palantes, de meridie ad posterum temulenti, ne armatu quidem sustinendo adsueti, sed impatientia laboris armis singillatim omittendis in velitum atque funditorum modum seminudi. Another example, the 'letter' in *SHA, Avidius Cassius*, 5, 5–12, is probably fictitious, but the general impression is almost certainly correct.

363  Tacitus, *Ann*. I 20: diu manipularis, dein centurio, mox castris praefectus, antiquam duram militiam revocabat.

364  Tacitus, *Ann*. XI 18: legiones operum et laboris ignavas, populationibus laetantis, veterem ad morem reduxit, ne quis agmine decederet nec pugnam nisi iussus iniret. stationes vigiliae, diurna nocturnaque munia in armis agitabantur; feruntque militem quia vallum non accinctus, atque alium quia pugione tantum accinctus foderet, morte punitos. quae nimia et incertum an falso iacta originem tamen e severitate ducis traxere; intentumque et magnis delictis inexorabilem scias cui tantum asperitatis etiam adversus levia credebatur.

365  For the fullest account of the *fustuarium* cf. Polybius VI 38, 2. Instances during the Civil Wars are by Caesar (Dio XLI, 35, 5), Domitius Calvinus (Dio XLVIII, 42, 2: the men of two centuries), Mark Antony (Frontinus, *Strat*., IV 1, 37; Plut., *Ant*., 39; Dio XLIX, 27, 1).

366  Cf. Polybius, *ibid*., Suetonius, *Div. Aug*. 24, 2. see below p. 126.

367  Dio XLIX, 38, 4; Suetonius, *ibid*.

368  Tacitus, *Ann*. III 21: raro ea tempestate et e vetere memoria facinore.

369  Suetonius, *Cal*. 48, 1.

370  Suetonius, *Galba* 12, 2; cf. Boissevain's *Dio*, LXIV, 3, 2.

371  Tacitus, *Hist*. I 31: legioni classicae diffidebatur, infestae ob caedem commilitonum, quos primo statim introitu trucidaverat Galba.

372  *CIL* XVI 7, 8 and 9.

373  Tacitus, *Ann*. XIV 44, 6: at quidam insontes peribunt, nam et ex fuso exercitu cum decimus quisque fusti feritur, etiam strenui sortiuntur. habet aliquid ex iniquo omne magnum exemplum quod contra singulos utilitate publica rependitur.

374  For the power of the army commander to execute without appeal cf. A. H. M. Jones, 'I appeal unto Caesar', *Studies in Roman Government and Law* (1960), 51 ff.: 'Soldiers were not, under the early principate at any rate, a privileged class. They were on the contrary, in the interest of military discipline, denied some of the rights of Roman citizens. The *ius gladii* will therefore have been in origin a power granted to army commanders to execute Roman soldiers, but not citizens under their jurisdiction.'

375  *Digest* XLIX 16, 5 (Arrius Menander): non omnes desertores similiter puniendi sunt, sed habetur et ordinis stipendiorum ratio, gradus militiae vel loci, muneris deserti et anteactae vitae: sed et numerus, si solus vel cum altero vel cum pluribus deseruit, aliudve quid crimen desertioni adiunxerit: item temporis quo in desertione fuerit: et eorum, quae postea

gesta fuerint. sed et si fuerit ultro reversus, non cum necessitudine, non erit eiusdem sortis.

376 *Digest* XLIX 16, 3, 9 (Modestinus): si plures simul primo deseruerint, deinde intra certum tempus reversi sint, gradu pulsi in diversa loca distribuendi sunt. sed tironibus parcendum est: qui si iterato hoc admiserint, poena competenti adficiuntur.

377 *Digest* XLIX 16, 3, 1 (Modestinus): poenae militum huiuscemodi sunt: castigatio, pecuniaria multa, munerum indictio, militiae mutatio, gradus deiectio, ignominiosa missio. nam in metallum aut in opus metalli non dabuntur nec torquentur.

378 Tacitus, *Ann.* XIII 35, 9: nec enim, ut in aliis exercitibus, primum alterumque delictum venia prosequebatur, sed qui signa reliquerat, statim capite poenas luebat.

379 For a date *c.* AD 130 see Eric Birley, *Roman Britain and the Roman Army* (1953), 20–30. For the evidence of tiles found at Nijmegen of probable Hadrianic date and the resultant conclusion that IX *Hispana* was not lost in Britain, see J. E. Bogaers, 'Die Besatzungstruppen des Legionslagers von Nijmegen im 2. Jahrhundert nach Christus', *Studien zu den Militärgrenzen Roms* (1967), 54 ff.

380 For Curio's action see Frontinus, *Strat.* IV 1, 43: C. Curio consul bello Dardanico circa Dyrrachium, cum ex quinque legionibus una seditione facta militiam detractasset securamque se temeritatem ducis in expeditionem asperam et insidiosam negasset, quattuor legiones eduxit armatas et consistere ordinibus detectis armis velut in acie iussit. post hoc seditiosam legionem inermem procedere discinctamque in conspectu armati exercitus stramenta coegit secare, postero autem die similiter fossam discinctos milites facere, nullisque precibus legionis impetrari ab eo potuit, ne signa eius summitteret nomenque aboleret, milites autem in supplementum ceterarum legionum distribueret. Octavian's disbandment of the Tenth is recorded by Suetonius, *Div. Aug.* 24, 2: decimam legionem contumacius parentem cum ignominia totam dimisit, item alias immodeste missionem postulantes citra commoda emeritorum praemiorum exauctoravit.

381 Suetonius, *Div. Iul.* 69: non enim cessit umquam tumultuantibus atque etiam obviam semper iit; et nonam quidem legionem apud Placentiam, quamquam in armis adhuc Pompeius esset, totam cum ignominia missam fecit aegreque post multas et supplicis preces, nec nisi exacta de sontibus poena, restituit. Cf. Dio XLI, 26–36, and Appian II 47, neither of whom mention the disbandment.

382 Suetonius, *Div. Iul.* 70: decimanos autem Romae cum ingentibus minis summoque etiam urbis periculo missionem et praemia flagitantes, ardente tunc in Africa bello, neque adire cunctatus est, quamquam deterrentibus amicis, neque dimittere; sed una voce, qua 'Quirites' eos pro militibus appellarat, tam facile circumegit et flexit, ut ei milites confestim responderint et quamvis recusantem ultro in Africam sint secuti; ac sic quoque

seditiosissimum quemque et praedae et agri destinati tertia parte multavit.
Cf. Appian II 94; Dio XLII, 52–5; Tac., *Ann.* I 42; Frontinus, *Strat.* IV 5, 2
(cf. also I 9, 4); Polyaenus VIII 23, 15.

383 *Bell. Afr.* 46, 4: qua ex re Caesar commotus eos quos in stationibus cum
longis navibus apud Thapsum custodiae causa in salo esse iusserat ut suis
onerariis longisque navibus praesidio esset, ob neglegentiam ignominiae
causa dimittendos ab exercitu gravissimumque in eos edictum proponen-
dum curavit. For the dismissal of the tribunes C. Avienus and A. Fonteius,
and of the centurions T. Salienus, M. Tiro and C. Clusinas see *Bell. Afr.* 54.

384 Not that this was a primary reason for the measures of AD 6, which were
principally due to the men's unwillingness to continue their service
beyond the period prescribed. Cf. G. R. Watson, 'Discharge and resettlement in the Roman Army: the praemia militiae', *Neue Beiträge zur
Geschichte der alten Welt*, II (1965), 147 ff.

385 Cf. *Digest* III 2, 2, 2 (Ulpian): multa genera sunt missionum. est honesta,
quae emeritis stipendiis vel ante ab imperatore indulgetur: est causaria,
quae propter valetudinem laboribus militiae solvit: est ignominiosa.
ignominiosa autem missio totiens est, quotiens is qui mittit addit nomina-
tim ignominiae causa se mittere. . . . est et quartum genus missionis, si
quis evitandorum munerum causa militiam subisset: haec autem missio
existimationem non laedit, ut est saepissime rescriptum. Cf. also *Digest*
XLIX 16, 13, 3 (Macer) missionum generales causae sunt tres: honesta
causaria ignominiosa. honesta est, quae tempore militiae impleto datur:
causaria, cum quis vitio animi vel corporis minus idoneus militiae renuntiatur: ignominiosa causa est, cum quis propter delictum sacramento
solvitur.

386 *Digest* III 2, 2, 2 (Ulpian): semper enim debet addere, cur miles mittatur.
sed et si eum exauctoraverit, id est insignia militaria detraxerit, inter
infames efficit, licet non addidisset ignominiae causa se eum exauctorasse.
XLIX 16, 13, 3 (Macer): et si sine ignominiae mentione missi sunt, nihilo
minus ignominia missi intelleguntur.

387 *CIL* XVI 10 (= McCrum and Woodhead, 397): causari, qui militaverunt
in leg. II Adiutrice Pia Fidele, qui bello inutiles facti ante emerita stipendia
exauctorati sunt et dimissi honesta missione.

388 *CIL* VI 3373: d.m. Aurelius Dassius militavit in leg(ione) II Part(hica)
Antoninian(a) Ae(terna) Pi(a) [F(elici)] Fi(deli) annis XVIIII ex c[ausa]
miss(us) hon(esta) m(issione) ex leg(ione) s(upra) s(cripta) vixit annis L
m(ensibus) III d(iebus) XXVI . . . Contrast *CIL* XIII 2948 (Agedincum):
Valerius [Bas?]sus cau(s)ari[us] ex milite pretorian[o].

389 Macer in *Digest* XLIX 16, 13, 3; Ulpian in *Digest* III 2, 2, 2. For the texts
cf. n. 385.

390 The definition *est honesta, quae emeritis stipendiis vel ante ab imperatore
indulgetur* implies that premature discharge with *honesta missio* is not a
right, but a privilege that can be granted under certain circumstances.

391 Cf. *CIL* XVI 10, n. 2: Causariis missio datur honesta, non, ut exspectaveris, causaria. . . . Ex Ulpiani verbis (*Dig.* 3, 2, 2, 2) scimus honestam missionem etiam ante emerita stipendia dari potuisse. Etenim solummodo eorum, qui *bello inutiles facti* sunt, hic mentio fit, cum missio causaria non imprimis ad eos spectare videatur, qui bello laesi sunt, sed ad eum, *cum quis vitio vel animi vel corporis minus idoneus militiae renuntiatur* (*Dig.* 49, 16, 13, 3).

392 *BC* III 74: hac habita contione non nullos signiferos ignominia notavit ac loco movit. For this punishment applied to a commanding officer cf. Frontinus, *Strat.* IV i 37: legatum cum ignominia dimisit. This was by Antony in 36 BC. Similarly, Cotta had reduced to the ranks P. Aurelius, a kinsman of his (*ibid.* 31): idem P. Aurelium sanguine sibi iunctum, quem obsidioni Lipararum, ipse ad auspicia repetenda Messanam transiturus praefecerat, cum agger incensus et capta castra essent, virgis caesum in numerum gregalium peditum referri et muneribus fungi iussit. Cf. Val. Max. II vii 4: C. Cotta consul P. Aurelium Pecuniolam sanguine sibi iunctum, quem obsidioni Liparitanae ad auspicia repetenda Messanam transiturus praefecerat, virgis caesum militiae munere inter pedites fungi coegit, quod eius culpa agger incensus, paene castra erant capta.

An example in the Empire is of the reverse process. Vitellius on his arrival in Lower Germany restored to their commands a number of broken centurions and cancelled their disgrace: Tacitus, *Hist.* I 52: redditi plerisque ordines, remissa ignominia, adlevatae notae. Cf. Suetonius, *Vit.*, 8: Castra vero ingressus nihil cuiquam poscenti negavit atque etiam ultro ignominiosis notas, reis sordes, damnatis supplicia dempsit.

393 *BGU* II 696 (= *CPL* 118, *Documenti* 9.) Cf. R. O. Fink, *AJPh* LXIII (1942), 61–71, for the view that the *pridianum* was normally a report made on 31st December, the *pridie par excellence*, but that since the Egyptian year ended near the end of August, an additional *pridianum*, with the date naturally fixed at the end of the Roman month, was made for the use of the provincial administration in Egypt.

394 *Contra* Fink, *op. cit.*, 66, who prefers to think that the man in question, Vespasianus, had previously served in the *cohors I Lusitanorum*, was then transferred to the *ala I Thracum*, perhaps after service in other corps, and is now being returned, with promotion to the decurionate, to his former cohort. But cf. Mommsen, *Ges. Schrift.* VIII 563 f., Domaszewski-Dobson 57, Lesquier, *op. cit.* in n. 168, 228.

395 ii 13–21. The context indicates that they remained *gregales*. Acceptance of service in an inferior arm at the same rank could, however, be explained on other grounds, such as easier discipline, more congenial companions, etc. A considerable sacrifice of pay would be involved.

396 Dio LXXIX, 3, 5. Cf. Groag in *PIR*[2] II 172 n. 795, for the date of Attalus' governorship of Thrace.

397 Polybius VI 37, 8; *Digest* XLIX, 16, 3, 1. Cf. Paulus, *epit. Festi*, p. 61 L: dirutum aere militem dicebant antiqui, cui stipendium ignominiae causa

non erat datum quod aes diruebatur in fiscum, non in militis sacculum. Cf. Nonius, p. 853 L, and also Cato *apud* Gell. XI 1, 6: nam in quarto originum verba haec sunt: Imperator noster, si quis extra ordinem depugnatum ivit, ei multam facit.

398 Frontinus, *Strat.* IV i 46: cum ab Liguribus in proelio Q. Petilius consul interfectus esset, decrevit senatus, uti ea legio in cuius acie consul erat occisus tota infrequens referretur, stipendium ei annuum non daretur, aera reciderentur. Val. Max. II vii 15: legioni neque stipendium anni procedere neque aera dari voluit, quia pro salute imperatoris hostium se telis non obtulerant.

399 Livy XL 41, 11: causa ignominiae uti semenstre stipendium in eum annum esset ei legioni decretum: qui miles ad exercitum non redisset, eum ipsum bonaque eius vendere consul iussus.

400 See above p. 122 and n. 382.

401 Tacitus, *Ann.* I 23: et centurio Lucilius interficitur cui militaribus facetiis vocabulum 'cedo alteram' indiderant, quia fracta vite in tergo militis alteram clara voce ac rursus aliam poscebat.

402 Suetonius, *Div. Aug.* 24: centuriones statione deserta, itidem ut manipulares, capitali animadversione puniit, pro cetero delictorum genere variis ignominiis adfecit, ut stare per totum diem iuberet ante praetorium, interdum tunicatos discinctosque, nonnumquam cum decempedis vel etiam caespitem portantes. Cf. Polyaenus, VIII 24, 3, who 'improves' the description by having the offenders made to carry bricks, not turf. A *praefectus equitum* had been similarly punished by the consul L. Calpurnius Piso in the Sicilian slave rising of 133 BC, cf. Val. Max. II vii 9: iussit eum toga laciniis abscisis amictum discinctaque tunica indutum nudis pedibus a mane in noctem usque ad principia per omne tempus militiae adesse. Cf. Frontinus, *Strat.* IV i 27: Sulla cohortem et centuriones, quorum stationem hostis perruperat, galeatos et discinctos perstare in principiis iussit.

403 Frontinus, *Strat.* IV i 28: Domitius Corbulo in Armenia Aemilio Rufo praefecto equitum, quia hostibus cesserat et parum instructam armis alam habebat, vestimenta per lictorem scidit eidemque ut erat foedato habitu perstare in principiis donec emitteretur imperavit.

404 Livy X 4, 4: cohortes quae signa amiserant extra vallum sine tentoriis destitutas invenit. Val. Max. II 7, 15: cum magnum captivorum civium suorum numerum a Pyrrho rege ultro missum recepissent, decreverunt ut ex iis, qui equo meruerant, peditum numero militarent, qui pedites fuerant, in funditorum auxilia transcriberentur, neve quis eorum intra castra tenderet, neve locum extra adsignatum vallo aut fossa cingeret, neve tentorium ex pellibus haberet. (Cf. Frontinus, *Strat.* IV i 18, and Eutropius II 13.) Frontinus, *Strat.* IV i 19: Otacilius Crassus consul eos, qui ab Hannibale sub iugum missi redierant, tendere extra vallum iussit, ut immuniti adsuescerent periculis et adversus hostem audentiores fierent. Livy XXVII 13, 9: cohortibus quae signa amiserant hordeum dari iussit, centurionesque

manipulorum quorum signa amissa fuerant destrictis gladiis discinctos destituit.

405 Tacitus, *Ann.* XIII 36: quod graviter Corbulo accepit increpitumque Paccium et praefectos militesque tendere extra vallum iussit; inque ea contumelia detenti nec nisi precibus universi exercitus exsoluti sunt. Frontinus, *Strat.* IV i 21: Domitius Corbulo in Armenia duas alas et tres cohortes, quae ad castellum Initia hostibus cesserant, extra vallum iussit tendere, donec adsiduo labore et prosperis excursionibus redimerent ignominiam.

406 Frontinus, *Strat.* IV i 25: legionibus, quae Punico bello militiam detractaverant, in Siciliam velut relegatis per septem annos hordeum ex senatus consulto datum est. For another instance cf. Livy, *loc. cit.*, and Plutarch, *Marcellus* 25.

407 Polybius VI 38, 3.

408 Suetonius, *Div. Aug.* 24: cohortes, si quae cessissent loco, decimatas hordeo pavit. Cf. Dio XLIX, 38, 4 and Polyaenus VIII, 24, 2. Antony had acted similarly, cf. Frontinus, *Strat.* IV i 37: duarum cohortium militem decimavit et in singulos ex his centuriones animadvertit, legatum cum ignominia dimisit, reliquis ex legione hordeum dari iussit. (Cf. Plutarch, *Ant.* 39.)

409 Vegetius I 13: ita autem severe apud maiores exercitii disciplina servata est, ut et doctores armorum duplis remunerarentur annonis et milites, qui parum in illa prolusione profecerant, pro frumento hordeum cogerentur accipere, nec ante eis in tritico redderetur annona, quam sub praesentia praefecti legionis, tribunorum vel principiorum experimentis datis ostendissent se omnia quae erant in militari arte complere. See also n. 117.

410 Cf. Tacitus, *Ann.* I 21: Blaesus paucos, maxime praeda onustos, ad terrorem ceterorum adfici verberibus, claudi carcere iubet.

411 An *optio carceris* is attested for the praetorians in *ILS* 9060: mil. chor. II praet. optioni carcaris; and perhaps in *AE* 1914, 250: optio Gargaris (?). For the urban cohorts cf. VI 531, IX 1617, XIII 1833 (Lugdunum). The *vigiles* had a *carcerarius*, attested as KARC in VI 221, a 7, 4. An *optio custodiarum* is recorded on legionary inscriptions in *CIL* XIII 6739 (Moguntiacum) and *CIL* III 15191 (Carnuntum: AD 201). P. *Dura* 101, xxi, 3, a roster of *cohors XX Palmyrenorum* of AD 222, had the marginal notation *custod*.

412 *CIL* III 15190 (Carnuntum: AD 201) and 15192. *CIL* III 14507 (Viminacium: AD 195), *dextr.* v. 7 reads: M. Aur. Firmus cl cas. The abbreviation *cl* is expanded by Bormann as *cl(avicularius)*, but by Domaszewski as *c(ornicularius) l(egati)*.

413 Domaszewski-Dobson 46.

# RELIGION AND MARRIAGE

414 For a dedication to a large group of deities cf. n. 20 above. Dedications to Cocidius are common in Cumberland and the surrounding area: *RIB* 966

(Netherby), 985–6, 988–9, 993 (Bewcastle), 1577–8, 1583, 1633 (House-steads), 1683 (Chesterholm), 1955–6 (Bankshead), 2015, 2020, 2024 (near Carlisle). Somewhat further away is *RIB* 602 (Lancaster). For the cult of Coventina at Carrawburgh see the series *RIB* 1522–35.

415 Tertullian, *Apol.* 16: religio Romanorum tota castrensis signa veneratur, signa iurat, signa omnibus deis praeponit. Cf. also Tertullian, *ad nat.* I 12: (castrensis religio) . . . signa adorat, signa deierat, signa ipsi Iovi praefert . . . sic etiam in cantabris atque vexillis, quae non minore sanctitate militia custodit; and Minucius Felix, *Octav.*, 29, 6–7: vos plane, qui ligneos deos consecratis, cruces ligneas ut deorum vestrorum partes forsitan adoratis. nam et signa ipsa et cantabra et vexilla castrorum quid aliud quam inauratae cruces sunt et ornatae?

416 A. von Domaszewski, 'Die Religion des römischen Heeres', *Westdeutsche Zeitschrift für Geschichte und Kunst* XIV (1895), 1–121, believed Tertullian to be right for the early Empire, though he thought that by Tertullian's own day the worship of the Emperor had begun to supplant the cult of the standards. Cf. Domaszewski, *op. cit.*, 13 and n. 59.

417 For bibliography see no. 84 in Appendix C.

418 Cf. the remarks by A. S. Hoey in *YCS* VII, 203 f.

419 The character of the Dura garrison is shown by the soldiers' nomenclature to be a mixture of Greek, Hellenized Oriental, and Oriental. Cf. *Dura* V, 37 f.

420 Hoey (*op. cit.*, 206 ff.) argues that by the date of the *Feriale* the provincial-ization and barbarization both of the *Offizierkorps* and of the rank and file of the army had so far advanced that a policy of Romanization was all the more necessary. This may be so, but there is no reason to suppose that a *Feriale* would have been any less Roman during the previous century.

421 Tacitus, *Ann.* II 17: interea pulcherrimum augurium, octo aquilae petere silvas et intrare visae imperatorem advertere. exclamat irent, sequerentur Romanas avis, propria legionum numina.

422 The eagles of the legions involved in the Varian disaster were recovered separately in AD 15, 16 and 41.

423 Velleius Paterculus, II 97: sed dum in hac parte imperii omnia geruntur prosperrime, accepta in Germania clades sub legato M. Lollio, homine in omnia pecuniae quam recte faciendi cupidiore et inter summam vitiorum dissimulationem vitiosissimo, amissaque legionis quintae aquila vocavit ab urbe in Gallias Caesarem.

424 The identification with V *Alaudae* is supported by E. von Nischer in Kromayer-Veith, *Heerwesen*, 518. Alternatively, the existence of a legio V *Gallica* has been presumed. Syme (*JRS* 1933, 17 ff.) prefers to hold that the legion continued to exist and is to be identified with V *Alaudae* or, preferably, V *Macedonica*. Cf. also A. Passerini *s.v.* 'legio' in *Diz. epigr.* IV (1949) 556.

425 Suetonius, *Vesp.* 4: id de imperatore Romano, quantum postea eventu

paruit, praedictum Iudaei ad se trahentes rebellarunt caesoque praeposito legatum insuper Syriae consularem suppetias ferentem rapta aquila fugaverunt. Cf. also Josephus, *BJ* II 18, 9 and 19, 7.

426 Cf. Parker, *RL*, 36 and M. Marin y Peña, *Instituciones militares romanas*, 61, para. 107, for the institution of the *aquila*. For the *aquilifer* cf. nn. 206-7 above.

427 For the silver eagle of the Republic cf. Cicero, *Cat.* I 9, 24: aquilam illam argenteam; Appian, *BC* IV 101; Dio XLIII 35. For the thunderbolts of gold cf. Dio, *ibid.*

428 Cf. Dio XL 18; Herodian IV 7, 7; Dexippus *frag.* 24 (= Jacoby, *FGrHist* II A 100).

429 Cf. Parker, *RL*, 37 ff.

430 Dio XL 18.

431 Tacitus, *Ann.* I 39: ingerunt contumelias, caedem parant, Planco maxime, quem dignitas fuga impediverat, neque aliud periclitanti subsidium quam castra primae legionis. illic signa et aquilam amplexus religione sese tutabatur, ac ni aquilifer Calpurnius vim extremam arcuisset, rarum etiam inter hostis, legatus populi Romani Romanis in castris sanguine suo altaria deum commaculavisset.

432 *ILS* 2293 (= *CIL* II 6183): I(ovi) o(ptimo) m(aximo) vexillatio [l]eg(ionis) VII G(eminae) f(elicis) sub cura [I]uni Victo[r]is 7 leg(ionis) ei[u]sd(em) ob na[t]alem aquilae.

433 *P. Dura* 54, ii 8: VI. [– – u]s Maias ob Rosalias Sign[o]rum suppl[icatio]; ii 14: Pr[i]d[ie] Kal(endas) Iunias ob Rosalias Signorum suppl[i]catio. The editors comment that the space available in line 8 perhaps favours the reading *VII Idus*, but since that was the first day of the Lemuria, an ill-omened festival of the dead, perhaps *VI* should be read. In favour of *VII* is the possibility that this was one of the soldiers' three pay days in the year at that time. Cf. R. O. Fink, *YCS* VII (1940), 70 ff. Against this, J. F. Gilliam, *HThR* XLVII (1954), 190 ff., shows that the papyri provide substantial grounds for believing that the three *stipendia* were paid or fell due on the Kalends of January, May and September, but give no reason for connecting them with a date beginning *VII Idus*. It is, of course, possible that payments were due on the Kalends, but were actually made a few days later. Fink has replied to Gilliam's arguments in *Dura* V, 203 ff.

434 A. S. Hoey, *HThR* XXX (1937), 15-35, esp. 30 ff., and *YCS* VII (1940), 115.

435 At least in Britain, though they are less uncommon in the Rhineland and along the Danube. Cf. Sir Ian Richmond, *AA* XXI (1943), 156.

436 e.g. *ILS* 2295 (= *CIL* III 7591), Novae: dis militaribus Genio Virtuti aquilae sanct(ae) signisque leg(ionis) I Ital(icae) Severianae M. Aurel(ius) Iustus domo Ho[r]rei Margensis m(unicipii?) Moesiae superioris ex (tre-cenario) p(rimus) p(ilus) d(ono) d(edit). dedic(atum) XII Kal. Oct. Iuliano II et Crispino cos. [pe]r Annium Italicum leg(atum) Aug(usti) pr(o) pr(aetore). 20 Sept. 224.

437 Cf. now Sheppard Frere, *Britannia* (1967), 326 f., for examples of *interpretatio Romana* in Britain.

438 See above, pp. 52, 79, 104 f.

439 Occasionally fourth-century restorers left only a pit-type strongroom, as at Chesterholm and Risingham. Cf. J. J. Wilkes, 'Early Fourth-Century Rebuilding in Hadrian's Wall Forts', *Britain and Rome* (ed. M. G. Jarrett and B. Dobson, 1965), 114 ff., esp. 116 f.

440 An almost parallel division would be between those gods worshipped inside the camp and those worshipped outside it.

441 For these deities cf. A. von Domaszewski, 'Die Religion des römischen Heeres', *Westd. Zeitschr. f. Gesch. u. Kunst* XIV (1895), esp. 1–40. *Minerva*, in addition to her general functions as a member of the Capitoline triad, had a special interest for regimental clerks. British examples of dedications to her from such personnel are *RIB* 1101 and 1134, dedicated by an *actarius* and a *librarius* respectively.

442 For *Urbs Roma* cf. *P. Dura* 54 ii 5: X̣[I K]ạḷ(endas) Maịạṣ ob natalem Urbis [R]omaẹ [A]ẹṭẹ[rnae U(rbi) R(omae) A(eternae) b(ovem) f(eminam)]. Examples of the cult from Britain are the dedications in *RIB* 812, 840 and 1270, the latter being set up on 21 April, the feast of the *Natalis Urbis Romae*. Cf. also *CIL* III 10470. The cult of *Disciplina* is common in Britain and Africa, but rare elsewhere. Richmond (*op. cit.*, 166 f.) explains this by the comparative isolation of Britain and Africa and the consequent need for more emphasis on this aspect of central authority. Significantly, both provinces supported Albinus. *Fortuna* is in Britain associated chiefly with bath-houses, cf. *RIB* 317 (Caerleon), 624 (Slack), 730 (Bowes), 968 (Netherby), 1210 (Risingham), 1449 (Chesters), 1537 (Carrawburgh), 1724 (Great Chesters), 2146 (Castlecary). For *Virtus* cf. n. 436 above; British examples are *RIB* 152 and 1466. For *Honos, Pietas* and *Bonus Eventus* cf. Domaszewski, *op. cit.*, 40–4.

443 Cf. Domaszewski, *op. cit.*, 49.

444 Cf. Tacitus, *Germania* 9: Herculem ac Martem concessis animalibus placant. Hercules in this context can only represent Donar. The same is true in *Ann.* II 12, 1: convenisse et alias nationes in silvam Herculi sacram.

445 Cf. Tacitus, *Hist.* I 36: haud dubiae iam in castris omnium mentes tantusque ardor ut non contenti agmine et corporibus in suggestu, in quo paulo ante aurea Galbae statua fuerat, medium inter signa Othonem vexillis circumdarent. Suetonius, *Tib.*, 48: et quaedam munera Syriacis legionibus, quod solae nullam Seiani imaginem inter signa coluissent.

446 For the goddess *Hammia* cf. *RIB* 1780. A prefect of the same unit set up *RIB* 1792 to the *dea Syria*. For *Mars Thincsus* and the *Alaisiagae* cf. *RIB* 1593, 1576, 1594. For *Viradecthis* cf. *RIB* 2108 and *ILS* 4759 (= *CIL* XIII 6486). For the sailors' attitude to *Serapis* cf. C. G. Starr, *The Roman Imperial Navy* (2nd edn., 1960), 87 f.

447 For Coventina's Well cf. *AA*, 2nd series, VIII, 45. Offerings were

apparently still being made right up to the final withdrawal of the Roman garrison.

448 For these three gods cf. Eric Birley, 'Maponus: the epigraphic evidence', *Dumfriesshire and Galloway Transactions*, 3rd series, XXXI (1954), 39–42.

449 For *Iuno* as consort cf. *ILS* 4320 (= *CIL* VI 413), 4321b (= VI 365), and 4322 (= VI 367).

450 Cf. *ILS* 4303 (= *CIL* III 1128): numini et virtutibu[s Iovis optimi maximi Dolicheni], nato ubi ferrum exor[itur]; *ILS* 4302 (= *CIL* VI 30947): Iovi optimo maximo Dolicheno ubi ferrum nascitur C. Sempronius Rectus 7 frumentarius d.d.; *ILS* 4301 (= *CIL* III 11927): I.O.M. Duliceno ubi ferum (*sic*) [nascit]ur.

451 Cf. Richmond, *op. cit.*, 180 f., and A. S. Hoey, *TAPhA* LXX (1939), 473.

452 For the story of the pirates cf. Plutarch, *Pompey* 24, 5. They instituted the cult at Olympus, a town in southern Asia Minor.

453 The dedications by prefects were made at Carrawburgh (*RIB* 1544, 1545, 1546), and at Rudchester (*RIB* 1395, 1396, and perhaps 1397). Centurions made dedications at Housesteads (*RIB* 1600) and Rudchester (*RIB* 1398), and the *beneficiarius consularis* at Housesteads (*RIB* 1599). The other dedication is *RIB* 1601 (Housesteads): D(eo) Soli Herion v(otum) l(ibens) m(erito).

454 Cf. my brief note on 'Christianity in the Roman Army in Britain', *Christianity in Britain 300–700* ed. by M. W. Barley and R. P. C. Hanson, (Leicester 1968), 51 ff.

455 Dio LX 24, cf. *BGU* I 114 (= *Negotia* 19, *Documenti* 3) and *BGU* I 140 (= *Leges* 78, *Documenti* 108).

456 *Digest* XXIV i 60-2 (Hermogenianus and Gaius): saepe enim evenit, uti propter sacerdotium vel etiam sterilitatem vel senectutem aut valetudinem aut militiam satis commode retineri matrimonium non possit: et ideo bona gratia matrimonium dissolvitur.

457 For the general position of equestrian officers cf. Eric Birley, 'The Equestrian Officers of the Roman Army', *Roman Britain and the Roman Army* (1953), 133–53, esp. the conclusion: 'Equestrian officers were technically civilians, except when holding specific establishment posts, so that an inefficient one need never constitute a permanent liability to the service; he could always be superseded and returned, without compensation, to civilian life. That is the most remarkable feature of the equestrian military system; it is perhaps a pity that it cannot be adopted in some modern armies.' For the ban on marriage with women of the province of service cf. *Digest* XXIII ii 63 (Papinian): praefectus cohortis vel equitum aut tribunus contra interdictum eius provinciae duxit uxorem, in qua officium gerebat: matrimonium non erit. *ibid.*, ii 65 (Paulus): eos, qui in patria sua militant, non videri contra mandata ex eadem provincia uxorem ducere idque etiam quibusdam mandatis contineri. Idem eodem. Respondit mihi placere, etsi contra mandata contractum sit matrimonium in provincia,

tamen post depositum officium, si in ea voluntate perseverat, iustas nuptias efficit: et ideo postea liberos natos ex iusto matrimonio legitimos esse.

458 Suetonius, *Div. Aug.* 24: disciplinam severissime rexit. ne legatorum quidem cuiquam, nisi gravate hibernisque demum mensibus, permisit uxorem intervisere.

459 Suetonius, *Gaius* 9: Caligulae cognomen castrensi ioco traxit, quia manipulario habitu inter milites educabatur.

460 Defined in the *Thesaurus Linguae Latinae* thus: 'in specie (vocabulum castrense); feminae quae quasi uxores cum militibus "concessa consuetudine" ad castra vivunt.'

461 For details of these measures see Hugh Last in *CAH* X 441 ff. For the action of Claudius cf. Dio LX 24, 3.

462 For this tax see J. F. Gilliam, 'The minimum subject to the *vicesima hereditatium*', *AJPh* LXXIII (1952), 397 ff., and the references there cited.

463 Cf. *BGU* I 140 (= *Documenti* 108), and *BGU* V 1210, 98–100 (= *Leges* 99, *Documenti* 107).

464 Cf. *P. Mich.* VIII 514, in which a mother writes of seeking to recover her deceased son's *deposita*. Cf. also no. 78 in Appendix C.

465 *BGU* I 114 + P. Cattaui. Cf. Mitteis 372, *Negotia* 19, *Documenti* 3.

466 Collected in *CIL* XVI, ed. H. Nesselhauf, 1936, with a supplement in 1955.

467 The crucial words read: ipsis liberis posterisque eorum civitatem dedit et conubium cum uxoribus, quas tunc habuissent, cum est civitas iis data, aut, si qui caelibes essent, cum iis quas postea duxissent dumtaxat singuli singulas.

468 The formula now becomes: (dimissis) civitatem Romanam, qui eorum non haberent, dedit et conubium cum uxoribus, quas tunc habuissent, cum est civitas iis data, aut cum iis quas postea duxissent dumtaxat singuli singulas. The change appears to have taken place between 15 February and 13 December, AD 140. Cf. Konrad Kraft, 'Zum Bürgerrecht der Soldatenkinder', *Historia* 1961, 120 ff.

469 Herodian III, 8, 5.

470 For the view that marriage was intended, see Wilmanns in *CIL* VIII p. 284; Lesquier, *L'armée romaine d'Egypte* (1918), 273; Nesselhauf in *CIL* XVI pp. 154 f. *Contra* Mommsen in *CIL* III pp. 2011 ff.

471 See the passages cited by Lesquier, *loc. cit.*, and by Erich Sander, *RhM* CI (1958), 154 f. The following seem conclusive:
   *Digest* XXIII, 2, 35 (Papinian): filius familias miles matrimonium sine patris voluntate non contrahit. This would be both otiose and absurd if a soldier could not marry even with his father's consent.
   *Digest* XLVIII, 5, 12 (11) *praef.* (Papinian): miles, qui cum adultero uxoris suae pactus est, solvi sacramento deportarique debet. Adultery presupposes marriage.
   *Digest* XLIX, 17, 16 (Papinian): dotem filio familias datam vel promissam in peculio castrensi non esse respondi. A *dos* implies marriage.

*Cod. Iust.*, VI, 21, 3, 1 (AD 213): nam cum pater familias filiam ex duabus unciis, uxorem ex uncia heredem scripserit, nec de residuis portionibus quicquam significaverit, in tres partes divisisse eum apparet hereditatem, ut duas habeat quae sextantem accepit, tertiam quae ex uncia est heres instituta. The whole section is entitled *de testamento militis.*

*Cod. Iust.*, IX, 9, 15 (AD 242): Imp. Gordianus A. Hilariano militi. Si quondam uxor tua, antequam crimine adulterii peteretur, provincia excessit, neque absens accusari potest neque in eam provinciam in qua stipendium facis transmitti iure deposcitur. sane cum per occupationes militares licuerit, accusare eam sollemniter poteris: nec enim tempus, quo muneribus militaribus occuparis, vindictam tibi, quam maritali dolore percussus reposcis, debet auferre. This describes how the normal procedure of litigation had to be adapted to suit the exigencies of the service.

*Cod. Theod.*, VII, 1, 3 (AD 349): quicumque militum ex nostra auctoritate familias suas ad se venire meruerint, non amplius quam coniugia liberos servos etiam de peculio castrensi emptos neque adscriptos censibus ad eosdem excellentia tua dirigi faciat. Sander points out the parallel with Herodian VI 7, 3, where the troops in the East were enraged because their families left behind at home had been slaughtered by the Germans.

472 Cf. Nesselhauf in *CIL* XVI p. 155: Quod ante a. 166 in militibus classiariis factum esse videmus, quasi praelusio est eorum, quae Septimius Severus innovavit. C. G. Starr, *The Roman Imperial Navy* (2nd edn., 1960), 92: 'If this be true, the first signs of a more liberal policy on the question of military marriage showed themselves in the navy, and the grant of *matrimonium* to the sailors by Marcus Aurelius presaged the certain bestowal of full marriage rights on soldiers under Septimius Severus.'

473 The old formula is retained in *Dipl.* 92 (AD 145) and *Dipl.* 100 (AD 152).

474 The new formula, first found in *Dipl.* 122 (30 April AD 166) reads: ipsis filiisque eorum, quos susceperint ex mulieribus quas secum concessa consuetudine vixisse probaverint, civitatem Romanam dedit et conubium cum iisdem, quas tunc habuissent cum est civitas iis data, aut si qui tunc non habuissent, cum iis quos postea duxissent dumtaxat singuli singulas.

475 Cf. Starr, *op. cit.*, 91 f. Five years before the publication of Starr's first edition Nesselhauf had been able to write in *CIL* XVI, p. 155: Qua formula non uxores matrimonio iuris peregrini legitimo ductas sed concubinas significari omnes consentiunt. But now cf. Erich Sander, *RhM* CI (1958), 161 f.: 'Die consuetudo wird jetzt concessa genannt. Das deutet darauf hin, dass den Angehörigen der prätorischen Flotten (nicht der Grenzflotten), die Ehe gestattet wird, zwar nicht nach römischen Recht, denn die nautae waren lateinischen Rechtes, wohl aber ex iure gentium.'

476 Starr, *op. cit.*, 92.

477 Praetorian guard, *Dipl.* 135, 136, 139, 140, 142, 143, 145, 147, 148, 149, 151, 153, 155, 156, 189. (The latest is *Dipl.* 156 of AD 298). Urban cohorts,

Dipl. 133 (Lugdunum, AD 192), 134, 137 (AD 216). *Equites singulares*, Dipl. 144 (AD 230), 146 (AD 237), Fleets, Dipl. 138, 152, 154 (AD 250). Doubtful, Dipl. 141, 150, 157 (AD 301?/5).

478 The praetorian guard, the *equites singulares*, and urban cohorts (except for the cohorts at Lyons and Carthage), were stationed at Rome, the fleet principally at Misenum and Ravenna.

479 *Legio II Parthica* was raised by Severus *c.* 197, and campaigned with him in the East. After its return to Italy its HQ remained at Albanum, though the legion saw service all over the Empire. Under Elagabalus it was honoured with the title *pia fidelis*.

480 Marcel Durry, *Les cohortes prétoriennes* (Paris 1938), 294–7. He makes use of *CIL* VI 32678: D(is) m(anibus). M. Varsilio Martiali vet(erano) ex coh(orte) IIII pr(aetoria) Varsilia Stacte patrono idem coniugi b(ene) m(erenti) fecit, cum qua vix(it) an(nis) XVI. His interpretation of this inscription is that Stacte, a slave, took the name Varsilia Stacte on being freed by Varsilius. He believes that Varsilius continued to be her *patronus* so long as he remained in service in the guard, and became her *coniux* in the strict sense only after his *honesta missio* had given him *conubium*. Even if all this is so, and the inscription is third-century, very little can be deduced. Permission to marry does not carry with it an obligation to marry, and the parties concerned may have been quite happy to continue in the patron-client relationship. For the marriage of sailors cf. J. Carcopino, *Mélanges Thomas* (1930), 97–8.

481 Starr, *op. cit.*, p. 93.

482 Dio (LII 24) allows to the praetorian prefects capital jurisdiction over all troops stationed in Italy with the exception of centurions and units commanded by officers of senatorial rank. This jurisdiction would cover all units in Italy except the urban cohorts. But note the reservations expressed by Durry, *op. cit.*, 165–71, and Passerini, *Le coorti pretorie* (Rome 1939), 226–45. Durry in *RE* XXII, 2 (1954), *s.v.* 'praetoriae cohortes', writes (p. 1622), 'Seit Commodus und dem Präfekt Perennis haben die *praef. praet.* faktisch alle Heere befehligt.' In practice, the military competence of the praetorian prefects in the third century was more closely analogous to that of the Chief of the General Staff.

483 Diplomas 138, 152 and 154 attest the 28-year period.

484 Dipl. 122.

485 Starr, *op. cit.*, 81.

486 Cf. P. Salway, *AA*[4] XXXVI (1958), 239: 'This alteration in the living arrangements of the troops has often been represented as part of a change from a mobile professional army to a peasant militia. Nothing could be further from the truth ... The change is, in fact, merely the introduction of a form of married quarters.' In a recent work, *The Frontier People of Roman Britain* (1965), 31 f., Salway retracts his former opinion and instead considers Severus's action to have been 'the simple reform of a legal

anomaly'. A different view is expressed by Ramsay MacMullen, *Soldier and Civilian in the Later Roman Empire* (1963), 127: 'On the other hand, the effect of the new policy should not be underestimated. Parts of forts were now given over to soldiers and their wives who chose to live "on the job" ... By the middle of the fourth century the authorities accepted soldiers' families as a necessary evil, and knowing how dangerous it was to separate the men from them, put at their disposal the public transportation to bring "only (!) their wives, children, and their slaves bought with their camp savings" to some new post of duty. This was what followed— though only over a span of several generations—from Septimius Severus's marriage policy.'

487 Cf. MacMullen, *loc. cit.* But J. J. Wilkes, 'Rebuilding in Hadrian's Wall forts', *Britain and Rome* (1965), 114–38, writes (130 f.): 'As regards the population dwelling within the fort (Housesteads) there is the possibility, not, it is true, supported by any evidence, that non-combatants were permitted to dwell within the forts.' He concludes: 'Because the remains of the forts of the *limitanei* do not compare with those of the earlier period, built under the supervision of legionary technicians with their fastidious attention to accuracy, there is no reason to infer that they did not carry out their duties effectively.' Contrast Sir I. A. Richmond, *Roman and Native in North Britain* (1958), 123 f.: 'The new work of AD 369 is clumsy botching. ... Even more markedly than the clumsy building, the planning diverges from military tradition. ... Civil settlements and forts are in fact merged, and the garrison, if it may be dignified by the name, is no longer a regular unit but a para-military community, comprising soldier-settlers and their families, gathered wholly within the protecting ring of the fort walls. ... It is not first seen in Britain: in North Africa, for example, it had been a commonplace on the Tripolitanian frontier for over a hundred years.'

488 For *canabae* see MacMullen, *op. cit.*, 119–25, and for the distinction between *vicus* and *canabae* see now Salway, *The Frontier People of Roman Britain* (1965), 9 ff.

489 *RIB* 899 (Old Carlisle): I.O.M. et V(u)lk(ano) pro salute d(omini) n(ostri) M. Anto(ni) Gordiani P(ii) F(elicis) Aug(usti) vik(anorum) mag(istri) aram a(ere) col(lato) a v(ikanis) d(edicaverunt).

*RIB* 1616 (Housesteads): Iul(ius) S[. . .] d(ecreto) vica(norum).

*RIB* 1700 (Chesterholm): pro domu divina et numinibus Augustorum Volcano sacrum vicani Vindolandesses curam agente [. . .]o[. . .] v(otum) s(olverunt) l(ibentes) [m(erito)].

*JRS* XLVII (1957), 229 f. no. 18 (Carriden): I.O.M. vikani consi[s]-tentes castel[lo] Veluniate cur[am] agente Ael(io) Mansueto v(otum) s(olverunt) l(aeti) l(ibentes) m(erito).

The inscription from Old Carlisle is securely dated to AD 238–44, those from Housesteads and Chesterholm probably belong to the third century also. Salway, *Frontier People*, 162, provisionally assigns Carriden to the second century. He adds that the discovery of a significant quantity of fourth-century pottery at Cramond has radically changed the previous picture, and that it now seems more likely 'that these coastal sites were held well after the abandonment of the Antonine Wall as a system—if not continuously, at least by successive commanders campaigning into Scotland.' He also points out (p. 68) that in the strip between Hadrian's Wall and the Vallum no civil buildings have yet been found that can be dated before the reign of Septimius Severus, and that the only *vici* in the area of Hadrian's Wall known to have existed before the third century are at Stanwix and at Housesteads *south* of the Vallum.

490 Cf. Sir I. A. Richmond in *Eburacum. Roman York, RCHM* (1962) xxxv ff. Britain was divided into two provinces not later than AD 220, though the earliest epigraphic evidence for the *colonia* of York is a dedication by a York merchant at Bordeaux in AD 237 (*JRS* XI, 1921, 102). The probabilities would seem to be in favour of the division having been made in the early years of Caracalla, in spite of Herodian III 8, 1–2. Cf. now A. J. Graham, 'The Division of Britain', *JRS* LVI (1966), 92 ff.

491 *Cod. Theod.*, VII, 1, 3 (AD 349), see n. 471 above. Cf. *Amm. Marc.*, XX, 4, 11: Iulianus contemplans rationabiles querelas, cum familiis eos ad orientem proficisci praecepit, clavularis cursus facultate permissa.

492 For the *limitanei* see now A. H. M. Jones, *The Later Roman Empire*, II (1964), 649–55, who disposes of the traditional view (most recently restated by MacMullen, *op. cit.*) that the *limitanei* were hereditary cultivators.

493 For the desertion of recruits cf. A. H. M. Jones, *op. cit.*, 618 f. Jones finds two main periods for desertion in general, 379–383, and 403–406. These periods correspond to the years immediately after Adrianople, to Alaric's first invasion of Italy, and to the aftermath of Radagaesus' invasion. (Cf. p. 648 and n. 94.) Britain had its own problems: the *barbarica conspiratio*, as Ammianus calls it (XXVII, 8, 1), led to a wave of desertion, and Count Theodosius had to grant an amnesty (XXVII, 8, 10): denique edictis propositis impunitateque promissa, desertores ad procinctum vocabat et multos alios per diversa libero commeatu dispersos. quo monitu rediere plerique, incentivo perciti.

# THE SOLDIER IN SOCIETY

494 Cf. Ramsay Macmullen, *Soldier and Civilian in the Later Roman Empire* (Cambridge, Mass. 1963), preface.

495 See above, pp. 77 f. and n. 182.

496 Cf. Ramsay MacMullen, *op. cit.*, 23 ff. and 'Roman Imperial Building in the Provinces', *Harvard Studies in Classical Philology* 1959, 214 ff.

497 For the career of an *architectus* who was legionary trained, transferred to the Praetorian Guard, and then given a higher post as an *evocatus*, cf. *CIL*

VI 2725 (= *ILS* 2034 add.): C. Vedennius C.f. Qui(rina) Moderatus Antio(chia) milit(avit) in leg. XVI Gal. a(nnos) X, tran(s)lat(us) in coh. IX pr(aetoriam), in qua milit(avit) ann(os) VIII, missus honesta mission(e), revocatus ab imp(eratore) fact(us) evoc(atus) Aug(usti) arc(h)itect(us) armament(arii) imp(eratoris), evoc(atus) ann(os) XXIII, donis militarib(us) donat(us) bis ab divo Vesp(asiano) et imp(eratore) Domitiano Aug(usto) Germ(anico). His working life thus lasted 41 years.

498 Pliny, *epp.* X 41, 3: superest ut tu libratorem vel architectum si tibi videbitur mittas. Trajan's reply (*ibid*, 42): poteris a Calpurnio Macro petere libratorem.

499 SHA, *Probus* 9, 3: extant apud Aegyptum eius opera, quae per milites struxit, in plurimis civitatibus. in Nilo autem tam multa fecit, ut vectigal frumentarium solus adiuverit. pontes, templa, porticus, basilicas labore militum struxit, ora fluminum multa patefecit, paludes plerasque siccavit atque in his segetes agrosque constituit.

500 *ibid.*, 9, 2: per milites, quos otiosos esse numquam est passus.

501 With unusual candour the author of the life of Probus admits that he has almost no literary evidence anyway (SHA, *Probus* 1, 3: scriptorum inopia iam paene nescimus). Cf. Sir Ronald Syme, *Ammianus and the Historia Augusta* (Oxford 1968), 98 and 102.

502 Cf. Hans Zwicky, *Zur Verwendung des Militärs in der Verwaltung des römischen Kaiserzeit* (Diss. Zürich 1944), 76 ff., who cites the relevant inscriptions.

503 Cf. Domaszewski-Dobson 108.

504 Inscriptions which attest the centurion's function as a technical expert are naturally rare, but cf. *ILS* 8716a: L. Aelio Caesare n. II et Balbino cos (AD 137), rationi urbicae, sub cur. Irenaei Aug. lib. proc., caesura Tulli Saturnini 7 leg. XXII Prim. *ILS* 8716b is almost identical.

505 *CIL* XI 707 (= *ILS* 2705), Bononia: Q. Manilio C.f. Cordo 7 leg. XXI Rapac., praef. equit., exact. tribut. Gall.

506 Cf. for instance *CIL* III 9864a (= *ILS* 5950), Vaganj (Dalmatia): L. Arruntius Camil[l]us Scrib[o]nianus le[g.] pro pr. C. [C]aesaris Aug. Germanici, iudicem dedit M. Coelium 7 leg. VII enter Sapuates et [La]-matinos, ut fines [reg]eret et terminus (*sic*) po[neret].

507 Tacitus, *Ann.* II 65: deligit centurionem qui nuntiaret regibus ne armis disceptaret. *ibid.*, XIII 9: accepitque eos centurio Insteius ab Vmmidio missus, forte prior ea de causa adito rege. *ibid.*, XV 5: Casperius centurio in eam legationem delectus apud oppidum Nisibin, septem et triginta milibus passuum a Tigranocerta distantem, adit regem et mandata ferociter edidit. *Hist.*, II 58: inde Cluvio Rufo metus, et decimam legionem propinquare litori ut transmissurus iussit; praemissi centuriones qui Maurorum animos Vitellio conciliarent. In *AE* 1903, 368 (= *ILS* 9200), from Heliopolis (Syria), we have the career of a *primus pilus* who combined a number of special duties with considerable active service: C. Velio Salvi f.

Rufo p.p. leg. XII Fulm., praef. vexillariorum leg. VIIII (sic): I Adiut., II Adiut., II Aug., VIII Aug., VIIII Hisp., XIIII Gem., XX Vic, XXI Rapac., trib. coh. XIII urb., duci exercitus Africi et Mauretanici ad nationes, quae sunt in Mauretania, comprimendas, donis donato ab. imp. Vespasiano et imp. Tito bello Iudaico corona vallar(i), torquibus, fa[le]ris, armillis, item donis donato corona murali, hastis duabus, vexillis duobus et bello Marcomannorum, Quadorum, Sarmatarum, adversus quos expeditionem fecit per regnum Decebali regis Dacorum, corona murali, hastis duabus, vexillis duobus, proc. imp. Caesaris Aug. Germanici provinciae Pannoniae et Delmatiae, item proc. provinciae Raetiae ius gla[d]i. hic missus in Parthiam Epiphanen et Callinicum regis Antiochi filios ad imp. Vespasianum cum ampla manu tributariorum reduxit.

508 Cf. Pliny's request to Trajan (X 77): Providentissime, domine, fecisti, quod praecepisti Calpurnio Macro, clarissimo viro, ut legionarium centurionem Byzantium mitteret. dispice an etiam Iuliopolitanis simili ratione consulendum putes . . . and Trajan's refusal (X 78): Ea condicio est civitatis Byzantiorum confluente undique in eam commeantium turba, ut secundum consuetudinem praecedentium temporum honoribus eius praesidio centurionis legionarii consulendum habuerimus. Si Iuliopolitanis succurrendum eodem modo putaverimus, onerabimus nos exemplo . . . .

509 These *beneficiarii* were normally detached from the governor's staff, as their titles *beneficiarius consularis* or *beneficiarius procuratoris* show. Cf. Zwicky, *op. cit.*, 83.

510 See above, p. 85.

511 Cf. W. G. Sinnigen, 'The origins of the *frumentarii*', *Memoirs of the American Academy in Rome* XXVII (1962), 213–24. He shows that there is no positive first-century evidence of their existence: *P. Gen. lat.* I recto ii, with the words *exit cum frum(entariis)*, is the strongest evidence, but even this depends upon the expansion to *frum(entariis)*, and *frum(ento)* remains possible. He concludes, however, that 'their use in the imperial administration, positively datable in Trajan's reign, probably began at a slightly earlier period in connection with the major changes in the army supply service made by Domitian.'

512 For the *castra peregrinorum* see T. Ashby and P. K. Baillie Reynolds, 'The Castra Peregrinorum', *JRS* XIII (1923), 152–67. Cf. also P. K. Baillie Reynolds, 'The Troops Quartered in the Castra Peregrinorum,' *JRS* XIII 168–9.

513 This is the view of W. G. Sinnigen, *op. cit.*, 213, and 'Two Branches of the Late Roman Secret Service,' *AJPh* LXXX (1959), 238–54, where he describes the activities of the *agentes in rebus* and the *notarii*. The importance of the former, however, is played down by A. H. M. Jones, *The Later Roman Empire* (Oxford 1964), 581 f.: 'The *agentes in rebus* have achieved a rather sinister reputation as a kind of secret police. It is based on the activities of certain members of the corps who made themselves notorious in

Constantius II's reign by ferreting out and denouncing treasonable plots, real and alleged. But they were by no means alone in exploiting that emperor's suspicious temper—several notaries gained as sinister a reputation—and there is no reason to believe that the *agentes in rebus* in normal times had any police functions except as inspectors of the post.'

514 *Res Gestae* 28: Italia autem XXVIII [colo]nias, quae vivo me celeberrimae et frequentissimae fuerunt, me[a auctoritate] deductas habet. For Augustus's policy in colonization see F. Vittinghoff, *Römische Kolonisation und Bürgerrechtspolitik unter Caesar und Augustus*, Abh. der Wiss. Mainz, Geist. und soz. Kl. 1951, 14 (Wiesbaden 1952). For the general question of discharge and resettlement, see also my comments in *Neue Beiträge zur Geschichte der alten Welt, Band II, Römisches Reich* (Berlin 1965), 147–62.

515 *Res Gestae* 17: et M. Lepido et L. Ar[r]unt[i]o cos. in aerarium militare, quod ex consilio m[eo] co[ns]titutum est, ex [q]uo praemia darentur militibus, qui vicena [aut plu]ra sti[pendi]a emeruissent, HS milliens et septing[e]nti[ens ex pa]t[rim]onio [m]eo detuli. Suetonius, *Div. Aug.* 49: quidquid autem ubique militum esset, ad certam stipendiorum praemiorumque formulam adstrinxit definitis pro gradu cuiusque et temporibus militiae et commodis missionum.

516 Dio LV 23.

517 Tacitus, *Ann.* I 17: ac si quis tot casus vita superaverit, trahi adhuc diversas in terras ubi per nomen agrorum uligines paludum vel inculta montium accipiant.

518 Tacitus, *Ann.* XIV 27: veterani Tarentum et Antium adscripti non tamen infrequentiae locorum subvenere, dilapsis pluribus in provincias in quibus stipendia expleverant; neque coniugiis suscipiendis neque alendis liberis sueti orbas sine posteris domos relinquebant. non enim, ut olim, universae legiones deducebantur cum tribunis et centurionibus et sui cuiusque ordinis militibus ut consensu et caritate rem publicam efficerent, sed ignoti inter se, diversis manipulis, sine rectore, sine adfectibus mutuis, quasi ex alio genere mortalium repente in unum collecti, numerus magis quam colonia.

519 It remained standard practice until the middle of the second century that men be discharged every other year, cf. A. Passerini s.v. 'legio' in *Diz. epigr.* IV 612, and *CIL* XVI p. 187. A. Alföldi jr., 'Zur Enstehung der Colonia Claudia Savaria,' *Archaeologiai Ertesitö* IV (1943), 81 n. 3, points out that Tacitus mentions only *diversis manipulis* and not different legions. But this makes nonsense of the spirit of the passage. It is not clear whether the *colonia* of 3000 legionaries which was established at Cyrene in the last year of Trajan was drawn solely from *legio* XV *Apollinaris*. Cf. *JRS* XL (1950), 84 and 87 f.; *PIR²* G 100; Syme, *Tacitus* 447, n. 4.

520 Cf. A. Passerini, *Le coorti pretorie*, 124, and G. Forni, *Il reclutamento delle legioni da Augusto a Diocleziano* (Milan 1953), 37.

521 The presence of veterans of these classes in *canabae* or *vici* does not imply that they received the *praemia* either in cash or in land.

522 *CIL* XVI, Dipl. 12–16.

523 Cf. C. G. Starr, *The Roman Imperial Navy* (ed. 2, Cambridge 1960), 94 and n. 110.

524 *CIL* XVI, Dipl. 10 and 17.

525 The view that non-citizens were not entitled to the *praemia militiae* has been expressed by Domaszewski, *Truppensold* 222, n. 2, and Vittinghoff, *op. cit.*, 23. Cheesman, *Auxilia* 34, left the matter uncertain.

526 P. A. Brunt, 'Pay and Superannuation in the Roman Army,' *PBSR* XVIII, NS V (1950), 66.

527 See above, p. 136.

528 Tacitus, *Ann.* I 8: praetoriarum cohortium militibus singula nummum milia, urbanis quingenos, legionariis aut cohortibus civium Romanorum trecenos nummos viritim dedit. Cf. Dio LVI 32. Passerini, *op. cit.*, 108, does not accept the view that equal consideration in respect of legacies was matched by equal consideration in respect of pay.

529 In *CIL* XVI, Dipl. 38 (13 July 93) the grant is recorded of citizenship and *conubium* to veterans of *cohors VIII voluntariorum civium Romanorum*, who are further defined as those *qui peregrinae condicionis probati erant*. This means that as early as AD 68 the *cohortes civium Romanorum* were being at least in part recruited from *peregrini*. If, as seems probable, it was Claudius who instituted the practice of issuing diplomas to ex-auxiliaries, it may have been his intention to standardize the position of the *auxilia*, and to eliminate the distinction between the *cohortes civium Romanorum* and the other cohorts.

530 See above, p. 104.

531 See n. 280 above.

532 See nn. 279 and 282 above.

533 Yet it is possible that my remarks in *Historia* V (1956), 337 could apply equally well to Praetorians: 'It is quite possible that in the same way as pay was standardized throughout the empire, so compulsory deductions for rations and other deductions for replacements of clothing and service requisites were made at a figure which took no account of local variations in the cost of living, but placed all similar units on terms of equality irrespective of station, whether this be on the Rhine, the Danube or the Nile.'

534 See p. 105 above.

535 See p. 44 above.

536 See n. 278 above and no. 139 in Appendix C. The amount is made up of 1459 *denarii* withdrawn from deposit in col. ii 28 and of 103 *denarii* withdrawn for arms in ii 44.

537 The figures are given in col. iii 72–75.

538 Columella (III 3, 8) suggests that a usual return was 6 per cent.

539 A. R. Burn, 'Hic breve vivitur: A Study of the Expectation of Life in the Roman Empire,' *Past and Present* IV (1953), 1–31.

540 *op. cit.*, 10.

541 *op. cit.*, 9 f. Cf. also the graph on p. 26 and the table on p. 20.

542 Burn's table (p. 23) yields the following comparisons for the military and civilian male population:
(i) At Lambaesis, of those alive at age 17, 55.2 per cent of the soldiers reached the age of 42, 19.6 per cent reached age 62, and only 2 per cent lived to be 82 years old. Of the civilians, 56.1 per cent reached age 42, 33.9 per cent reached age 62, and as many as 8.2 per cent lived to be aged 82.
(ii) In the Danubian provinces, the corresponding figures for soldiers are 45.4 per cent, 13.7 per cent, and 2.5 per cent; for civilians they are 53.4 per cent, 21.7 per cent, and 4.2 per cent. These figures are all lower than those for Lambaesis except that for soldiers over 82, which is very slightly higher.

543 See above, p. 140.

544 Cf. Peter Salway, *The Frontier People of Roman Britain* (Cambridge 1965), 29.

545 *CIL* V 5747 (= *ILS* 2465 and Smallwood, *Gaius* 290), Monza: C. Sertorius L.f. Ouf. Te[rtull] us veteranus leg. XVI civium Roman[or.] Moguntiaci——

546 Cf. Salway, *loc. cit.*

# APPENDIX A

*P. Gen. Lat. 1 recto I*

L ASINIO COS
Q IVLIVS PROCVLVS DAM

[Accepit]stip I an III do     dr ccxlviii
    Ex eis
[fae]naria     dr x
in v[ic]tum     dr lxxx
cal[i]gas fascias     dr xii
[saturna]licium k     dr xx
in [vesti]torium     dr lx
    Ex[pen]sas     dr clxxxii
[reliqua]s deposuit     dr lxvi
et habuit ex prio     dr cxxxvi
fit [s]umma     dr ccii

Accepit stip II anni eiusd     dr ccxlviii
    [E]x eis
f[a]enaria     dr x
in victum     dr lxxx
caligas fascias     dr xii
[ad]signa     dr iv
    Ex[p]ensas     dr c[vi]
reliquas deposuit     dr cxlii
[et h]abuit ex prior[e]     dr ccii
fit summa omnis     dr cccxl[iv]

A[c]ce[pit sti]p III a[nn]i
    [e]ius[d]     dr ccxlviii
    [E]x eis
faen[a]ria     [dr x]
[in victum     dr lxxx]
[caligas fascias     dr] xii
in vestim[en]t[i]s     [d]r [cxl]vi
    Expensas     [d]r ccxlviii
habet in deposito     dr cccxliv

C VALERIVS GERMANVS TYR

Accepit stip I an III do dr ccxlviii
    Ex eis
faenaria     dr x
in v[i]ctum     [d]r lxxx
caligas fascias     dr xii
saturnalicium k     dr xx
in vestimen[tu]m     dr c
    Expensas     dr ccxxii
reliquas depo     dr xxvi
et habuit     dr [xx]
fit summa omnis     dr [x]lvi

Accepit stip II anni eius dr ccxlviii
    Ex eis
faenaria     [d]r x
in victum     dr lxxx
caligas fascias     dr xii
ad signa     dr iv
    Expensas     dr cvi
r[eliq]uas deposuit     dr cxlii
et habuit ex priore     dr xlvi
fit summa omnis     dr cl[xxxviii]

Accepit stip III anni
    [eiusd     d]r ccxlviii
    Ex eis
faenaria     [d]r x
in victum     [d]r lxxx
caligas fascias     [d]r [x]ii
in vestimentis     dr cxlvi
habet in deposito     dr clxxxviii

RENNIVS INNOCENS

AD 81

| Q. Iulius Proculus of Damascus | dr | |
|---|---|---|
| Recd 1st pay of 3rd yr of our Lord | | 248 |
| Deductions: | | |
| Bedding? | 10 | |
| Food | 80 | |
| Boots and straps | 12 | |
| Regt. dinner? | 20 | |
| Clothing | 60 | |
| | — | |
| Total expenses | 182 | |
| Remainder on deposit | | 66 |
| Previous balance | | 136 |
| | | — |
| Present balance | | 202 |
| Recd 2nd pay of 3rd yr of our Lord | | 248 |
| Deductions: | | |
| Bedding? | 10 | |
| Food | 80 | |
| Boots and straps | 12 | |
| Burial club? | 4 | |
| | — | |
| Total expenses | 106 | |
| Remainder on deposit | | 142 |
| Previous balance | | 202 |
| | | — |
| Present balance | | 344 |
| Recd 3rd pay of 3rd yr of our Lord | | 248 |
| Deductions: | | |
| Bedding? | 10 | |
| Food | 80 | |
| Boots and straps | 12 | |
| Clothing | 146 | |
| | — | |
| Total expenses | 248 | |
| Present balance | | 344 |

*Rennius Innocens*

| C. Valerius Germanus of Tyre | dr | |
|---|---|---|
| Recd 1st pay of 3rd yr of our Lord | | 248 |
| Deductions: | | |
| Bedding? | 10 | |
| Food | 80 | |
| Boots and straps | 12 | |
| Regt. dinner? | 20 | |
| Clothing | 100 | |
| | — | |
| Total expenses | 222 | |
| Remainder on deposit | | 26 |
| Previous balance | | 20 |
| | | — |
| Present balance | | 46 |
| Recd 2nd pay of 3rd yr of our Lord | | 248 |
| Deductions: | | |
| Bedding? | 10 | |
| Food | 80 | |
| Boots and straps | 12 | |
| Burial club? | 4 | |
| | — | |
| Total expenses | 106 | |
| Remainder on deposit | | 142 |
| Previous balance | | 46 |
| | | — |
| Present balance | | 188 |
| Recd 3rd pay of 3rd yr of our Lord | | 248 |
| Deductions: | | |
| Bedding? | 10 | |
| Food | 80 | |
| Boots and straps | 12 | |
| Clothing | 146 | |
| | — | |
| Present balance | | 188 |

| APPENDIX B<br>P. Gen. lat. 1 verso V | 1<br>K<br>domiti[ | 2<br>VI nonis<br>domitiani | 3<br>V nonas<br>domitia[ |
|---|---|---|---|
| I     C DOMITIVS ÇE[LER] | | | |
| II    C AEMILIVS VALE[NS] | | ornatus | heli |
| III   C IVLIVS VAL[E]NS | harena 7 | phal | ad cuniç 7 |
| IV    L IVLIVS OCT[AV]IA[NVS] | — | | |
| V     P CLODIVS [S]ECVNDV[S] | pro | quin | ta |
| VI    M ARRIVS NIGER | | | in 7 |
| VII   L SEXTILIVS G[E]R[MA]N[VS] | stapor | signis | ballio |
| VIII  C IVLIVS F . . . . | | phal | specula |
| IX    Q CASSIVS RV[F]VS | insula | | |
| X     C IVLIVS LONGVS SIDO | pro | quin | ta |
| XI    C IVLIVS LONGVS AVSO | — | | exit cu[m] |
| XII   T FLAVIVS PRISCVS | | | |
| XIII  T FLAVIVS NIG[ER] | de.e.e | trib | — |
| XIV   M ANTONIVS CRI[SPVS] | ballio | fercla | in 7 |
| XV    . NVM . . . . . . | | sta princip | . . . |
| XVI   Q PETR[ON]IVS | | . . . . . . . .<br>arm . . . . | . . . |
| XVII  . CAR . . . . . . . . S | . . . | . | |

| 4 | 5 | 6 | 7 | 8 | 9 | 10 |
|---|---|---|---|---|---|---|
| IV no dom[ | III no dom[ | pr no do[ | nonis domit[ | VIII idus domitiani | VII idus dom[ | VI idus do[ |
| | | | | | b pref com | C |
| — | — | | goṣṣ[..].. | arma metor | ballio | in 7 |
| ad cal | arma mentạ | arma mentar | ba[l]lịọ | galeari ato | in 7 | ba[llio] |
| | in 7 | ballio | sta prin cipis | vianico | in 7 | pr . . . |
| ne | sio | | stapor | calcem | cal hel | |
| | strigiṣ | strigis | strigis | strigis | strigis | st[rigis] |
| phal | d d[ecri] 7 | d. decri 7 | d. decri 7 | d. decri 7 | d. decri 7 | d de[cri 7] |
| | ṣereni 7 | sereni 7 | sereni 7 | sereni 7 | sereni 7 | se[reni 7] |
| | | | | | | cal[ |
| ne | sio | in 7 heli | — | — | | in [7] |
| asin | ạḍ çạ[l] | . . . . | | | | |
| | stati ad terenu | | | | | |
| — | — | — | — | — | — | |
| pagano cultu | in 7 | | comẹs | tr | — | |
| | in 7 | in 7 | | vianico | in 7 | |
| ballio | ballio | pro | quin | ta n | ẹṣ[io] | |
| . . . | — | — | — | — | | |

| | | 1 | 2 | 3 |
|---|---|---|---|---|
| | | K<br>domiti[ | VI nonis<br>domitiani | V nonas<br>domitia[ |
| XVIII | Ç AEMILIVS ....... | | çọmesseṛ | ... |
| XIX | C VALERỊVṢ ...... | cọm pilị | ... cus | |
| XX | Ṭ FLAVIVS ...... | | | |
| XXI | Q FABIVṢ ḶABEṚ | [b]a[l]lio | stapor | |
| XXII | M MA[R]Ç[IVS] ÇLẸMENS | exit aḍ | horṃ. ... | ạeḷ |
| XXIII | C VALERIVS FELIX | çạeç. | — | |
| XXIV | C CERFICIVS FVSCVS | | | |
| XXV | Ṭ FVṚ[I]ṾṢ ......... | | | ... niç |
| XXVI | L GALL ......... | | | p̣ha[l] |
| XXVII | Q ANNỊṾ[S] | ṣcopariụs | | |
| XXVIII | Q V .......... ÇO | sṭ[a]prin | | |
| XXIX | Ṃ LONGINV[S] | | | |
| XXX | M DOMITIVṢ ..... Ọ | | | exit |
| XXXI | M LONGINVS A ...... | | | .. ṛ |
| XXXII | M IVLIVS FELỊX | çọmess | — | — |
| XXXIII | T FLAVIVS VALENṢ | | | |
| XXXIV | C SOSSIVS ÇELER | | | |
| XXXV | L VI ..... EIVS SERENVS | | | |
| XXXVI | Ṃ IṾLỊVS LONGVS | | | |

| 4 | 5 | 6 | 7 | 8 | 9 | 10 |
|---|---|---|---|---|---|---|
| IV no dom[ | III no dom[ | pr no do[ | nonis domit[ | VIII idus domitiani | VII idus dom[ | VI idus do[ |
| | | pro | quin | tane | s[io] | |
| | ... | d ḍecr[i 7] | d decri 7 | d [d]ec[ri 7] | | |
| b[allio] | ba[l]li[o] | ballio | s[t]apor | ... | | |
| b[al]li[o] | bạ[l]ḷiọ | ballio | balli[o] | [bal]li[o] | | |
| | | — | — | — | | |
| [sta]p[o]r | stạ[p]oṛ | ḅ .... | | [i]ṇ 7 | | |
| | ị ... | in 7 | arṃ[a] [m]ẹntạ | ... | | |
| | | | ... | via[ni]çọ | ... | |
| | | | st[apo]ṛ | | | |
| [ad fru | me]ṇtụ | m ṇeap | oḷi | | | |
| | | aḍ stercus 7 | | | | |
| — | — | stapor | — | — | | |
| | | | | | | |
| | | | | | | |
| | | | | | | |

| | | 1 Oct. | 2 Oct. | 3 Oct. |
|---|---|---|---|---|
| I | C DOMITIVS CE[LER] | | | |
| II | C AEMILIVS VALE[NS] | | Batman to Helius | |
| III | C IVLIVS VAL[ENS] | Training area | Tower? | Drainage |
| IV | L IVLIVS OCT[AV]IA[NVS] | As before | | |
| V | P CLODIVS [S]ECVNDV[S] | Camp | Market | Duty? |
| VI | M ARRIVS NIGER | | | In century |
| VII | L SEXTILIVS G[E]R[MA]N[VS] | Gate guard | Standards | Baths |
| VIII | C IVLIVS F.... | | Tower? | Watch |
| IX | Q CASSIVS RV[F]VS | Island | | |
| X | C IVLIVS LONGVS SIDO | Camp | Market | Duty? |
| XI | C IVLIVS LONGVS AVSO | As before | | On detach |
| XII | T FLAVIVS PRISCVS | | | |
| XIII | T FLAVIVS NIG[ER] | Departed without tribune? | | |
| XIV | M ANTONIVS CRI[SPVS] | Baths | Stretchers | In century |
| XV | . NVM...... | | HQ Guard | ... |
| XVI | Q PETR[ON]IVS | | ? | ... |
| XVII | . CAR........S | ... | . | |

| 4 Oct. | 5 Oct. | 6 Oct. | 7 Oct. | 8 Oct. | 9 Oct. | 10 Oct. |
|---|---|---|---|---|---|---|
| | | | | | Leave by Prefect's permission | |
| — | — | | Cotton guard? | Armoury | Baths | In century |
| Boots | Armoury | | Baths | Orderly | In century | Baths |
| | In century | Baths | HQ Guard | Road Patrol | In century | ? |
| | | | Gate Guard | Boots | Helius' boots | |
| | | Lines | Fatigue | | | |
| Tower? | Duty in D. Decrius' century | | | | | |
| | Duty in Serenus' century | | | | | |
| | | | | | | Boots |
| | | Duty in Helius' century | | | | In century |
| ment with Asinius for boots? | | | | | | |
| | Rampart Guard | | | | | |

| 4 Oct. | 5 Oct. | 6 Oct. | 7 Oct. | 8 Oct. | 9 Oct. | 10 Oct. |
|---|---|---|---|---|---|---|
| Plain Clothes | In century | | Tribune's escort | | | |
| | In century | In century | | Road Patrol | In century | |
| Baths | Baths | Camp Market Duty? | | | | |
| . . . | — | — | — | — | | |

| | | 1 Oct. | 2 Oct. | 3 Oct. |
|---|---|---|---|---|
| XVIII | C AEMILIVS ....... | | Escort to Serenus | |
| XIX | C VALERIVS ...... | Escort to Chief Centurion | ? | |
| XX | T FLAVIVS ...... | | | |
| XXI | Q FABIVS FABER | Baths | Gate Guard | |
| XXII | M MA[R]C[IVS] CLEMENS | | On detachment to | |
| XXIII | C VALERIVS FELIX | | Duty in Caecilius' | |
| XXIV | C CERFICIVS FVSCVS | | | |
| XXV | T FVR[I]VS ......... | | | Road Patrol? |
| XXVI | L GALL......... | | | Tower? |
| XXVII | Q ANNIV[S] | Street cleaning | | |
| XXVIII | Q V........... CO | HQ Guard | | |
| XXIX | M LONGINV[S] | | | |
| XXX | M DOMITIVS ..... O | | | On |
| XXXI | M LONGINVS A ...... | | | ? |
| XXXII | M IVLIVS FELIX | Escort to Serenus? | | |
| XXXIII | T FLAVIVS VALENS | | | |
| XXXIV | C SOSSIVS CELER | | | |
| XXXV | L VI...... EIVS SERENVS | | | |
| XXXVI | M IVLIVS LONGVS | | | |

| 4 Oct. | 5 Oct. | 6 Oct. | 7 Oct. | 8 Oct. | 9 Oct. | 10 Oct. |
|--------|--------|--------|--------|--------|--------|---------|
| | | Camp Market Duty? | | | | |
| | . . . | Duty in D. Decrius' century | | | | |
| Baths | Baths | Baths | Gate Guard | . . . | | |
| Baths | Baths | Baths | Baths | Baths | | |

harbours with Aelius?

| | | | | | | |
|--------|--------|--------|--------|--------|--------|---------|
| century? | — | — | — | | | |
| Gate Guard | Gate Guard | Baths? | | In century | | |
| | In century? | In century | Armoury | ? | | |
| | | | ? | Road Patrol | ? | |
| | | | | | | |
| | | | Gate Guard | | | |
| | | | | | | |

detachment to the granaries at Neapolis

| | | | | | | |
|--------|--------|--------|--------|--------|--------|---------|
| | | Latrines | | | | |
| — | — | Gate Guard | — | — | | |
| | | | | | | |
| | | | | | | |
| | | | | | | |
| | | | | | | |

I   9   b(eneficio) pref(ecti) com(meatus)
   10   C(ommeatus)
II  7   g[l]oss(ocoma) *Nicole* gos f *Nicole* goni *Premerstein*
        goss *Marichal* (*cf.* gossipion *Plin. NH XIX 2.*
        *6*) *sed*
        *ad stationes melius convenit* g[r]om(a) (*cf. Dura Final*
        *Report V Part I, p. 378*)
    9   *et passim* ballio *ad balneum refert Premerstein* (*cf.*
        *P. Dura 82, ii 9*)
III 2   phal(is) *vel* phal(aricis) *potius quam* phal(eris) *Morel*
    3   ad cunic *Morel* ad clinici *Nicole* ad cunic 7
        *Premerstein*
    6   armamenta *Nicole* armamentar(io) *Marichal*
    8   galeariatu *Nicole* galeariato *Marichal*
IV  7   *et passim* sta(tione) principi(i)s *Premerstein potius*
        *quam* sta(tione) principis *Morel*
    8   *et passim* via Nico(politana)
V 1–5   *et passim* pro quintanesio *ad ludum quintanum refert*
        *Premerstein*
    7   *et passim* sta(tione) por(tae)
    8   cal(ceamenta) Hel(i)
X       Sipo *Nicole* Sido(nius) *Marichal*
XI      Miso *Nicole* Auso(nius) *Marichal*
XII 5   stati[o]ad serenu *Nicole* stati(one) ad ter⟨r⟩enu(m)
        (aggerem) *Marichal*
XIII 1, 2  d. . . .e trib *Nicole* de nene trib *pro* de ⟨b⟩ene(ficio)
        trib(uni) *Premerstein* de.e.e trib (*vel* dessesse trib)
        *Marichal* sed *fortasse* des(cendit) sine trib(uno) *est*
        *legendum*
XIV 2   ferc(u)la(rio)
    4   pagane cultus *Nicole* pagano cultu *Morel*
XVI 2   pr. . . .us amenta *Nicole* (*cf.* III 5, 6?)
XVII 1, 2  com[e]s *Nicole*
    4   ballio *Nicole*
XVIII 2  . . . ones *Nicole* comes Ser(eni) *Marichal* C. Valerius
        . . . . . sus *Nicole*
XIX 1   com(es) (primi) pil(i)
    2   *cf.* XXXI 6?

| XX | 7 | papili *Nicole* pr(imi) pili *Morel* |
|---|---|---|
| XXII | 1–3 | exit vi No(nas) c̣uṃ . . . . . . ṛẹḷ . . . *Nicole* exit in om c . . . Ne(apoli)? *vel* in Oss . . . . Ne(apoli)? *Morel* exit ạḍ horṃ . . . . ạeḷ *Marichal, qui sic legendum esse suspicatur:* exit ad horm(os) cum Ael(io) |
| XXIII | 1 | gel *Nicole* Caec(ilii) (centuria) ? *Marichal* |
| XXV | | Ṭ FVRỊVS . . . . . . RVS . . . *Nicole* |
| XXIX | | Ṃ LONGINVṢ ṚVF̣VS Nicole |
| XXXI | 6 | in stercuss *Nicole* ad stercus *Lesquier* ad stercus 7 *Marichal* |
| XXXII | 1–5 | comes S(ereni)? |

# APPENDIX C

1 *Aegyptus* XII (1932) pp. 129 ff. AD 153, Greek. Evidence of the ill-treatment of a veteran by a *magister pagi*. *Sel. Pap.* II 254: *Negotia* 188.

2 XXIII (1945) pp. 153 ff. Second century. Greek. Soldier's receipt.

3 *BGU* I 4. Second-third century. Greek. Veteran's letter to tribune.

4 36. AD 101–2. Greek. Appeal to a centurion by a creditor assaulted by debtors. Mitteis 125; *Documenti* 82.

5 69. AD 120. Greek. Chirograph. Mitteis 142.

6 113. AD 140. Greek. Epicrisis of veterans. Wilcken 458; *CIL* XVI app. 4; *Negotia* 7a; *Documenti* 92.

7 114 + *P. Cattaoui*. Second century. Greek. Decisions in cases resulting from soldiers' illegal marriages. Mitteis 372; *Negotia* 19; *Documenti* 3.

8 140 AD 119. Greek. Letter of Hadrian concerning the rights of soldiers' children. Mitteis 373; *Sel. Pap.* II 213; Girard p. 194; *Leges* 78; *Documenti* 108; Smallwood, *Nerva* 333. Plates in *BGU* I and Schubart, *Papyri Graecae Berolinenses*, 22a.

9 142. AD 159. Greek. Epicrisis certificate of veteran of *cohors II Ulpia*, from Syria. (Cf. *PSI* X 1026). Wilcken 455; *Documenti* 99.

10 143. AD 159. Greek. Epicrisis of sailor. Wilcken 454.

11 161. = *BGU* II 448, *q.v.*

12 180. AD 172. Greek. Petition by veteran for exemption from liturgies. Wilcken 396; Sel. *Pap.* II 285; *Documenti* 105.

13 265 AD 148. Greek. Epicrisis of veterans. Wilcken 459; *CIL* XVI app. 5; *Negotia* p. 17 n. 3; *Documenti* 93.

14 266 AD 138. Greek. Requisition of camels. Wilcken 245; *Documenti* 57.

15 272. AD 138. Greek. Chirograph between veterans. Cancelled by a line across. Mitteis 143.

16 300. AD 148. Greek. Chirograph between veterans. Mitteis 345; *Negotia* 159.

17 326. AD 194. Greek. Copy of a veteran's Latin will. Mitteis 316; Girard pp. 805 ff.; *Sel. Pap.* I 85; *Negotia* 50.

18 344. Second-third century. Greek. List of names, some military.

19 II 378. AD 147. Greek. Petition. Mitteis 60.

20 423. Second century. Greek. Sailor's letter home. Wilcken 480; *Sel. Pap.* I 112; Deissmann, *Licht vom Osten*[2] 120 ff. Plate in Schubart, *Papyri Graecae Berolinenses*, 28.

21 435. Second-third century. Greek. Letter.

22 448. (= I 161). AD 150–3. Greek. Petition to the prefect by a veteran to have his parent's will opened. Mitteis 310.
23 454. 17 June 193. Greek. Denunciation for theft addressed to the centurion. Documenti 79.
24 455. First century. Greek. Chirograph.
25 515. 2 June 193. Greek. Denunciation for acts of violence addressed to the centurion. Wilcken 268, Documenti 78.
26 522. Second century. Greek. Petition by a widow to the centurion. Documenti 80.
27 600. ante AD 140? Greek. Deed with seven military witnesses. Cf. Deissmann, Nachtr. zu BGU II.
28 610. AD 140. Latin. List of ex-soldiers. CPL 115.
29 614. AD 217. Greek. Petition. Wilcken 37.
30 623. Early third century? Greek. Letter.
31 628 verso. First century. Latin. Copy of Edict of Octavian concerning veterans' privileges. Wilcken 462; Girard p. 172 f.; CIL XVI app. 10; Leges 56; Ehrenberg-Jones 302; Calderini 21; CPL 103; Documenti 100.
32 655. AD 215. Greek. Receipt for supply of leather for arms manufacture. Documenti 60.
33 696. AD 156. Pridianum of a cohors equitata. Latin. Schrifttafeln 6; Sel. Pap. II 401; AJPh LXIII (1942) 61–3; Écriture latine 24; CPL 118; Documenti 9. Cf. also Mommsen in EE VII (1892), 456–67 (= Ges. Schr. VIII, 553–66); R. O. Fink, 'Mommsen's Pridianum', AJPh LXIII (1942), 61–71; J. F. Gilliam, 'Paganus in BGU 696', AJPh LXXIII (1952), 75–8; Plates: Schrifttafeln 6; Pal. Soc., Ser. 2, vol. 2, no. 165; Ecriture latine, 24.
34 III 741. AD 143–4. Greek. Pignus. Mitteis 244; Negotia 119.
35 780. AD 154–6. Greek. Epicrisis certificate in red ink. CIL XVI, app. 6; Documenti 94.
36 807. AD 185. Greek. Receipt for military supplies. Schubart, Papyri Graecae Berolinenses, 266.
37 847. AD 182–3. Greek. Epicrisis certificate. Wilcken 460; CIL XVI app. 7; Documenti 96.
38 IV 1032. AD 173. Greek. Epicrisis certificate in red ink.
39 1033. Age of Trajan. Greek. Epicrisis certificate corrected in red ink.
40 1083. First century. Latin. Fragment of matricula. Ecriture latine 21; Calderini 50; CPL 109; Documenti 14.
41 1108. 5 BC. Greek. Contract. Ehrenberg-Jones 262.
42 V 1210. AD 150–61. Greek. Gnomon of the Idios Logos. W. G. Uxkull-Gyllenband, Der Gnomon des Idios Logos, zweiter Teil; Der Kommentar (Berlin 1934), 44 ff.; S. Riccobono, jr., Il Gnomon dell'Idios Logos (Palermo 1950); Sel. Pap. II 206; Leges 99; Documenti 1 and 107.
43 VII 1612. Third century. Greek. Receipt for requisition. Documenti 63.
44 1690. AD 131. Latin. Birth certificate of soldier's illegitimate child. Cagnat, Journ. des Sav., 1927, 197; Wilcken, Archiv VIII (1927), 293; Sanders,

*AJA* XXXII (1928), 329 and *Aegyptus* XVII (1937), 234 n. 161; Schulz, *JRS* XXXII (1942), 79, n. 14; Montevecchi, *Aegyptus* XXVIII (1948), 129 ff., no. 6; *Negotia* 5; *CPL* 160.

45 1695. 7 October 157. Latin. Sailor's will. Calderini 59; *CPL* 223.

46 *CIL* XVI app. 1. AD 122. Latin. Wooden tablet recording grant of *honesta missio* to an *eques*. Wilcken 457; *ILS* 9060; Calderini 58; *CPL* 113; *Documenti* 88.

47 *CR* XXXIII (1919) pp. 49–53. Second century. Greek. Ostraca containing receipts for rations.

48 *JRS* XXVII (1937), pp. 30–6. 25 April 127. Birth certificate of soldier's illegitimate child. Latin. H. I. Bell, 'A Latin registration of birth', *JRS* XXVII (1937), 30–6; Wilcken, *Archiv*. XIII, (1939), 152 f.; Schulz, *JRS* XXXII (1942), 78–91 and XXXIII (1943), 55–64, and *Bull. Ist. Dir. Rom.* 'Vittorio Scialoja', N.S. 15 (1951), 170–206; O. Montevecchi, *Aegyptus* XXVIII (1948), 129–67; Volterra, 'Un'osservazione in tema di tollere liberos', *Festschrift Fr. Schulz* (Weimar 1951), I, 338–98; *CPL* 159.

49 O. *Fay*. 19, 21, 50. Third–fourth century. Greek. Military receipts.

50 O. *Milne* 103. AD 77–8. Greek. Receipt for hay. J. G. Milne, *Theban Ostraca*, Part III, Greek Texts, 1913; *Documenti* 50.

51 104. AD 88–9. Greek. Receipt for hay. *Documenti* 51.

52 108. AD 166 Greek. Receipt for hay for the heating of the baths. *Documenti* 53.

53 O. *Strassb*. 445. AD 145. Greek. Receipt for hay for the camels of a cohort. *Documenti* 52.

54 O. *Tait* II 2020. Second century. Greek. Receipt issued to a *cibariator* by a *cornicen*. *Documenti* 45.

55 O. *Tell. Edfou* 196–204, 209, 324–5, 472–5. First century. Latin. G. von Manteuffel, *Tell. Edfou 1937: Fouilles franco-polonaises*, Cairo, I (1937), II (1939), III (1950). Cf. H. C. Youtie, 'Records of a Roman Bath in Upper Egypt', *AJA* 1949, 268–70; *CPL* 283–98.

56 O. *Wâdi Fawâkhir*. First–second century. Latin. Soldiers' letters. O. Guéraud, 'Ostraca grecs et latins de l'Wâdi Fawâkhir'. *BIFAO* XLI, 1942. 141–96. *CPL* 303–9.

57 O. *Wâdi Hammamat*. Second century. Latin. Mention of *Cohors I Apamenorum*. J. Schwartz, *Chronique d'Egypte* (1956), 118 f. *CPL* 310.

58 O. *Wilb.-Brk*. 73. AD 145. Greek. Receipt for chaff for an *ala*. Claire Préaux, *Les Ostraca grecs de la Collection Charles-Edwin Wilbour au Musée de Brooklyn* (1955).

59 O. *Wilcken* 905–6, 914, 927, 951, 1011–12, 1014, 1128–46, 1223, 1258, 1265, 1372, 1447, 1458, 1464, 1475–6, 1487. Mainly second century. Greek. Receipts.

60 1266. Second century? Latin. Receipt. *CPL* 299.

61 O. *Würzburg* 19 June 18 BC. Latin. Receipt for *frumentum*. U. Wilcken, *Archiv*. I (1901), 372, n. 2; *CPL* 282.

62 *P. Aberdeen* 21. Third–fourth century. Greek. Account of corn assigned to soldiers.

63 61. AD 48–9. Latin. Receipt for first payment. H. A. Sanders, *Class. Phil.* 1941, 63 f.; Calderini 62; *Negotia* 146; *CPL* 185.

64 133. AD 192–6. Latin. Part of same document as *P. Berlin* 6866, *q.v. CPL* 123.

65 149. Late second– early third century. Greek. Nature uncertain, possibly the earliest mention of the *praefectus montis Berenicidis*.

66 150. Second–third century. Latin. Fragment of *matricula*? *CPL* 127; *Documenti* 18.

67 170. AD 187. Greek. Soldier's receipt for barley.

68 *P. Amherst* II 107. AD 185. Greek. Receipt for barley issued by *duplicarius* of the *ala Heracliana*. Wilcken 417; *Sel. Pap.* II 387; *Documenti* 54.

69 108. AD 185–6. Greek. Receipt of similar form to the preceding.

70 109. AD 185–6. Greek. Receipt issued by village elders to acknowledge payment by government collectors for barley supplied to *ala*. On *verso* a list of villages in a different hand. Wilcken 418.

71 173–8. AD 185–6. Greek. Incomplete receipts similar to *P. Amherst* II 107. No. 177 is perhaps a duplicate of 175.

72 182. AD 287–304. Bilingual. Unpublished. Parts of four lines of military document. *CPL* 141.

73 *P. Antinoopolis* I 41. Third century. *Matricula*? Latin. On the *verso* a fragment, perhaps a Greek letter. *CPL* 135; *Documenti* 24.

74 *P. Berlin* 6866 + *P. Aberdeen* 133. Dated to AD 192 by R. O. Fink, *Synteleia Vincenzo Arangio-Ruiz* (Naples 1964), 233. Latin. R. Marichal, *L'Occupation romaine de la Basse Egypte* (Paris 1945); J. Lesquier, *L'armée romaine d'Egypte d'Auguste à Dioclétien* (Cairo 1918), 252 f.; A. Passerini, 'Il papiro berlinese 6866 e il soldo militare al tempo di Commodo', *Acme* I (1946), 366 and 'Gli aumenti del soldo militare da Commodo a Massimino', *Athenaeum*, n.s. XXIV (1946), 145–59; R. Marichal, 'La solde des armées romaines d'Auguste à Septime-Sévère d'après les P. Gen. lat. 1 et le P. Berlin 6.866', *Mélanges Isidore Lévy* (Brussels 1955), 399–421; *Ecriture latine* 27; *CPL* 122; *Documenti* 35. (For *P. Aberd.* 133 cf. *CPL* 123.)

75 *P. Berlin* 11649. Third century. Latin letter of recommendation. W. Schubart, *Amtl. Berichte* 1917, 334–8; *Aegyptus* 1920, p. 97 n. 527; *Ecriture latine* 22; Calderini 64; *CPL* 257.

76 *P. Bibl. Un. Giss.* 15. Second–third century. Greek. Requisition by a centurion. *Documenti* 71.

77 *P. Cattaoui* + *BGU* I 114, *q.v.*

78 *P. Columbia inv.* 325. AD 143. Greek. Mother's receipt for *deposita* of deceased soldier. J. F. Gilliam, 'The Deposita of an Auxiliary Soldier', *Bonner Jahrbücher* 167 (1967), 233–43.

79 *P. Dura* 26. AD 227. Greek with Latin subscriptions. Deed of sale. C. B. Welles, *Archives d'Histoire du Droit Oriental* I (1937), 261 ff. *Negotia* 138; *CPL* 344.

80 30. AD 232. Greek with Latin subscriptions. Marriage contract.

81 32. AD 254. Greek with Latin subscriptions. Divorce.

82 43. AD 238–44. Greek. Contract.

83 46. Early third century. Greek. Private letter from a soldier.

84 54. AD 225–35, possibly 225–7. Latin. The *Feriale Duranum*. *YCS* VII (1940) 1–222; A. D. Nock, 'The Roman Army and the Roman Religious Year', *HThR* XLV (1952) 187–252; J. F. Gilliam, 'The Roman Military Feriale', *HThR* XLVII (1954) 183–96; J. Mallon, *Paléographie Romaine* (1952), p. XVII, 4; *CPL* 324.

85 55. AD 218–22. Greek and Latin. File of letters. Breaches of discipline and desertions.

86 56. AD 208. Latin. Letters from Provincial Headquarters, assigning mounts. *YCS* XI (1950) 171–89; *Eos* XLVIII (*Symbolae R. Taubenschlag Dedicatae*, 1957) 209 f.; *CPL* 330.

87 58. *c.* AD 240–50. Latin. Copy of letter assigning mounts. *YCS* XI (1950) 187–9; *CPL* 343.

88 59. Prob. AD 241. Latin. Letter from a Governor of Syria. *CPL* 329.

89 60. *c.* AD 208. Latin. File of circular letters. *CRAI* 1933, 315–23; *AE* 1933, 107; *Écriture latine*, 28; *CPL* 327.

90 61. *c.* AD 216. Latin. Letter concerning *frumentationes*.

91 63. AD 211. Latin. Fragmentary correspondence. *CPL* 332.

92 64. AD 221. Latin. Letters to the Tribune from a Praepositus. *CPL* 337.

93 66. AD 216. Greek and Latin. Correspondence file of Postumius Aurelianus, dealing mainly with personnel. A *tomos synkollesimos*, containing parts of over fifty letters.

94 67. *c.* AD 223–5. Latin. Copy of letter with lists of names and centuries and *turmae*. *CPL* 338.

95 69. AD 235–51. Latin. Roster?

96 81. *c.* AD 250. Latin. Fragment of the copy of a letter. Cf. R. O. Fink, *AJPh* 1967, 84 f.

97 82. *c.* AD 233. Latin. Morning report. *YCS* XI (1950) 209–46; *CPL* 326.

98 83. AD 233. Latin. Morning report. *ibid. CPL* 339.

99 85. *c.* AD 230. Latin. Morning report (?)

100 87. *c.* AD 230 (?) Latin. Morning report (?)

101 88. AD 238–44 (?) Morning report. *YCS* XI (1950) 209–37, 252. *CPL* 340. Latin.

102 89. AD 239. Latin. Morning report. *YCS* XI (1950) 215–37, 248–52, *CPL* 331.

103 91. *c.* AD 225–35. Latin. Tabulation or Morning report.

104 92. *c.* AD 225–35. Latin. Tabulation.

105 93. AD 230–40? Latin. List of *Principales*. *TAPhA* LXXVI (1945), 277 f.; *CPL* 341.

106 94. *c.* AD 240. Latin. Parchment. Summary of dispositions of soldiers. *Monuments Piot* XXVI (1923) 40–3; *Fouilles* 314–17, no. VI. *CPL* 345.

107  95. AD 250 or 251. Latin. Strength report.
108  96. c. AD 245–55. Latin. List of names with ranks.
109  97. AD 251. Latin. List of men and mounts. *YCS* XI (1950) 189–209; *CPL* 325.
110  98. c. AD 218. Latin. Roster. *CPL* 333.
111  100. AD 219. Latin. Roster. *CPL* 335.
112  101. AD 222. Latin. Roster. *CPL* 335.
113  102. AD 222–4. Latin. List of names by centuries. *CPL* 338.
114  103. c. AD 224. Latin. List of cavalrymen.
115  104. Perhaps c. AD 235. List of names. Latin.
116  105. AD 250–6. Latin. Roster.
117  106. AD 235–40. Latin. Guard roster.
118  107. c. AD 240. Latin. Guard roster.
119  108. AD 235–40. Latin. Guard roster (?)
120  109. AD 242–56. Latin. Parchment. Guard roster.
121  110. Prob. AD 241. Latin. Parchment. Guard roster.
122  112. AD 241 or 242. Latin. Parchment. Guard roster (?)  Centuries and numerals.
123  114. AD 225–35. Latin. List of names.
124  115. AD 232. Latin. List of names by *turmae* and centuries. *CPL* 334.
125  116. AD 236. Latin. Names and notations by centuries and *turmae*: list of *principales*?
126  117. AD 236. Latin. List of names by centuries, with numerals.
127  118. AD 255 (?) Latin. List of names.
128  119. AD 230–40? Latin. Parchment. List of names.
129  120. Prob. AD 233–5. Latin. List of names by centuries, with dates by day and month.
130  121. Prob. AD 241. Latin. Record of accessions by transfer.
131  122. c. AD 241–2. Latin. List by centuries of soldiers of the same year.
132  123. After AD 225. Greek with Latin influence. List of names.
133  125. AD 235. Latin. Decision of a tribune. *Dura* V, 298; *CPL* 328.
134  126. AD 235. Greek. Decision of a tribune. *Dura*. V, 298.
135  128. Prob. c. AD 245. Fragments of an official journal. Greek with Latin notations. *CPL* 336.
136  129. AD 225. Greek. Receipt of money for purchase of barley.
137  130. AD 215–45. Latin. *Tituli* of rolls. *YCS*, XI (1950, 172 n. 5; *CPL* 342.
138  *P. Fay.* 38. Second-third century. Greek text with Latin date. Order from a centurion. *ChLA* III 207, *CPL* p. 437 n. 26; *Documenti* 70.
139  105. c. AD 175. Latin. Pay accounts of an *ala*. R. Marichal, *L'Occupation romaine de la Basse Egypte* (Paris 1945), 42 ff.; *CPL* 124; *ChLA* III 208; *Documenti* 34.
140  *P. Fay. Barns* 2. AD 92. Latin. Declaration of eligibility for legionary service. J. Barns, 'Three Fayum Papyri', *Chronique d'Egypte* XXIV (1949), 295–304, no. 2; cf. Forni, *Reclutamento*, 103 ff.; R. Cavenaile, 'Le P. Mich. VII

432 et l'*honesta missio* des légionnaires,' *Studi in onore di A. Calderini et R. Paribeni*, II (Milan 1957), 245; *CPL* 102; *Documenti* 2.

141 *P. Flor.* II 278. AD 203. Greek with Latin notations. *Liber epistularum missarum* in Greek, with marginal notations in Latin of the *acta* of a *familia* of gladiators, and on the *verso* accounts in Greek. D. Comparetti, *Mélanges Nicole*, I (1905), 57–83; *CPL* 145; *Documenti* 64.

142 *P. Fouad* I 21. AD 63. Greek. Minutes of an audience before the prefect in a case concerning veterans' rights. *Negotia* 171a; *Documenti* 101; Smallwood, *Gaius* 297a. Cf. *P. Oslo inv.* 1451 and *SB* V 8247.

143 45. AD 153. Latin. Loan in the form of a chirograph. Main text in Latin with simplified Greek version in second hand, and signatures in Greek and Latin with Greek subscriptions. *Negotia* 121; Calderini 61.

144 72. Third century. Greek. List of names.

145 *P. Gen.* 17. AD 207. Greek. Wife reports husband missing to the centurion and the decurion. *Documenti* 73.

146 35. AD 161. Greek. Woman gives receipt to the decurion of the *ala veterana Gallica* for payment for two camels. *Documenti* 56.

147 *P. Gen. lat.* 1. AD 81–90. Latin. Military archives.
    (i)   individual pay-accounts.
    (ii)  employment of men on special duty.
    (iii) excerpt from *matricula?*
    (iv) daily parade-state.
    (v)  duty roster.

    J. Nicole and Ch. Morel, *Archives militaires du Ier siècle* (Geneva 1900); A. von Premerstein, 'Die Buchführung einer ägyptischer Legionsabteilung', *Klio* III (1903), 1–46; R. Marichal, *ChLA* I 7; *CPL* 106; *Documenti* 10 and 30; McCrum and Woodhead 405.

148 4. AD 84. Latin. Individual pay account. J. Nicole, 'Compte d'un soldat romain', *Archiv* II (1903), 63–9; R. Marichal, *ChLA* I, 9; *CPL* 107; R. Marichal, 'Le papyrus latin 4 de Genève', *Studi in onore di A. Calderini e R. Paribeni*, II (Milan 1957), 225–41; *Documenti* 31.

149 *P. Grenf.* I 48. AD 101. Greek. Receipt by an *eques* of the *ala Gallica* for *frumentum emptum*. Wilcken 416; *Documenti* 55.

150 II 51. AD 144. Greek. Receipt by a *duplicarius* of the *ala veterana Gallica* for four goat-skins. *Documenti* 58.

151 108. AD 167. Latin. *Receptum nautae*. Mitteis 339; *Ecriture latine* 26; *Negotia* 154; Calderini 45; *CPL* 191.

152 110. AD 293. Latin. Military document. *Ecriture latine* 30; *CPL* 142.

153 *P. Hamb.* I 4. AD 87. Greek. Oath to remain for trial. *Negotia* 168.

154 31. AD 103. Greek. Epicrisis. In red ink. *CIL* XVI app. 2; *Documenti* 90.

155 31a. AD 126–33. Greek. Epicrisis. In red ink. *CIL* XVI app. 3; *Documenti* 91.

156 39. AD 179. Greek. Receipt book of the *ala veterana Gallica*. *Sel. Pap.* II 369; *Documenti* 40.

157 *P. Hunt.* AD 110–17. *Pridianum of cohors I Hispanorum veterana quingenaria*

*equitata.* Latin. A. S. Hunt in *Raccolta Lumbroso*, 265–72; G. Cantacuzène in *Aegyptus* IX (1928), 63–96; Calderini 56; *Pal. Soc.* IInd Ser., 186; *CPL* 112; R. O. Fink in *JRS* XLVIII (1958), 102–16; Ronald Syme in *JRS* XLIX (1959), 26–33. *ChLA* III 219; J. F. Gilliam 'The Moesian *pridianum*', *Hommages à A. Grenier* (Brussels 1962), 747–56. See pl. 2 p. 34 above.

158 *P. Lond. inv.* 229 = *Archaeologia* 58 (1895), 433 ff. AD 166. Latin text and signatures with registration in Greek. Girard 852; *Ecriture latine* 25; *Negotia* 132; Calderini 23; *Jur. Pap.* 37; *CPL* 120.

159 *P. Lond.* II 256a. AD 15. Greek. Carriage of military foodstuffs. Wilcken 443; S. Daris, 'Osservazioni ad alcuni papiri di carattere militare', *Aegyptus* XXXVIII (1958), 156–7; *Documenti* 67.

160 384. AD 179. Greek text with Latin notations. Veteran's appeal to the prefect. *ChLA* III, 201; *Documenti* 106.

161 482. AD 130. Latin. Receipt for hay supplied to the *ala veterana Gallica* by the *conductores. Ecriture latine* 18; *ChLA* III 203; *CPL* 114; *Documenti* 38.

162 III 1171*v.* AD 42. Greek. Edict forbidding improper requisitioning. (Cf. *PSI* V 446 and *SB* V 8248). Wilcken 439; Smallwood *Gaius* 381.

163 *P. Mich.* III 159. AD 41–68. Latin. Decision in a case of intestacy. *Negotia* 64; Calderini 27; *CPL* 212.

164 161. Second century. Latin. Military receipt. V. Arangio-Ruiz, *Studi Solazzi*, 261; *CPL* 128.

165 162. Dated to AD 193–7 by R. O. Fink, *Synteleia Vincenzo Arangio-Ruiz* (Naples 1964), 233 f. Latin. List of soldiers with places of origin and dates of enrolment. H. I. Bell, *JEA* XVII (1931), 268 f.; Wilcken, *Archiv* X (1930), 277; *CPL* 129; *Documenti* 16.

166 163. Third century. Latin. Military list. J. F. Gilliam, 'P. Mich. 163', *Class. Phil.* LXI (1956) 96–8; *CPL* 130; *Documenti* 22.

167 164. AD 242–4. Latin. Roll of promotions. J. F. Gilliam, 'The *ordinarii* and *ordinati* of the Roman army', *TAPhA* LXXI (1940), 127–48; 'The appointment of auxiliary centurions (P. Mich. 164)', *TAPhA* LXXXVIII (1957), 155–68; *CPL* 143; *Documenti* 27.

168 175. 18 April 193. Greek. Request to the centurion. *Documenti* 77.

169 203. Age of Trajan. Greek. Letter of a soldier stationed at Pselchis.

170 VII 432. End of first century. Latin. Certified copy of an edict of Domitian by which the *civitas* and the *conubium* is granted to veterans of *legio XXII Deiotariana*. E. G. Turner, *CR* LXII (1948), 147; J. F. Gilliam, *AJPh* LXXI (1950), 432; R. Cavenaile, 'Le P. Mich. VII 432 et l'*honesta missio* des legionnaires', *Studi in onore di A. Calderini et R. Paribeni*, II, (Milan 1957), pp. 243–51; *CPL* 105; *Documenti* 89.

171 433. AD 110. Latin. Certificate of the adoption of the *toga pura. CPL* 165.

172 *P. Mich.* VII 435 + 440. Second century. Latin. Military records of inheritance. J. F. Gilliam, *AJPh* LXXI (1950), 432 ff.; 'The minimum subject to the *vicesima hereditatum*', *AJPh* LXXIII (1952), 397–405; *CPL* 219 and 190; *Documenti* 37. R. O. Fink, *Bull. Am. Soc. Pap.* I (1963–4), 39 ff.

173  436. AD 138. Latin. Birth certificate of a soldier's illegitimate child. *CPL* 161.

174  438 AD 140. Latin. Chirograph. *CPL* 188. V. Arangio-Ruiz, *Chirografi*, 255; J. F. Gilliam, *AJPh* LXXI (1950), 433 f.

175  441. AD 156–61. Latin. Bronze tablet. S. Daris, 'Note per la storia dell' esercito romano in Egitto, I', *Aegyptus* XXXVI (1956), 240 ff.; *CIL* XVI suppl. 184; *CPL* 119; *Documenti* 87.

176  442. Second century. Latin. Deed concerning a dowry with witnesses' signatures in Greek. H. A. Sanders, *Proceedings of the American Philological Society* LXXXI (1939), 581–90; R. O. Fink, 'The *sponsalia* of a *classiarius*', *TAPhA* LXXII, 109–24 and 'P. Mich. VII 442 (inv. 4703): Betrothal, Marriage or Divorce?', *Essays in honor of C. Bradford Welles, American Studies in Papyrology* I (1966), 9–17; V. Arangio-Ruiz, *Parerga* (Naples 1945) 24–39; *Negotia* 20; *CPL* 210.

177  433. Second century. Latin. Soldier's petition? E. G. Turner, *CR* LXII (1950), 147; J. F. Gilliam, *AJPh* (1950), 435; *CPL* 177.

178  445. End second century. Latin. Contract between soldiers. V. Arangio-Ruiz, *Chirografi*, 262; J. F. Gilliam, *loc. cit.*; *CPL* 194.

179  446. End second century. Latin. Soldier's will. V. Arangio-Ruiz and A. M. Colombo, *Journ. Jur. Pap.* IV (1950), 122–3; *CPL* 226.

180  447. Second century. Latin. Military list. *ChLA* III, 218; *Ecriture latine* 40; *CPL* 121; R. O. Fink, 'P. Mich. VII 447', *AJA* LXVIII (1964), 297–9; *Documenti* 26.

181  448. End second century. Latin. Military record. *CPL* 131.

182  450 + 455. Third century. Latin. *Acta diurna?* J. F. Gilliam, *AJPh* 1950, 436; *CPL* 132–3; *Documenti* 12.

183  454. Third century. Latin. List of accessions, J. F. Gilliam, *loc. cit.*; S. Daris, *Aegyptus* XXVI (1956), 235–46; *CPL* 146; *Documenti* 20.

184  VIII 465. AD 107. Greek. Soldier's letter home. Cf. Cl. Préaux, *Phoibos* V (1950–1), 123 ff.; Smallwood, *Nerva* 307a.

185  466. AD 107. Greek. Soldier's letter home. Cf. Préaux, *ibid.*; Smallwood, *Nerva* 307b.

186  467. Early second century. Latin. Tiberianus archive. Sailor's letter home. A. Calderini, 'La corrispondenza greco-latina del soldato Cl. Tiberiano e altre lettere del II sec. d. Cr. nel recente vol. VIII dei papiri del Michigan', *Rendiconti 1st. Lombardo, Classe di lettere e scienze morale e storiche* LXXXIV (1951), 155–66; Rita Calderini, 'Osservazioni sul latino del P. Mich. VIII 467–72', *ibid.*, 250–62; *CPL* 250; *Documenti* 6.

187  468. Early second century. Latin. Tiberianus archive. Cf. preceding letter. *CPL* 251; *Documenti* 7.

188  469. Early second century. Latin. Tiberianus archive. (Cf. no. 186.) *CPL* 252. Address in Greek.

189  470. Early second century. Latin. Tiberianus archive. (Cf. no. 186.) *CPL* 253.

190 471. Early second century. Latin. Tiberianus archive. (Cf. no. 186.) *CPL* 254.

191 472. Early second century. Latin. Tiberianus archive. (Cf. no. 186). *CPL* 255.

192 473. Early second century. Greek. Tiberianus archive. (Cf. no. 186.)

193 474. Early second century. Greek. Tiberianus archive. (Cf. no. 186.)

194 475. Early second century. Greek. Tiberianus archive. (Cf. no. 186.)

195 476. Early second century. Greek. Tiberianus archive. (Cf. no. 186.)

196 477. Early second century. Greek. Tiberianus archive. (Cf. no. 186.)

197 478. Early second century. Greek. Tiberianus archive. (Cf. no. 186.)

198 479. Early second century. Greek. Tiberianus archive. (Cf. no. 186).

199 480. Early second century. Greek. Tiberianus archive. (Cf. no. 186.)

200 481. Early second century. Greek. Tiberianus archive. (Cf. no. 186.)

201 483. Age of Hadrian. Greek. Letter of a centurion. *Class. Phil.* XXII (1927), 247–9; *SB* IV 7335.

202 484. Second century. Greek. Letter to a soldier by the writer of the preceding.

203 485. Second century. Greek. Letter to a *signifer*.

204 490. Second century. Greek. Letter of a recruit to the navy. Similar to *BGU* II 423.

205 491. Second century. Greek. Letter of a recruit to the navy. A later letter than the preceding. *SB* IV 7353; *Sel. Pap.* I 111.

206 509. Second–third century. Greek. Brief letter to a soldier.

207 514. Third century. Greek. Isidora to Sarapias. The writer's son, a soldier, has died, and she is having difficulty in recovering his *deposita*. *Documenti* 36.

208 *P. Oslo* II 30. BC 20. Greek. Declaration before the centurion. *Documenti* 72.
208a III 122. AD 235–42? Latin. List of cavalry *principales*. R. O. Fink, 'A fragment of Roman military papyrus at Princeton', *TAPhA* LXXVI (1945), 275; *CPL* 139; *Documenti* 23.

209 *P. Oslo inv.* 1451 = *Aegyptus* XLII (1962) p. 125. Greek. Claim for veterans' rights. (cf. *P. Fouad* I 21 and *SB* V 8247). A. Traversa, 'Documenti greci inediti della collezione papirologica osloense', *Symbolae Osloenses* XXXVII (1961), 100–31; *Documenti* 102.

210 *P. Oxy.* I 32. Second century. Latin. Letter of recommendation to a tribune. *Sel. Pap.* I, 122; Calderini 63; *CPL* 249.

211 39. AD 52. Greek. Certificate of exemption on medical grounds (?). Corrected in *P. Oxy.* II p. 319. Wilcken 456. See also *P. Oxy.* XII p. 152.

212 43. AD 295. Greek. Accounts of the watchmen of Oxyrhynchus. W. Ensslin, 'Zu Pap. Oxyrhynchus I 43 recto', *Aegyptus* XXXII (1952), 163–78.

213 65. Third century? Greek. Order for arrest. *Sel. Pap.* II, 232.

214 II 276. AD 77. Greek. Receipt for grain, with mention of military escort. S. Daris, 'Osservazioni ad alcuni papiri di carattere militare', *Aegyptus* XXXVIII (1958), p. 156; *Documenti* 68.

215 IV 735. AD 205. Latin nominal roll with Greek receipt. Cf. *P. Oxy.* V p. 315; Lesquier, *Armée d'Egypte*, 97; J. F. Gilliam, 'Two Latin Letters from Dura-Europos of AD 221', *Etud. Pap.* VIII, p. 51 n. 1; *CPL* 134; *Documenti* 39.

216 VII 1022. AD 103. Latin. Certified copy of a letter of the prefect of Egypt concerning recruits. Wilcken 453; *Sel. Pap.* II 421; *ChLA* III 215; Calderini 57; *CPL* 111; J. F. Gilliam, 'Enrollment in the Roman Imperial Army', *Eos* XLVIII (1957), 207–16; S. Daris, 'Osservazioni ad alcuni papiri di carattere militare', *Aegyptus* XXXVIII (1958), 151–8; *Documenti* 4.

217 XII 1481. Early second century. Greek. Soldier's letter home.

218 1508. Second century. Greek. Extracts concerning a veteran.

219 1511. Before AD 247. Latin. Fragment of a *liber epistularum missarum*? Cf. *P. Flor.* II 278. *CPL* 140.

220 XIV 1637. AD 257–9. Greek. Division of property by a *princeps praetorii*.

221 1657. Late third century. Greek. List of utensils. Military?

222 1666. Third century. Greek. Letter concerning a recruit in a legion, who wanted to transfer to an *ala*. *Sel. Pap.* I, 149; *Documenti* 8.

223 *P. Princeton* II 57. Second–third century. Greek. Account of expenditure on arms.

224 *P. Princeton G. D. inv.* 7532. Third century. Latin. *Matricula* of *principales* of II *Traiana*? R. O. Fink, 'A fragment of a military papyrus at Princeton', *TAPhA* LXXVI (1945) 271–8; *CPL* 138; *Documenti* 21.

225 *P. Ryl.* II 79. AD 144–50. Latin. Naval nominal roll. R. O. Fink, *ibid.*; J. F. Gilliam, 'A Roman naval roster, P. Ryl. 79' *Class. Phil.* XLVIII (1953), 97–8; *CPL* 125; *Documenti* 28.

226 85. AD 185. Greek. Receipt for military supplies.

227 141. AD 37. Greek. Denunciation to the centurion. *Documenti* 76.

228 223. Second century. Latin. Military account? Calderini 55; *CPL* 312.

229 273a. Second century. Latin. Fragment of pay account. *CPL* 126; *Documenti* 32.

230 274. AD 185. Greek. Receipt similar to no. 226.

231 275. Greek. Fragment of similar receipt.

232 IV 608. First–second century. Latin. Letter of recommendation to a procurator. *CPL* 248; *Cod. lat. ant.*, II 228.

233 609. AD 505. Latin. Mobilization letter. *CPL* 274.

234 611. AD 87–8. Latin. Declaration by a veteran. *CPL* 176.

235 *PSI* III 184. AD 292. Greek. Notice to the decurion of a fire. *Documenti* 75.

236 222. Third century. Greek. Denunciation to the decurion. *Documenti* 81.

237 V 446. AD 133–7. Greek. Decree of the prefect forbidding improper requisitioning by soldiers. *Sel. Pap.* II 221; *Documenti* 49. Cf. *P. Lond.* 1171 V and *SB* 8248.

238 465. AD 265. Greek. Acknowledgment to an *optio* of II *Traiana Fortis* for supplies. *Documenti* 61.

239 VI 729. AD 77. Latin. Purchase of a horse by an *eques* of the *ala Apriana* from a centurion of *leg. XXII Deiotariana*. Girard-Senn, p. 920, no. 7; *Ecriture latine* 15; *Negotia* 136; Calderini 60; *CPL* 186. Cf. J. F. Gilliam, 'Military Papyri from Dura', *YCS* XI (1950), 181, n. 56.

240 VII 797. AD 232. Greek. Requisitions for army. Cf. *PSI* VI 683 of AD 199. *Documenti* 59.

241 IX 1026. AD 150. Latin. Veterans' petition. A. Degrassi, *Aegyptus* X (1929), 242 ff. and *Riv. di fil.* XII (1934), 194 ff.; U. Wilcken, *Archiv.* IX (1930), 80 f. and *Atti del IV congr. intern. di papirol.* (1935), 109; W. Seston, *CRAI* 1932, 311 ff. and *Rev. de Phil.* LXIX (1933), 373 ff.; R. Cavenaile, 'Le P. Mich. VII 432 et l'honesta missio des légionnaires,' *Studi in onore di A. Calderini e R. Paribeni*, II (Milan 1957), 243 ff.; S. Daris, *Aegyptus* XL (1960), 67 ff.; V. Arangio-Ruiz, *Chirografi*, 260, n. 34; *CIL* XVI app. 13; *CPL* 117; *Documenti* 83 and 98, Smallwood *Nerva* 330.

242 1063. AD 117. Greek. Receipts for *deposita tironum*. Cf. J. F. Gilliam, 'An Egyptian cohort in A.D. 117', *Beiträge zur Historia-Augusta-Forschung*, Band 3 (Bonn 1966), 91 ff.; *Sel. Pap.* II 368; *Negotia* 126; *Documenti* 33.

243 XIII 1307. First century. Latin. *Acta diurna*. Cf. J. F. Gilliam, 'Notes on PSI 1307 and 1308', *Class. Phil.* XLVII (1952), 29 ff.; S. Daris, *Aegyptus* XXXVIII (1958), 157. Cf. *P. Dura* 82. *CPL* 108; *Documenti* 11.

244 1308. Second century. Latin. Naval nominal roll. J. F. Gilliam, *ibid.*; *CPL* 144; *Documenti* 29.

245 *P. Tebt.* II 333. AD 216. Greek. Denunciation to the centurion. *Sel. Pap.* II 336; *Documenti* 74.

246 *Par. d. Pass.* LV (1957), 305. First-second century. Latin. Nominal roll of auxiliaries. R. O. Fink, 'Two fragments of Roman military rosters in Vienna', *Parola d. Passato* LV (1957), 298 ff.; *Documenti* 15.

247 *Par. d. Pass.* LV (1957), 300. *c.* AD 215. Latin. Nominal roll with places of origin and dates of enlistment. R. O. Fink, *ibid.* and *Synteleia Vincenzo Arangio-Ruiz* (Naples 1964), 235 f.; *Documenti* 19.

248 *SB* III 6304. Second century. Latin in Greek characters, with a section in Latin characters. Purchase of a slave girl. *Negotia* 134; Calderini 24; *CPL* 193.

249 6957. Second century. Greek. Ostracon. Receipt for wine issued. Cl. Préaux, *Chronique d'Egypte* XXVI, 121 ff.; *Documenti* 41.

250 6961. Second century. Greek. Ostracon. As for preceding. *Documenti* 42.

251 6963. Second century. Greek. Ostracon. As for preceding. *Documenti* 43.

252 6967. Second century, Greek. Ostracon. Receipt for lentils, salt and vinegar received from a *cibariator*. *Documenti* 44.

253 7181. AD 220. Greek and Latin. Receipt for supplies. M. Norsa, *Raccolta di scritti in onore di G. Lumbroso* (Milan 1925), 319 ff.; *Negotia* 142; Calderini 56; *Documenti* 65; *CPL* 137.

254 IV 7362. AD 188. Greek. Epicrisis. A veteran presents not the usual diploma but a Latin letter from the prefect. A. E. R. Boak, *Ann. Serv.* XXIX

(1929), 58 n. 5; S. Daris, *Aegyptus* XL (1960), 70 ff.; *Sel. Pap.* II 315; *CIL* XVI app. 8; *Negotia* 7b; *Documenti* 97.

255 V 8247. AD 63. Greek. Claim for veterans' rights. Cf. *P. Fouad* I 21 and *P. Oslo inv.* 1451. C. B. Welles, *JRS* 1938, 41 ff.; *Negotia* 171b; *Documenti* 103; Smallwood, *Gaius* 297b.

256. 8248. AD 48–9. Greek. Decree of prefect forbidding improper requisitioning. Cf. *P. Lond.* 1171v and *PSI* V 446. *CIG* 4956; *IGRR* I 1262; *Documenti* 48; Smallwood, *Gaius* 382.

257 VI 9118. Second century. Greek. Ostracon. Order to a *curator praesidii* concerning an *eques*. H. C. Youtie, 'Greek ostraca from Egypt', *TAPhA* LXXXI (1950), 99 ff.; Cl. Préaux, *Chron. d'Egypte* XXVII (1952), 293; J. F. Gilliam, 'Ostr. Skeat 11', *TAPhA* 1952, 51–5; *Documenti* 5.

258 9202. Third century. Greek. Supply of barley to a centurion, a *duplicarius*, a *sequiplicarius* and a *signifer*. H. G. Gundel, *Kleine Beiträge zum römischen Heerwesen in Aegypten* (*P. Giss. Bibl. inv. 282*) (Giessen 1940); *Documenti* 46.

259 9223. BC 2. Greek. Inscribed vase. Mention of soldiers of *legio* XXII *Deiotariana*. O. Guéraud, 'Un vase ayant contenu un échantillon de blé', *Journ. Jur. Pap.* IV (1950), 107–11; S. Daris, 'Osservazioni ad alcuni papiri di carattere militare', *Aegyptus* XXXVIII (1958), 156–7; *Documenti* 66.

260 9227–8. AD 159. Greek. Epicrisis of veterans. A. Bataille, 'Un papyrus Clermont-Ganneau appartenant à l'Académie des Inscriptions', *Journ. Jur. Pap.* IV (1950), 327–40; S. Daris, 'Note per la storia dell'esercito romano in Egitto, II', *Aegyptus* XL (1960), 71; *Documenti* 95.

261 9248. Second century. Latin and Greek. Receipt for grain. Cf. *P. Oxy.* IV 735. A. Bataille, 'P. Clermont-Ganneau 3–5', *Journ. Jur. Pap.* VI (1952), 186–8; *CPL* 136; *Documenti* 47.

262 9290. Second century. Greek with Latin date. Order from the centurion. E. C. Baade, 'Two Yale papyri dealing with the Roman army in Egypt', *Mitteilungen aus der Papyrussammlung der Oesterreichischen National-bibliothek*, n.s. V (1956), 23–7; *Documenti* 69.

263 *Stud. Pal.* XXII 92. Third century. Greek. Receipt for javelins of palm-wood, issued by a *signifer*. *Documenti* 62.

264 *Tablette Keimer.* AD 142. Latin with Greek subscriptions. Will of an *eques*. P. Jouguet and O. Guéraud, *Etudes de Papyrologie* VI (1940), 1–20; J. Macqueron, *NRHD* 1945, 123–70; A. Berger, *NRHD* 1948, 337; *Rev. Arch.* 1949, 168; V. Arangio-Ruiz, 'Il testamento di Antonio Silvano e il senatoconsulto di Nerone', *Studi in onore di Emilio Albertario* (Milan 1950), 203–12; S. von Bolla, 'Zum römischen Militärtestament', *Studi in onore di V. Arangio-Ruiz* (Milan 1953), I 273–8; E. Weiss, 'Procurator ex testamento', *ibid.* IV 61–70; *Negotia* 47; *CPL* 221.

265 *TAPhA* XC (1959), 139–46. (= *P. Cornell inv.* I 64). AD 136. Greek. A veteran looks for a house. Naphtali Lewis, 'A Veteran in Quest of a Home', *TAPhA* XC (1959), 139 ff.

266 Wessely, *Schrifft.* 7 (= *P. Lond. inv.* 229, *q.v.*)

267 8. Second century. Latin. Nominal roll from *legio III Cyrenaica. Ecriture latine* 17; *CPL* 110; *Documenti* 13.

268 9. Second century. Latin. List of soldiers with dates of enlistment, perhaps with details of location. *Stud. Pal.* XIV, viii inf.; *Ecriture latine* 20; *CPL* 116; *Documenti* 17.

269 11. Second–third century. Latin. Fragment of account. Military? *Stud. Pal.* XIV viii.

270 23. Third–fourth century. Latin. *Acta diurna? Stud. Pal.* XIV ix; *CPL* 322; *Documenti* 25.

271 Wilcken, *Chrest.* 463. AD 94. Latin. Edict of Domitian concerning veterans' rights. G. Lefebvre, *Bull. de la Soc. d'Arch. d'Alexandrie* III (1910), 39–52; F. Schehl, 'Zum Edikt Domitians über die Immunitäten der Veteranen', *Aegyptus* 1933, 137–44; *CIL* XVI app. 12; *CPL* 104; *Documenti* 104.

# SOURCES OF ILLUSTRATIONS

1, 6, 15, 16, Mansell-Alinari; 2, 3, 4, 12, Trustees of the British Museum; 5, Society for the Promotion of Roman Studies; 7, 8, Crown Copyright, Royal Commission on Historical Monuments; 9, The Dean and Chapter, Cathedral Library, Durham; 10, Muzeul de Istoria Cluz, Rumania; 11, Toledo Museum of Art, gift of Edward Drummond Libbey; 13, Nottingham University Museum; 14, Archives Photographiques; 17, 18, 20, 21, 22, Professor I. Florescu and the British School of Archaeology at Rome; 19, Dr E. A. Johnson and Malcolm Todd; 23, Professor I. Florescu and the Society for the Promotion of Roman Studies; 24, 26, Crown Copyright, Ministry of Public Buildings and Works; 25, Professor Eric Birley and the Cumberland and Westmorland Antiquarian and Archaeological Society.

# INDEXES

## PEOPLE

## 2 DEITIES

## 3 PLACES

## 4 GENERAL

## 5 INSCRIPTIONS